PATIENTS WITH SUBSTANCE ABUSE PROBLEMS

A Norton Professional Book

PATIENTS WITH SUBSTANCE ABUSE PROBLEMS

Effective Identification, Diagnosis, and Treatment

Edgar P. Nace, M.D. and Joyce A. Tinsley, M.D.

W. W. Norton & Company

New York • London

All table and figures were created by the authors or are in the public domain, unless credited otherwise.

For information about permission to reproduce selections from this book, write to Permissions, W. W. Norton & Company, Inc., 500 Fifth Avenue, New York, NY 10110

Manufacturing by Haddon Craftsmen
Book design by MidAtlantic Books & Journals
Production Manager: Leeann Graham

Library of Congress Cataloging-in-Publication Data

Nace, Edgar P., 1939–
    Patients with substance abuse problems : effective identification, diagnosis, and treatment/ Edgar P. Nace and Joyce A. Tinsley.
        p. cm.
    "A Norton professional book."
    Includes bibliographical references (p. 195).
    ISBN-13: 978-0-393-70511-9
    ISBN-10: 0-393-70511-0
        1. Substance abuse. I. Tinsley, Joyce A. II. Title

RC564.N327 2007
616.86—dc22

                                                                                        2006046649

ISBN 13: 978-0-393-70511-9
ISBN 10: 0-393-70511-0

W. W. Norton & Company, Inc., 500 Fifth Avenue, New York, N. Y. 10110
www.wwnorton.com
W. W. Norton & Company Ltd., Castle House, 75/76 Wells St., London W1T 3QT
1   2   3   4   5   6   7   8   9   0

We dedicate this book to the American Academy of Addiction Psychiatry, an organization that aims to promote excellence in the clinical practice of addiction psychiatry.

Contents

Acknowledgments

We acknowledge the National Institute on Alcoholism and Alcohol Abuse and the National Institute on Drug Abuse for the materials they make available to advance the public's understanding of substance abuse.

PATIENTS WITH SUBSTANCE ABUSE PROBLEMS

Introduction

If you want to learn how to help patients with substance abuse problems, this book is for you. We believe that nonspecialists in both primary care and psychiatric practices can treat addicted patients. This book provides basic information on addiction as a brain disease, shows how to recognize a substance use disorder, and introduces therapeutic strategies. The terms *addiction* and *substance dependence* are used interchangeably throughout the text. Some health care professionals find addicts among their least rewarding patients. One reason is pessimism about patients' potential for recovery. Another reason is that physicians and other clinicians may be uneasy when they do not know how to solve a patient's problem.

We begin to highlight reasons for optimism in Chapter 1. In part, this optimism rests upon an improved scientific understanding of drug and alcohol dependence. Compared to the slow pace of research in the past, knowledge about the brain's role in addictive diseases has accumulated rapidly during the past 20 years. Psychotherapeutic and pharmacological interventions have expanded as well. Comfort levels in treating these patients should improve as practitioners understand them better.

An initial approach to substance abuse treatment involves identifying and accurately diagnosing patients with substance use disorders. Misdiagnosis can be costly in both directions: Underdiagnosis may lead to serious and expensive health or social complications, and overdiagnosis may lead to costly treatment with interventions that miss the patient's primary problem. The initial chapters review important aspects of patient evaluation, including the use of collateral sources, laboratory testing, and screening tools.

Two special populations are featured in this book: those at opposite ends of the age spectrum. Adolescence and late life are both times of change. The adolescent struggles to become an independent adult; the older person struggles to accept the accomplishments and failures of adulthood. Whether angst or growth is the predominant emotional experience depends on many factors. Substance abuse is one factor that can thwart healthy development.

Terms for describing the misuse of substances are not uniform, which can be confusing. We provide readers with definitions from the *Diagnostic and*

Statistical Manual of Mental Disorders IV–Text Revision (American Psychiatric Association, 2000); however, throughout the book we also use language that is better known among the general public. The most common terms for more severe forms of excessive substance use are *substance abuse, substance dependence, addiction, alcoholism,* or *alcohol dependence,* and the once popular term *chemical dependence.* Outside the addiction field, the term *substance abuse* is sometimes used interchangeably with *substance dependence.* However, strictly speaking, the term refers to a less advanced condition. One of the best indicators that a patient suffers from dependence on drugs or alcohol is the inability to consistently control its use.

Why do they do what they do?

Substance abuse and dependence are complicated and fascinating subjects about which volumes have been written. Their etiology is multifaceted. Given that a strong genetic component has been demonstrated for alcoholism, part of the answer to why a person drinks when it leads to big problems may be found through the study of genetics. Other etiologies are believed to include psychological, social, and cultural factors.

There is a growing body of knowledge about the function of brain neurotransmitters in addiction. The second chapter addresses addiction as a disease, presented in a simple way that focuses on the reward system in the brain. The reward pathway (or the pleasure pathway, as some call it) is a rich source of dopamine receptors. Dopamine is a "feel good" chemical. Most people boost their dopamine levels through the legitimate satisfaction of natural appetites. Those with severe addictions find that nothing transcends the euphoria of bingeing on their drug of choice. However, addiction becomes a frustrating and often tragic way to gain satisfaction. Unfortunately, the urge to use the cherished substance can seem irrepressible.

It is not only through biology that substances fail the user. The addict engages in psychological gymnastics in order to hide from the truth of his or her substance dependence. Chapter 3 explains the role of pathological defenses such as denial and discusses how an understanding of a patient's defensiveness prepares us to advance the clinical process. Denial, which is a common defense among substance abusers, is one of their most frustrating characteristics. It can be difficult for clinicians to understand why they do not change self-destructive behaviors. This chapter presents ideas about how to deal with a patient's entrenched defenses.

2

How big is the problem of substance abuse?

Substance use disorders are harmful to the patient, and as if that patient threw a pebble into a pond, ripples extend outward to families and communities. Usually the substance abuser's trouble is obvious; the family's suffering is less apparent. Communities shoulder relatively hidden consequences in the form of highway crashes, crimes, and homelessness. We review the established data documenting the prevalence of substance use disorders in the general population and in the clinical settings of primary care and psychiatry.

In the United States, an estimated 15.1 million people have an alcohol use disorder, and around 10 million abuse illicit drugs or are dependent on them (National Household Survey on Drug Abuse, 1999). The number of citizens who abuse prescription medications is not known; however, a quarter of Americans—adults and adolescents—use nicotine (Greenfield, Manwani, & Nagiso, 2003). The overall financial cost of abusing substances is tremendous, and there is no doubt that the abuse of alcohol and drugs is a significant cause of morbidity and mortality, not only in the United States but also abroad.

The World Health Organization, in conjunction with Harvard University, evaluated the impact of a variety of diseases on disability through the Global Burden of Disease study (Murray & Lopez, 1996). The study developed a measurement factor called *disability adjusted life years* (DALYs), which quantifies the years of healthy life lost due to either premature death or disability. This measure was used to define disease burden. Using DALYs, data from 1990 showed that alcohol use was responsible for 4.7% of the disease burden in established market economies, and illicit drug use was responsible for 1.5%. In other words, alcohol use was the fourth leading cause of disease burden (meaning, premature death or disability), preceded by (in ascending order) ischemic heart disease, unipolar major depression, and cardiovascular disease. However, when gender was used as a sorting variable, alcohol use was found to be the leading cause of disability for men.

What works?

Some people who are faced with the consequences of their substance abuse develop an intention to change their behavior and are able to do that. Others have trouble quitting or are not convinced a change is necessary. A professional who understands the biological and psychological underpinnings of substance dependence is in a good position to help strengthen a patient's resolve to change. Motivational techniques have been proven to help facilitate change. Alcoholics Anonymous was an early psychological intervention, and it continues to be effective for many patients. Additional psychological therapies such as cognitive behavioral therapy, motivational enhancement, and 12-step facilitation have been shown to have beneficial effects in the treatment of this heterogeneous group of patients (Project MATCH Research Group, 1998).

Nicotine dependence is an area in which a combination of medication management and psychological therapy is important to the treatment process. Clinicians who have learned to help patients quit smoking have developed an important set of skills, some of which they can generalize to other addicted patients.

Until recently, the only medication available in the United States for the treatment of alcohol dependence was disulfiram (Antabuse), a serendipitously discovered drug that has been used since the mid-1940s. More recently, medications have been developed that target areas of pathology. Acamprosate is an example of such a medication, developed on the basis of neuroscience research into alcohol dependence.

Clinicians will be more confident in discussing the problems of alcohol and drug dependence with patients if they know about state-of-the-art treatments. Nevertheless, patients may not accept our assessment and may not follow our treatment recommendations. Fortunately, some thwarted results are eventually overcome by continuing effort, patiently applied. In instances where the clinician's best efforts fail to prevent a negative outcome, it is reassuring to know that he or she has done all that reasonably could be expected and has remained available to the patient.

How can this book help you help them?

Clinicians from both medical and mental health arenas can use this handbook as a quick reference source for the basics of identification, assessment, diagnosis, and treatment in cases involving substance abuse or dependence. This book is divided into 10 chapters. Part I describes the medical basis for addictive disease; Part II deals with the clinician's interaction with the patient around issues of diagnosis and intervention, including how to begin working with a patient by using motivational strategies; and Part III addresses specific topics involving potentially thorny problems.

Each chapter begins with several bulleted highlights that itemize key points. Brief vignettes are used to illustrate concepts, and tables or figures

4

are included to clarify material. At the back of the book is a glossary that defines some of the terms used here as well as in the addiction field. Specifically:

Chapter 1. Substance abuse is a pervasive problem whose costs in dollars and in emotional damages are staggering. Health-care professionals at every level, including students and trainees, encounter addicted patients, and each encounter is an opportunity to make a positive impact on a substance-abusing patient. This first chapter, therefore, explains the challenges of treating substance abusers.

Chapter 2. This chapter provides an overview of the reward pathway in the brain and discusses the proposed role of dopamine in a patient's overwhelming desire to use their drug of choice, be it nicotine, alcohol, cocaine, or heroin. The graphic on page 22 comes from work sponsored by the National Institute on Drug Abuse (NIDA). Please visit the NIDA website for more information: *www.drugabuse.gov.*

Chapter 3. Why do patients continue self-destructive patterns that harm loved ones, conflict with their values, and prevent success in basic life roles? This chapter addresses the common psychological process that keeps the addict stuck: denial.

Chapter 4. Substance abuse is often difficult to detect. This chapter explores how to find clues when substance abuse is a diagnostic possibility. Patients are often ambivalent about wanting help and may hope the clinician can produce a remedy without fully understanding the extent of their condition.

Chapter 5. Here the focus is on making an objective diagnosis. The category of substance use disorders encompasses substance *abuse* and substance *dependence.* Medical criteria from the *Diagnostic and Statistical Manual of Mental Disorders IV—Text Revision* (American Psychiatric Association, 2000), is presented in table form. These are the generally accepted criteria for making diagnoses. The chapter also contains information on psychiatric disorders that are common in cases of substance abuse and dependence.

Chapter 6. This chapter explains the several types of treatments that are available, the differences among them, and what makes a patient fit into one type of program rather than another. Motivational strategies are also discussed.

Chapter 7. Adolescent substance abusers can be an intimidating group for those who are not accustomed to dealing with them. This chapter provides background information and practical tips for professionals to use when working with teenagers. Also included are considerations for parents who want to talk to their children about drugs.

Chapter 8. The geriatric substance abuser is sometimes forgotten. However, intoxication in late life can lead to serious physical and emotional consequences. Alcohol and prescription drugs are the substances of choice for this age group. This chapter contains vignettes about specific problems in older adults.

Chapter 9. Everyone knows that smoking kills. Nonetheless, physicians and other clinicians have more work to do in motivating their smoking patients to quit. This chapter covers how to determine the severity of nicotine dependence, how to talk to patients about quitting, and how to use the treatments that work best.

Chapter 10. Pharmacological agents that are efficacious or promising in the treatment of addictive disorders are covered here. Medication should be used as one part of a recovery plan and not as the only component of treatment.

Understanding and treating patients who struggle with substance use disorders can be rewarding. This is an exciting time to work in the addiction field because the amount of information available to pass along to our patients has never been greater. Likewise, more therapeutic options are available. Patients and families have reasons to believe their lives can be manageable. We hope those who read this book will find it useful, and that some readers will follow it up by additional study on the subject of how to help patients with substance abuse problems.

Part 1
Medical Overview

1

Facing the Challenge
Patients with Substance Abuse Problems

"It is the burden of doctors to have great responsibility
in a sea of doubt and uncertainty."
—Cassell, 1991, p. 18

Highlights

• Substance abuse costs more than $200 billion per year to the American economy and absorbs a large portion (20–25%) of public health dollars.

• Years of life lost from alcoholic liver disease far exceed years of life lost from cancer and heart disease.

• 6% of Americans in a given year have a substance use disorder, with the rate 4–5 times higher in primary care settings.

• Physicians can effectively screen for substance use disorders but may lack confidence in intervention and treatment.

We begin by briefly reviewing the cost and prevalence of substance use disorders. Data on these topics enable us to appreciate the social importance of treating patients who have substance abuse problems. Further, it becomes obvious how extensive these problems are and that any clinician is likely to encounter substance-abusing patients.

Then we face questions on every clinician's mind:

- Do patients with drug and alcohol problems get better?
- Can the primary care physician or mental health practitioner make a difference?

Cost of Substance Abuse

A review of the costs of substance use disorders cannot but impress us with the scope of economic loss (not to mention human misery) in the United States as a result of alcohol and drug problems.

- Alcohol abuse is estimated to cost the United States $184.6 billion a year (Harwood, 2000). More than 70% of this amount comes from lost productivity, deaths, or alcohol-related illnesses. Health-care costs of alcoholism are about $26.3 billion a year, and most of this cost ($18.9 billion) is for treating the medical complications of alcoholism. The cost of treating alcoholism, itself, is considerably lower ($7.5 billion). Years of life lost for an individual's death from cancer is estimated, on the average, to be 2 years; from heart disease 4 years; but from alcoholic liver disease, 9–22 years.
- The cost of drug abuse, in general, to the United States is estimated to be $109.8 billion (U.S. Department of Health and Human Services, 1998). Medical costs in 1998 were $6.0 billion, lost earnings from premature deaths were $16.2 billion, and $20.4 billion went to costs associated with crime, crashes, and fires.
- Health-care expenses in 1995 for substance abuse problems absorbed 20% of Medicaid costs and 25% of Medicare costs, according to the Robert Wood Johnson Foundation (AHA News, 2001).

There is no certainty that such costs will diminish. Alcohol and drug use among adolescents, positive attitudes among youth toward drug and alcohol use, and availability of alcohol and drugs all suggest a continuing—if not growing—problem.

Prevalence in the General Population

The National Comorbidity Study (NCS; Kessler et al., 1994) provided an epidemiological profile of substance abuse in the U.S. population (ages 18–54). This study, along with the earlier Epidemiologic Catchment Area (ECA) Wave 2 study (Regier et al., 1993), found that nearly one in four adults will have a substance use disorder (either abuse or dependence) in their lifetime. NCS (Kessler et al., 1994) data indicate the following:

- Alcohol dependence occurs in 14% of Americans—20% of men and 8% of women.
- Drug dependence has reached a lifetime prevalence of 7.5% of Americans—9% of men and 6% of women.
- Abuse of alcohol occurs in an additional 9% of the population.
- Abuse of drugs occurs in an additional 4% of the population.

These statistics are both enlightening and alarming. The need for skills in recognizing substance use disorders and initiating treatment is obvious. Looking at the NCS study from a 12-month perspective, we find that in a given year nearly 11% of men will be currently alcoholic (i.e., alcohol dependent) and an additional 3% will abuse alcohol. The comparable figures for women in a 12-month period are 8% dependent and 4% abusing. Drug dependence and drug abuse in a 1-year time frame will occur, respectively, in 4% and 1% of men and in 2% and less than 1% (0.3%) of women.

A recent reanalysis of ECA and NCS data using "clinical significance criteria" found that in the U.S. population, ages 18 years and older, 6% will have a substance use disorder in a given year, 5.2% will have either alcohol abuse or dependence, and 1.7% drug abuse or dependence (Table 1.1; Narrow et al., 2002).

Do these figures, which are based on large standardized surveys of the U.S. population, have any bearing on what the primary care physician, psychiatrist, or mental health practitioner finds in his or her office? That is, given the extensive presence of substance use disorders, in general, what can we expect to find in clinical populations in settings where clinicians work?

Table 1.1
A Conservative Estimate of Substance Use Disorders
in the General Population in a Given Year

Alcohol abuse and alcohol dependence: 5.2%

Drug abuse and drug dependence: 1.7%

Adult (18 years and older) prevalence of any substance use disorder: 6.0%

From Narrow et al., 2002.

Prevalence in Primary Care Patients

Depending on the study, up to 30% of patients in primary care settings have alcohol-related problems (Barry et al., 1993; Rydon et al., 1992).

- A study (Fleming et al., 1997) that screened over 17,000 patients from primary care practices found that 16% were problem drinkers (as defined by a positive CAGE score of 2 or more (see Table 4.4 on page 48; Ewing, 1984), binge drinkers, or consumers of more than 14 drinks per week for men (or 11 drinks per week for women); 4% of the total sample met all of the above three criteria.
- More than 20% of patients presenting to emergency departments are abusing alcohol (Crawford et al., 2004). A University of Michigan Hospitals study found that 30% of admissions met criteria for alcohol dependence (Chermock et al., 1998).
- Although drinking declines after age 65, studies have found that 4–10% of older adult outpatients are actively alcoholic (Adams et al., 1996).

It is obvious that substance use disorders occur in primary care settings in percentages beyond that found in general population studies. Can we expect that this potential clinical need is being addressed? In a survey of primary care physicians (Wechsler et al., 1996), more than 90% reported asking patients "routinely" about alcohol and cigarette use. One-half asked patients about illicit drug use, diet, or exercise. Most of these physicians stated they were prepared to counsel patients on illicit drug use, but only a small minority (4–13%) described themselves as being "very successful" in helping patients actually change their behavior.

Doctors express a willingness to intervene in alcohol or drug problems, but such sentiments usually are not reflected in clinical practice. A lack of confidence in actually identifying substance-abusing patients (Geller et al., 1989) and pessimism regarding outcome are major barriers to physician effectiveness (Rohman et al., 1987). Lack of patient forthrightness can be an additional problem. For example, primary care patients (Koback et al., 1997) were detected 15% of the time as having alcohol abuse when "interviewed" by a computer, but only 7.5% when interviewed by clinical staff. Screening tests may double the detection of "alcohol misuse" over that detected by routine nursing and medical care (Sharkey et al., 1996).

Obviously, underdiagnosis of substance abuse problems is occurring. For example, 42% of patients with a suspected alcohol problem were not recognized by primary care physicians (Spitzer et al., 1994). In a hospitalized sample, 25% of patients had alcohol-related problems, but house staff and faculty detected these problems in less than 25% of cases in surgery and between 25 and 50% in medicine and neurology (Moore et al., 1989). A study of patients who were intoxicated when arriving at an emergency department found that 90% of these patients had evidence of chronic alcohol abuse (Reynaud et al., 2001), yet such patients may be identified by staff as having a drinking problem in less than 10% of cases (Cherputel et al., 1996). Table 1.2 summarizes the prevalence of substance use disorders in primary care settings.

A report from The Institute of Medicine (Grant et al., 1990) summarized the problem: Practitioners spend much time treating consequences of drug and alcohol abuse, but rarely attempt to focus on the drug-taking behavior itself.

Table 1.2
Estimate of Substance Use Disorders in Primary Care Settings

Problem drinkers (Fleming et al., 1997)	16%
Alcohol-related problems (Barry et al., 1993)	30%
General hospital patients (Chermock et al., 1998)	30%
Eldery adult (> 65 years) outpatients (Adams et al., 1996)	4–10%

Prevalence in Patients with Psychiatric Disorders

There is a high prevalence of substance use in patients who have psychiatric disorders. The presence of an addiction in conjunction with another psychiatric illness is common, and the term "dual diagnosis" is used to describe this co-occurrence. Patients who have a mental illness as well as the additional burden of a substance use disorder typically have a poorer prognosis than those who do not abuse substances.

Over a decade ago, the ECA study provided convincing evidence that patients who have a psychiatric disorder are more likely to abuse alcohol and drugs (Regier et al., 1993). Among individuals with any lifetime mental disorder

- 22.3% had a lifetime history of alcohol abuse or dependence.
- 14.7% had a history of another drug abuse or dependence.
- 28.9% had a lifetime history of either addictive disorder.

These findings were contrasted with the finding that 13.2% of individuals with no lifetime mental disorder had a history of either addictive disorder.

When compared to individuals in the general population, patients with schizophrenia were 4.6 times more likely to have a substance use disorder. Patients with an anxiety disorder or with depression were almost 2 times more likely to have a substance use disorder, and those with bipolar illness were 6 times more likely to have a substance use disorder than individuals in the rest of the population.

More recent studies have continued to show that individuals with psychiatric illnesses are at high risk for drug and alcohol abuse. In 1997 the American Psychiatric Association sponsored an observational study that collected detailed information from practicing psychiatrists to determine the characteristics of psychiatric patients (Pincus et al., 1999). The study reported on 1,226 systematically selected patients. Although psychiatrists listed a substance-related disorder as the first or primary diagnosis for only 4% of their patients, a history of substance abuse was reported for 42%. Looking more closely at the findings, we find that 12% of patients were reported as having a diagnosis of alcohol abuse or dependence, even though it was not necessarily listed as the primary diagnosis, and only 2.5% of current patients had a primary diagnosis of alcohol abuse or dependence. Compared to other treatment-based studies, these numbers are low. The authors speculated that patients and psychiatrists may not be reporting alcohol problems; health care reimbursement may have driven addicted patients into nonpsychiatric settings; and systematic assessment for alcohol-related problems may be lacking.

It is important for clinicians to be aware of the strong association between substance abuse and psychiatric illness, and of the adverse effect that substance abuse has on the outcome of psychiatric disorders.

As many as half of patients with psychiatric illness may experience diagnosable substance abuse at some point in their lives. Schizophrenic patients are nearly 5 times more likely to have a substance use disorder during their lives than the general population (Regier et al., 1993); bipolar patients are 6 times more likely. The prognosis of patients with psychotic, mood, and anxiety disorders is worse in the context of drug or alcohol abuse. (Table 1.3 summarizes the rates of substance use disorders in psychiatric patients.) However, prognosis improves when patients stop using, even for those with severe mental illness. More information on the co-occurrence of substance use disorders and psychiatric illness is presented in Chapter 5.

Table 1.3
Psychiatric Patients and Substance Use Disorders

Individuals with a lifetime history of mental disorders:

22% will experience alcohol abuse or dependence

15% will experience drug abuse or dependence

30% will have a lifetime history of either an alcohol or drug disorder

Increased rates of substance use disorders by diagnosis:

Bipolar disorder: 6 times more likely to have substance use disorder than general population

Schizophrenia disorder: 4.6 times more likely to have a substance use disorder than general population

Anxiety and depressive disorders: 2 times more likely to have a substance use disorder than general population

From Regier et al., 1993.

Do Substance-Abusing Patients Get Better?

Substance use disorders are chronic illnesses, and treatment outcomes must be viewed from that perspective. Both intensity and length of treatment improve results. For example:

- 35% of alcoholic patients who received either inpatient or intensive outpatient treatment, followed by aftercare, were found to be continuously abstinent after 1 year of treatment.
- An additional 46% were abstinent at the 9- to 12-month follow-up appointment.
- 7% were drinking moderately 12 months after treatment, without experiencing any problems.

Clients who received less intensive treatment had continuous abstinence for 1-year following treatment in 20% of cases, and an additional 30% were not drinking at the 9- to 12-month follow-up (Project MATCH Research Group, 1998). Further, the treatment of opiate dependence and cocaine dependence is successful 6 months after treatment in 50–80% of patients (O'Brien, 1996).

The success of treatment depends on the population being treated and the type of drug involved. The employed, including professionals, can be expected to have better results than those with no job prospects or those who are poorly educated.

Even though relapses often occur following treatment, the overall reduction in drug and alcohol use is usually substantial. Further, the improvement in health and social functioning is impressive, as documented by a California study wherein benefits of treatment outweighed the costs of treatment by at least fourfold (Gerstein et al., 1994).

So, yes, patients with substance use disorders can be expected to get better, and as with other chronic illnesses, patience, persistence, and tolerance of relapse are necessary.

Can Physicians and Clinicians Not Specializing in Substance Abuse Make a Difference?

The answer is an unqualified "yes." Research as well as clinical experience supports the importance of clinicians' involvement and understanding. To bolster this assertion, we briefly describe an effective, data-based intervention and then highlight the importance of the doctor–patient relationship and maintaining its constancy.

Brief Intervention

Rehabilitation programs or other intensive or extended treatments are not available to, or are refused by, many patients. This fact does not preclude, however, implementing other meaningful interventions. An extensive literature has emerged over the past decade documenting the effectiveness of brief interventions (Bien et al., 1993). Brief interventions typically involve a 15-minute counseling session with a physician. Variations on this model abound, but overall results document that this effort in primary care settings yields positive health and social outcomes that are greater than no intervention at all (Fleming et al., 2002).

For example, a study involving 64 primary care physicians found that brief interventions, compared to merely providing health literature, resulted in 20% fewer emergency department visits and 32% fewer days of hospitalization for the group receiving the brief intervention (Fleming et al., 2002). Over 4 years significant differences in drinking reduction occurred in the experimental group compared to the controls. Men in the experimental group reduced their drinking from 21 drinks per week at baseline to

14 drinks, and women showed a reduction from a baseline of 15 drinks per week to 8 drinks per week.

The model used by Fleming et al. (2002), which provides one example of a brief intervention technique, consists of the following:

1. General health information booklet given to each patient.
2. Two 15-minute sessions with a physician scheduled 1 month apart. (Physicians followed a scripted workbook and gave patients tasks to complete at home).
3. Two 5-minute follow-up phone calls from an office nurse.

Another successful approach consisted of a consultation with the physician every 3 months, a monthly gamma glutamyl transferase (GGT), and monthly contact with a nurse. Patients received letters with their GGT results, containing advice on how to cut down (Kristenson et al., 1983).

Staying with the Patient

By *staying with the patient* we mean remaining constant and hopeful when relapses occur or when the patient is noncompliant. By being there to help patients restart their program following a relapse or cope with a painful consequence of their addiction, we are modifying, inadvertently, the self-castigation experienced by most patients who struggle with a substance use disorder. Further, *staying with the patient* implies that we are part of the treatment and not just dispensers of pharmaceuticals. Our relationship with the patient is a fulcrum for beneficial change. We use this leverage to counter the patient's frustration, discouragement, or despair with determination to learn from "failure," outline the next course of treatment, and communicate our belief in the patient's capacity for change.

The decision on our part to remain committed to the treatment process is not simply a matter of sustaining an optimistic outlook. The commitment is rooted in a realistic appraisal of the patient's clinical status. If that status turns ominous, our fears and concerns should be made explicit to the patient and his or her family. Just as a surgeon outlines the risks when faced with a high-risk operation, a physician must share his or her perception of risks and probable outcomes to the noncompliant or relapsing chemically dependent patient. Such disclosures are not a "scare tactic" but an honest response to destructive patterns of behavior. The patient often will identify with the clinician's anxiety and thereby more fully appreciate the need for continuing treatment or for accepting more intensive help.

We now shift to a consideration of specific advances in understanding addiction at the neurobiological level. These advances can be expected to lead to improved understanding and treatment of addictive conditions.

2

Addiction
A Disease of the Reward Pathway

Highlights

- Dopamine is a neurotransmitter within the brain-reward circuitry that mediates pleasurable feelings.

- The primary structures that make up the reward pathway are the ventral tegmental area, the nucleus accumbens, and the amygdala, with projections into the prefrontal cortex.

- Addictive substances change the intrasynaptic transmission of neurotransmitters, produce neuroplastic changes, and alter gene transcription activity.

- Addictive substances are sought because they produce rewards (positive reinforcement) and relieve discomfort (negative reinforcement). In addition, the brain becomes "incentivized" to use addictive substances when exposed to substance-related cues.

- Medications for addiction treatment are increasingly linked to neuroscientific discoveries.

Addiction is a disease. Experts in the addiction field accept this premise largely because of advances in neuroscience. In addition, genetic studies suggest that heritability is a factor in determining who develops an addiction.

19

Some question whether it is reasonable to apply disease terminology to a condition that has moral, social, and legal ramifications. The addict's inappropriate and dangerous behavior is difficult to understand. These actions raise questions about the wrongdoer's personal culpability, the role of willpower in self-control, and the choice of pleasure over responsibility. If we accept that a disease is present when a part of the body fails to function as it should, then addiction is a disease.

Current research shows that the brains of addicts are different from the brains of people without addiction. The disease of addiction, medically called *substance dependence*, prevents the addict from behaving predictably. Another question that is frequently raised considers the addict's accountability while intoxicated. Society ultimately determines the accountability of its citizens. However, regardless of society's judgment on breaking its laws, there are personal consequences for irresponsible actions. These actions usually occur in the areas of family, occupational, legal, and health problems. In the end, it is up to the addict to get the help needed to control his or her disease. Sobriety, however, is a struggle for most. Health care professionals can help with this struggle. Physicians, clinicians, and families who understand addiction are in the best position to help. In this chapter we present information about the disease of addiction.

Research on Addictions

Craving for alcohol or drugs is similar to the strong natural cravings for food or sex. One alcoholic described his urge to drink as similar to great thirst, hunger, and sexual desire combined. This man's description was very close to a hypothesis that would be tested in research laboratories: specifically, that addiction is an artificially induced drive. Dopamine, one of many neurotransmitters found in the brain, is the implicated endogenous chemical. A healthy dopamine-rich pathway becomes activated by naturally pleasurable stimuli. Substance use can also activate it. However, with excessive substance-induced stimulation, the pathway becomes diseased, which perpetuates a forceful urge to use substances. Elegant studies have identified a reward pathway in the mesolimbic and corticolimbic areas as being substantially responsible for the powerful effects of alcohol and addictive drugs through the activation of dopamine. The key structures in these areas include the ventral tegmental area (VTA), the nucleus accumbens, the extended amygdala, and the prefrontal cortex (orbitofrontal cortex and anterior cingulate gyrus).

In one study certain parts of a rat's brain were stimulated to release dopamine (Kalivas & Volkow, 2005). Trained rats pressed a lever that produced a tiny electrical jolt in the part of the brain that contained an electrode. When the electrode was placed in the nucleus accumbens of the rat and the rat pressed the lever, dopamine was released, providing a pleasurable sensation. When the electrode was placed outside the reward pathway where there was no dopamine, the rat stopped pressing the lever because it learned that no pleasurable sensation followed. Dopamine levels were increased in the reward pathway when sites along its track received stimulation that led to pleasurable feelings. Dopamine is a powerful reinforcer within the synaptic space of neurons located along the reward pathway. Glutamate, the brain's major excitatory neurotransmitter, is also involved; glutamatergic pathways from the prefrontal cortex to the nucleus accumbens constitute a "final common pathway" for initiation of drug seeking (Kalivas & Volkow, 2005). If glutamate release is blocked, drug seeking is reduced (McFarland et al., 2003). In addition, other neurotransmitters, such as serotonin, norepinephrine, and endogenous opiates, contribute to the process of addiction.

Research has determined that chronic drug use leads to changes in the structure and function of the mesolimbic dopamine system. The neurons of this system may be altered for months or years after alcohol or drug use has stopped. The engine of activity in the mesolimbic reward system is the ventral tegmental area, located near the base of the brain. The VTA projects to the nucleus accumbens, a structure deep below the prefrontal cortex. Drugs such as cocaine, amphetamines, alcohol, nicotine, and opiates stimulate the ventral tegmental area to release dopamine at its axons, which are projected into the nucleus accumbens. In turn, the nucleus accumbens releases additional dopamine, which stimulates other parts of the brain. For example, when the amygdala is stimulated, it determines whether the experience is pleasurable or painful and whether it should be avoided or pursued. Projections to the hippocampus stimulate memories and record memories of the drug-induced experience. Finally, the prefrontal cortex is stimulated, and this stimulation mediates behaviors that often lead to further pursuit of drugs.

Dopamine has been referred to as a "feel good" neurotransmitter. Figure 2.1 visualizes the reward pathway beginning in the ventral tegmental area where dopamine is stored, extending to the nucleus accumbens where dopamine is released, and then upward to the prefrontal cortex where there is further release of dopamine. Although chemically distinct, the commonly abused substances (alcohol, nicotine, cocaine, and heroin) all affect neuro-

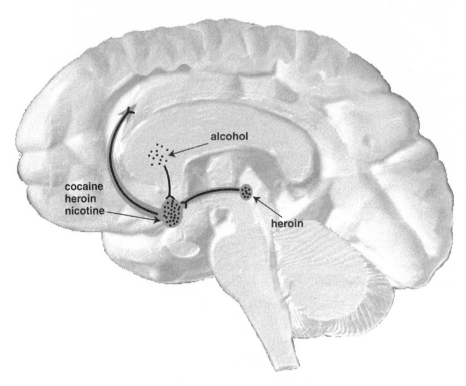

Figure 2.1 Commonly abused drugs activate neuroreceptors along the reward pathway.
(Reprinted with permission of NIDA, 1997.)

receptors along this same pathway. Our depiction is a simplified one, and other pathways or foci are likely activated as well. The use of each of these substances results in a greater availability of dopamine within the synaptic spaces of neurons along the pathway. Each drug has unique properties, including the degree to which it stimulates dopamine and other neurotransmitters. For instance, cocaine strongly stimulates dopamine as well as serotonin and norepinephrine. Opiates bind to opiate receptors and activate the endogenous opiate system. Alcohol is a complex substance that involves glutamate, an excitatory neurotransmitter, and gamma-aminobutyric acid (GABA), an inhibitory system (Secretary of Health and Human Services, 2000).

Factors That Perpetuate Substance Abuse

It is difficult for the person without addiction to understand why someone continues to seek drugs or alcohol when it causes serious problems in that person's life. It may help to consider the concept of *salience*, which refers to the importance of a particular substance for an individual. The way in which salience develops is complex. In short, the continuous exposure of nerve cells to addicting substances changes the morphology of the neurons. For example, the nucleus accumbens has signal-receiving projections called *spines*. When a cocaine addiction is established, these spines, or dendritic branches, change in appearance to look more like brushes. The remodeling of these neurons increases the sensitivity of the cell to the signals it receives from the ventral tegmental area, which is believed to increase drug sensitivity. The increase in drug sensitivity probably accounts for the salience of the drug experience, the tendency of the addicted individual to relapse easily upon re-exposure to drug-related cues, and the tendency to seek the drug experience in spite of known adverse consequences.

The reference to salience requires further explanation. Addiction has sometimes been explained as the result of negative reinforcement. That is, the addict uses drugs to avoid withdrawal symptoms—a state of discomfort or pain. There is no doubt that this dynamic contributes to drug use, but it is clearly only a small piece of the puzzle. Positive reinforcement is another possible explanation for continued drug use. This term refers to the well-established fact that if behavior is followed by a pleasurable or desirable experience, then that behavior is likely to be repeated. This mechanism would seem to be an explanation for the rat's continued pressing of the lever that releases dopamine. However, experience with people who are addicted demonstrates that the pleasurable aspect of addiction fades with time and is only partially recaptured as the addiction continues. Therefore we might ask, "Why does use continue if it is no longer intensely pleasurable?" The answer is that there is a difference between "drug liking" and "drug wanting" (Robinson & Berridge, 2000).

Addictive drugs have the ability to produce long-lasting adaptations in neurosystems, as described above. One of these critical adaptations is a hypersensitivity to those drugs. In addition, stimuli such as environmental or emotional factors have been associated with drug use. The brain systems that become sensitized are likely to be different from the brain systems that mediate pleasurable or euphoric feelings; these sensitized regions may mediate a *wanting* for the drug even though the *liking* of the drug may have greatly diminished. This wanting versus liking constitutes the profound dilemma in people who are dependent on alcohol or drugs. In spite of their intention to stop using substances and their appreciation of the harmfulness of using, a *wanting* continues to prevail. This wanting may reflect an underlying *incentive sensitization.* That is, the brain has become sensitized to cues connected to drug or alcohol use, and this sensitization is expressed as an incentive, or wanting, to use. This phenomenon of incentive sensitization has been documented in a wide range of studies (Robinson & Berridge, 2000). The neurocircuitry involves the nucleus accumbens, the hippocampus, and possibly cholinergic mechanisms in the prefrontal cortex, which could alter attentional capacities (Robinson & Kolb, 1997).

As physicians and clinicians appreciate the phenomenon of wanting or incentive sensitization, their capacity to empathize with people who are addicted to drugs should increase. It may help to remind those who fail to understand the dilemma of the addict what it is like to quit cigarette smoking. Intentions can be sincere, serious, and determined, yet a large majority of people who attempt to stop smoking relapse several times before they succeed in fully quitting. Thus we are not in a position to consider the addict to be an individual who is selfishly seeking pleasure or who merely wants to avoid every possible discomfort in life. Rather, it is important to appreciate that complicated neural systems mediate not only the positive reinforcing aspects of drug use but also the long-term changes in sensitization and the incentive to return to the pattern of addiction.

Drugs of abuse not only act by releasing neurotransmitters from the axon terminal and stimulating postsynaptic receptor sites, but they have profound intracellular consequences as well. For example, cyclic adenosine monophosphate (cAMP) is increased within the cell, and this signaling molecule activates a protein called CREB (cAMP response element binding). This protein is called a *transcription factor* and binds to DNA to activate specific genes. The increased formation of CREB and its action on specific genes correlates with the development of tolerance (see glossary). Delta FosB is a second signaling protein that results from dopamine's impact on the nucleus accumbens. Delta FosB shuts off a protein called *dynorphin*, which ordinarily inhibits dopamine release. The shutting down of dynorphin by delta FosB's action at the dynorphin gene keeps the neuronal structures of the reward system activated. Further, genes that are activated by delta FosB produce proteins that are likely to account for the structural changes in the dendritic spines, which we referred to above, with the result that the individual remains persistently sensitive to cues associated with drug use (Nestler, 2001b).

It is reasonable to believe the brain-reward circuitry, or the reward pathway, can become diseased and fail to function properly, as do other parts of the brain and body. The familiar drives for water, food, and sex are beautifully de-

24

signed to ensure human survival. The problem seems to occur when the pathway is compulsively stimulated, leading to an abnormal frequency and amount of dopamine release. Repeated and frequent drug use results in an inability to maintain normal reward functions. Self-reported craving for drugs correlates with increased metabolic activity in specific areas of the cerebral cortex ("gray matter") called the orbitofrontal and anterior cingulate cortices (Volkow et al., 1999). Yet natural reward cues, such as sexually evocative cues, fail to stimulate these centers in addicts. These brain changes affect decision-making tasks. The bottom line is that the addict is challenged with a brain that is exceptionally sensitive to drug-related cues but relatively inhibited in response to natural rewards or to cognitive control over drug-seeking behavior (Volkow et al., 2004).

As drug use and the associated stress hormones, particularly stimulation of corticotropin-releasing function (CRF), activate the brain to cause dysregulation of neuronal systems, it becomes increasingly difficult for the brain to experience any reward. This difficulty, which is a product of neuronal and hormonal changes that come about because of the abnormal stimulation of drug use, further drives drug-seeking behavior (Koob, 2003). The recipient of the reward wants to continue being rewarded but finds reward difficult to achieve. In order to perpetuate the intensity of the reward, the rat continues to press the lever or the addicted user continues to use. Frequently the drive becomes so powerful that it takes supremacy in the drug user's life, sometimes successfully competing with the natural drives for adequate hydration, food, and sex. Certainly, the drive to use drugs can override the user's value system and rival his or her interest in close personal relationships.

Because it is apparent from neurobiological research that addictive substances tamper with basic biological mechanisms, it is apt to consider the addicted individual to have acquired an artificially induced drive that is strong enough to overpower the natural biological drives. Much of this research has investigated the effects of cocaine. Cocaine blocks the reuptake of dopamine, thereby overstimulates the nervous system with this neurotransmitter. Drugs such as alcohol and opiates also enhance dopamine release at the ventral tegmental area and nucleus accumbens by inhibiting neurons that would otherwise dampen or inhibit a dopamine-secreting neuron. It is important to appreciate that numerous neurotransmitter systems are involved in the orchestra of addiction; for example, the ventral tegmental area and nucleus accumbens are more sensitive to glutamate as a result of the cascade of events summarized above. Glutamate-binding receptors are increased on cellular membranes as the addictive process unfolds and play a role in the long-term potentiation of memory. This is yet another possible mechanism for the salience, or predominance, of a drug experience that the individual is doomed to carry for weeks, months, or years, and which facilitates the process of relapse.

Neuroimaging studies involving functional magnetic resonance imaging (fMRI) and positron emission tomography (PET) have provided evidence that the frontal cortex is involved in the reinforcing properties of drugs and alcohol. Some reinforcing cues are thoughts, actions, and emotions that coincide with states such as intoxication and withdrawal (Goldstein et al., 2002). The frontal cortex mediates the execution of self-directed behaviors, and decreased frontal lobe function may lead to neurobehavioral disinhibition. Symptoms of this brain disinhibition process include affective lability, inattention, and impairment in planning and following through. The importance of frontal lobe impairment in addiction is being increasingly appreciated. Decreased metabolism in the orbitofrontal cortex and the anterior cingulate gyrus has been documented (Volkow et al., 1993). These metabolic changes help us understand the term "impaired-response inhibition and salience attribution," used by Goldstein and Volkow (2002) to summarize the addiction mechanism. Let us break down this term: The changes in the frontal cortex result in a decreased ability to inhibit impulses, and the sensitization and salience phenomena facilitate and prolong destructive substance use. Stimuli associated with drug reinforcement states gain priority, and the salience attributed to these stimuli leads to bingeing and compulsive use. Self-monitoring capacities are threatened, and the relative anhedonia that follows withdrawal is a stimulus for returning to drug or alcohol use.

Medications

Medications used to treat addiction are being developed on the basis of neuroscientific understanding. This is a much different approach to the development of therapeutics than the approach that led to the discovery of disulfiram (Antabuse), which was first used in the 1940s when it was surreptitiously found to cause an unpleasant reaction in the presence of alcohol. Naltrexone, an opioid antagonist, is an interesting example of a discovery based on this new approach. Opioid *agonists* produce the effects we associate with opioid drugs, such as analgesia, euphoria, and respiratory depression. Naltrexone, an opioid *antagonist*, blocks the effects of opioids. One of these effects important to addicts is euphoria and the sense of well-being. Based on this explanation of the actions of naltrexone, it is clear that it blocks the euphoria opioid addicts get from a drug such as heroin. However, we might be surprised to learn that naltrexone can also reduce the urge to drink alcohol. Because opioids and alcohol stimulate some of the same reward areas in the brain, it makes sense that an opioid antagonist might dull the desire for alcohol (see Figure 2.1). It is postulated that opioid antagonists modulate some aspect of the mesolimbic dopamine reward circuitry, either presynaptically or postsynaptically. Indeed, studies provide evidence for this mechanism of action. One example is a study in which naloxone (similar to naltrexone, but shorter-acting) prevented alcohol-induced dopamine release from the nucleus accumbens (Benjamin et al., 1993). Clinically, naltrexone has been shown to outperform placebo in preventing relapse in people with alcoholism (O'Malley et al., 1996; Volpicelli et al., 1992).

Acamprosate is the first medication in a decade to be approved by the Federal Drug Administration (FDA) for the treatment of alcoholism in the United States. A French company produces it under the trade name Campral. The chemical structure of acamprosate is similar to the major inhibitory neurotransmitter GABA. The GABA system is prominent in the actions of sedative/hypnotics and alcohol. The use of alcohol relaxes the person and depresses brain activity, in part through stimulating GABA. In biological terms, if an organism senses that GABA is more plentiful—as would be the case if a GABA-like compound such as acamprosate is in one's system—then that organism would have little reason to consume a GABA-enriching substance such as alcohol. Acamprosate also has a binding site on glutamate and inhibits release of this excitatory neurotransmitter. These neurotransmitters are thought to play significant roles in how acamprosate reduces the craving for alcohol (Littleton, 1995).

Future Directions

Advances in technologies provide compelling reasons to believe that our knowledge will grow at a fast pace. More research is needed to fully comprehend the neurobiology of addiction, including the mystery of why some who abuse substances become addicted while others do not. Epidemiological studies have established that strong familial patterns exist in alcohol, cocaine, and opiate dependence, with genetic risk estimated at 40–60% (Kendler et al., 2000). Genes could influence vulnerability to addiction by altering levels of normal proteins; another possibility is that genes could produce mutant proteins that change the structure, sensitivity, or functioning of neural circuits (Nestler, 2000). Environmental factors are also rich areas of study. For example, stress may alter the responsiveness of neural circuitry exposed to drugs (Jacob et al., 2001). Medications show promise in improving the rates of recovery from the devastating effects of substance dependence. Addiction is a disease, to which there are almost certainly genetic predispositions, environmental vulnerabilities, and neurochemical changes that make it difficult for addicts to consistently control the use of drugs or alcohol. As each piece of research is linked to another, we increase the likelihood of solving the puzzle that lies within the brains of our addicted patients.

3

Denial
Does the Patient Know Something Is Wrong?

Highlights

• Drug and alcohol dependence are characterized by the presence of pathological defenses, usually summarized as denial.

• Denial emerges within the process of an addiction secondary to both neurochemical processes and psychological experience.

• Neurochemical mechanisms include excessive dopamine stimulation, hypofunctioning of the frontal lobe, and acquisition of an artificial drive.

• Psychological experiences and trauma resulting from addictive behavior adversely impact self-esteem through emotions of shame, guilt, and worthlessness.

Those close to the alcohol- or drug-abusing patient witness the harm of substance abuse. This is frightening and confusing. They, as well as their health care providers, ask "Why doesn't [he or she] see what is happening? Why doesn't [he or she] agree with us? Why is the need for help denied?"

Why indeed is this option to drink or use drugs so important? The answer to this question brings us to the essence of addiction. Drinking or using drugs is vitally important to the person who is chemically dependent. In ways not fully understood, the brain of the dependent individual is sensitized to want the drug over and over again (Robinson et al., 2000), even when the initial reinforcers of use have diminished (e.g., the person doesn't get as high or the need for relief has lessened). The neurochemical underpinnings of this "drive" for more of the drug are gradually being understood (Nestler, 2001a), as we noted in Chapter 2.

The Composition of Denial

Biochemical alterations within and between neurons impact behavior and thinking; the changes in behavior are what we observe. But we also observe, as noted above, a denial by the patient of his or her deteriorating behavior. Denial is considered an unconscious defense mechanism characterized by a refusal to acknowledge painful realities, thoughts, or emotions. Denial is not conscious deceit or lying, but these elements are often operative. Denial blocks the consequences of addiction from being processed by good judgment, rational thinking, and insight. However, it is never complete; there are always cracks in its surface, or pathways around its bulwarks. One of our tasks as doctors and mental health professionals is to widen the cracks or circumvent the bulwarks. We can do this by understanding the processes out of which denial emerges and the purpose it serves in the mental economy of the patient.

First, let's take a look at three processes out of which denial emerges (Figure 3.1 below).

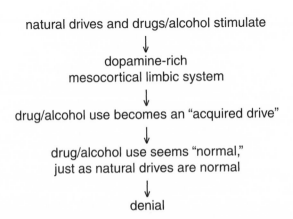

natural drives and drugs/alcohol stimulate

↓

dopamine-rich
mesocortical limbic system

↓

drug/alcohol use becomes an "acquired drive"

↓

drug/alcohol use seems "normal,"
just as natural drives are normal

↓

denial

Figure 3.1 The shared pathway of natural drives and drugs/alcohol leading to use as an "acquired drive."

1. Compulsive use of alcohol and drugs reflects an *acquired drive* involving the same brain circuits as natural drives such as thirst, hunger, or sex (Kreek & Koob, 1998). The same mesolimbocortical pathways mediate both the urge for, and the reinforcement from, drugs and alcohol as well as natural drives. Just as satisfaction for natural drives seems normal, seeking satisfaction from alcohol or drugs comes to seem "normal," and the inappropriateness of drug-seeking behavior is no longer appreciated.

2. Use of alcohol and drugs *depresses the frontal lobes (hypofrontality*; Goldstein & Volkow, 2002). PET studies show the acute effects of psychoactive drugs on brain metabolism and mood (Volkow et al., 1999). As a result, profound behavioral changes occur—changes that typically are at variance with the person's usual standards and expectations. These behavioral changes include decreased control of impulses, failure to delay gratification, and failure to anticipate the consequences of actions. The inevitable conflict between these impaired drug- and alcohol-driven behavioral patterns and what the user, as well as others, expect results in guilt, shame, and feelings of worthlessness in the chemically dependent person. These painfully negative emotions are managed not by constructive changes but by the mental defense of denial.

3. The dependence on alcohol or drugs *impacts thinking* (cognitive processes) just as it impacts behavior. These changes, however, are subtle. The cognitive changes constitute psychological dependence (as opposed to physical dependence, which is manifested by tolerance and withdrawal symptoms) and can be outlined as follows:

- *Inability to abstain* ("I can't quit"). Chemically dependent patients have a fear that they won't be able to quit. They have tried before and it did not work. If they keep drinking or drugging, they know (because it has been pointed out to them many times) that worse problems lie ahead: divorce, disease, jail, even death. Their situation is hopeless if they can't quit; their only hope for a healthy life is to quit. But the disease of alcoholism or addiction has, by now, impressed them sufficiently to believe that they cannot quit, and they feel hopeless. This is a very painful emotional state, and relief would be welcomed. The relief arrives in the form of denial and other possible defenses (e.g., rationalizations, blaming of others). "If it's not as bad as they are saying, then I really don't have to quit (and am spared the fearful possibility that I *can't* quit)."

  As physicians and clinicians we help these individuals realize that their fear (usually not consciously acknowledged) is unfounded as we build a treatment plan for staying sober and drug free—"one day at a time." Each sober day makes a lie out of the withering fear that "I can't quit."

• *Self-doubt* ("I can't cope without alcohol or drugs"). Chemically dependent individuals have come to believe that, without drugs or alcohol, daily misery is assured—not simply the distress of withdrawal symptoms but the more enduring pain of anxiety, depression, disappointment, guilt, shame, failure, and so on. Their confidence in coping has been eroded by the chronic boost from alcohol and drugs. Having to cope with or tolerate painful feelings and circumstances without a drug or alcohol seems too difficult. Alcohol and drugs have been faithful companions.

Our job as physicians and clinicians is to assist these patients in regaining confidence in their capacity to cope without intoxicants. Sometimes this capacity may need bolstering from antidepressants or antianxiety medication, but it always requires a supportive, encouraging, and tolerant attitude from professionals.

• *Fear of loss* ("Alcohol is my best friend"). Chemically dependent people fear that living without alcohol or drugs will be boring or monotonous. It seems unfair—they expect to be excluded, to be left out of the fun, to be deprived of sophisticated experiences. The feelings of loss and grief about giving up alcohol or drugs highlight the influence such chemicals exert on individuals' perceptions and emotions. With time the "loss" of intoxication is replaced with subtler but enduring daily pleasures.

As physicians and clinicians we can reassure these patients that the initial feelings of deprivation will wane and the rewards of better health and improved relationships will emerge.

• *Priority problem*. Chemically dependent patients have lived in a miasma of conflicting priorities. The desire and need for drugs takes precedence over social and occupational goals. Early in the course of alcoholism, for example, individuals are concerned about whether a few drinks at lunch will interfere with their completing the afternoon schedule; later, their concern focuses on whether their schedule will interfere with getting a drink. Put simply, using the drug becomes increasingly compelling and acquires priority over family, occupation, or social responsibilities. This shift in priorities does not take place without an emotional price. Shame, guilt, and feelings of worthlessness accompany this process. Now dependent on the drug, these individuals sense how they have changed—and if they have any doubts, there are always those rebukes from those who depend on them. Figure 3.2 summarizes how the experience of drug or alcohol dependence affects self-esteem (Nace, 1987).

As physicians and clinicians we can point out to addicted patients that the changes in their behavior and priorities are a function of the disease of addiction and not of their basic values. Fear of inability to abstain, self-doubt, sense of loss, and the priority or primacy given the addicting substance all constitute psychological dependence. Because of this dependence, the person experiences a growing sense of helplessness and hopelessness if the substance is not available. As we understand the origins and utility of denial for individuals with an addiction, we can then help them to overcome this process.

Another characteristic of human (and animal) behavior is worthy of consideration in our efforts to better understand the behavior of the addicted individual. It is well established that processes that "pay off" quickly (e.g., the

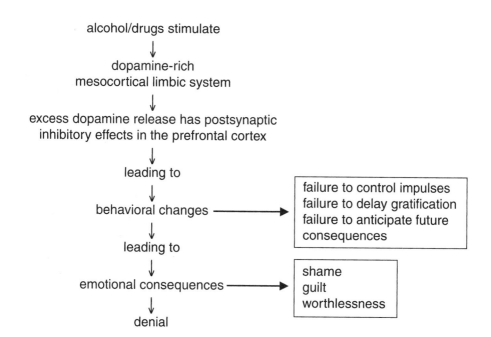

Figure 3.2 The behavioral chain of effects from alcohol/drug addiction to shame, guilt, and worthlessness.

euphoria of a drug) tend to be more compelling and therefore more difficult to resist than more enduring but slower-paying processes (e.g., sobriety; Ainslie, 2001). This principle helps to account for the failure of "will power" so commonly observed in addictions. Patients can benefit from appreciating this behavioral principle in the sense that "forewarned is forearmed." Avoidance of the quick payoff may be achieved by physically avoiding the reward; making cognitive efforts not to think about it; attempting to reverse the emotional valence of the reward (e.g., becoming repulsed by the sight of alcohol); or by turning a choice into a personal rule (i.e., the refusal of a drink is linked to the grander concept of personal sobriety; Ainslie, 2001).

Addressing Denial

What can be done about denial? We see its effects on the patients—a disavowal of the problem, the need to change, or the need for help. We may experience its effects, as well, when we become frustrated, impatient, or angry as the patient discounts our diagnosis, concern, or recommendations. We prefer to avoid these emotional tensions in our interactions with patients. In fact, one way to avoid these tensions is to not "see" (or to overlook) evidence of a substance use disorder, or, if seen, assume we can't do much about it and therefore avoid the expenditure of energy involved in identification, diagnosis, and assessment. Is there any way out of this ineffective pattern?

Clearly, action on the clinician's part is necessary. Two approaches can be taken. First, *denial must be directly challenged by the facts*. That is, the behavioral changes observed must be made explicit. For example, "You said you were going to have one glass of wine at the reception, but you were drunk before dinner started" (loss of control); "I came home last week and the kids hadn't had dinner. They said you were sick, and I found you in bed with a bottle of vodka on the floor" (value conflict). The confrontation can be conducted by family members, possibly with the help of their physician or a substance abuse counselor, and may involve friends or significant people in the chemically dependent individual's life. Each participant writes down his or her observations and directly, but kindly, presents these realities to the chemically dependent person. This process clearly points out to the alcoholic person the consequences of his or her drinking, and will frequently weaken the patient's denial system. As a result of this lowering of defenses, the capacity to rationally accept the need for help arises. Recommendations for evaluation and treatment should be prepared in advance and implemented as soon as possible—often the same day.

The second approach is to *establish hope that change is possible*. This is accomplished by demonstrating that the cognitive changes that create the state of psychological dependence (Figure 3.3) are manifestations of the chemical dependency and do not reflect the individual's abilities or the reality of their everyday existence. For example, each day that the chemically dependent person does not drink or drug but puts up with stress, frustration, disappointment, or other painful feelings demonstrates that his or her doubts about coping without the crutch of a drug are not well founded. Similarly, each day that the person does not drink or drug but experiences satisfaction, pleasure, contentment, or other positive experiences indicates that the sense of loss expected with abstinence will be transitory. Similarly, the fear of not being able to quit will gradually diminish as the person learns to abstain one day at a time.

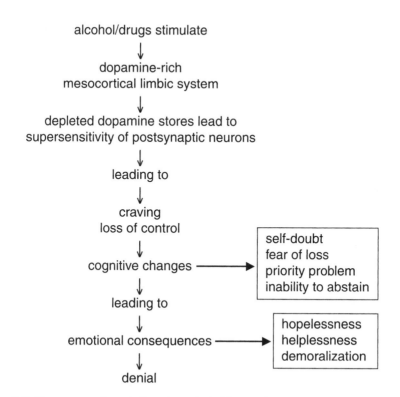

Figure 3.3 The cognitive chain of effects from alcohol/drug addiction to hopelessness, helplessness, and demoralization.

In summary, our obligation as physicians and clinicians is to confront the chemically dependent patient with the facts of his or her dependency— medical findings, family problems, work, or legal consequences. Simultaneously, we explain that addiction is a treatable disease, and that we can help the person get started. This two-pronged approach—reality-based and hope-focused—tells the patient that you know what's going on with him or her (therefore, the patient is less likely to try to deny the problem with you) and that you will help him or her turn this problem around.

How Much Does the Patient Know?

To return to the question at the center of this chapter: "Does the patient know that something is wrong?" Yes, the patient does know that something is wrong. However, there are varying degrees of clarity as to what is wrong. For example:

- The patient fully knows that she is an alcoholic, recognizes her need for alcohol, doesn't know what to do about it, hopes to hide it or hopes it will go away (i.e., return to previous benign social drinking). Also, she has a fear of being found out and is ashamed of being in this condition.
- The patient knows that he is using "extra" hydrocodone and more alprazolam than was prescribed. He recognizes that he takes these pills even before pain or tension is apparent. But they've been prescribed by a doctor, and the back pain is still there. He needs relief and he needs sleep. It's not right to be getting these from more than one doctor, but he has to be able to function. He doesn't like worrying about keeping a supply of pills available, and he feels bad about how irritable he becomes with his family if the medicine is not there.
- The patient is angry—tired of his wife's complaining about him, especially if he drinks. She's turned the kids against him. There is no problem! He could cut back if he wanted to. Why bother if everyone is going to accuse him of drinking anyway. Besides, the hassles he has to put up with every day entitle him to a time-out.

Whether the awareness is clear or clouded by rationalization and denial, patients with chemical dependency are troubled by what is happening. As we know, they often are troubled at first by the response they receive from others about their use of alcohol or drugs. Even when patients present with such a superficial attitude, our exploration of changes in the quantity of use, when they use, how often they use, the effects of not using (e.g., withdrawal symptoms), and the effects of using (e.g., accidents, arguments, poor health) will reveal that they are uneasy about the impact of alcohol or drugs on their lives. If, at first, they express concern that you, as a clinician, are putting too much emphasis on alcohol or drugs, they will eventually come around to respect and appreciate your persistent attention and be relieved that they have someone to whom they can talk about drinking or drug use.

With these points in mind, we can now explore the steps involved in identifying the problem and making and presenting a diagnosis.

Part II

Diagnostic and Treatment Issues

Steps to Identification

Highlights

• Being alert to the possibility of a substance use disorder in patients is a first step in identification.

• Screening questionnaires can help identify patients with substance use disorders.

• There are clues that point to substance abuse as a problem in a patient's history, physical exam, laboratory data, and family interviews.

• Family members typically want to be helpful; however, they may unintentionally perpetuate the addiction.

• Family members can also function as detectives in identifying the substance use problem.

• Family members also need to take steps to care for their own well-being.

Physician as Detective

In advanced cases of alcohol and drug dependence, the diagnosis is painfully clear. There is no doubt about the diagnosis of alcohol dependence in a patient with a history of multiple emergency room visits for intoxication who is finally admitted to the hospital for management of complicated alcohol withdrawal. Neither is there doubt that illicit drugs are central to the problems of the homeless patient who has track marks on his arms and legs. More often, however, substance abuse and dependence are not at all obvious. Physicians and other clinicians not trained to recognize substance abuse probably see, but do not recognize the significance of, subtle presentations of medical and psychiatric complaints that are related to the misuse of drugs or alcohol. Common alcohol-related symptoms that may stump the practitioner are gastrointestinal complaints, hypertension, insomnia, sexual dysfunction, depression, injuries, and anxiety.

A patient does not go to the doctor saying that he has dyspepsia because of his daily consumption of a six-pack of beer, or that she cannot sleep because of her longstanding habit of consuming several drinks in the evening. The patient may not think information about substance use is important. Because this crucial information is unlikely to come from patients unsolicited, the clinician needs to know when to suspect that symptoms are related to substance abuse. Case 1 illustrates a dramatic medical symptom. The physician

---

Case 1

Mr. A, a 43-year-old businessman, was referred for evaluation of a first-time seizure that occurred one evening after a family picnic. Several laboratory tests were abnormal (MCV = 102 fl; GGT = 92 U/L; LDL cholesterol = 256 mg/dl; triglycerides = 475 mg/dl). The day after the seizure, an electroencephalogram (EEG) and magnetic resonance imaging (MRI) of the brain were normal. The patient reported that he was a social drinker. The doctor spoke to the patient's wife who confided her concern about her husband's daily drinking, which tended to be greater on weekends. The patient was told that alcohol withdrawal was the most likely explanation for his seizure and that the recommendation was to discontinue all alcohol use. The physician encouraged the patient's wife to tell her husband what worried her about his drinking. In the presence of the physician, she was able to speak to her husband about the impact of the patient's drinking on their family. Mr. A decided to follow the recommendation to enter an outpatient alcohol treatment program.

---

suspected that alcohol caused the medical problem after laboratory data was obtained and collateral information was gathered.

Sometimes, as in Case 1, the physician must act as a sleuth, uncovering information that will solve a case. The physician knows that alcohol withdrawal is among the possible causes of seizure. She conducted a medically sound seizure workup and found that the only abnormal laboratory data were consistent with excessive alcohol use. In particular, the MCV, GGT, and serum triglycerides were abnormal. The patient's report was not consistent with the doctor's suspicion of a drinking problem; however, she knew that collateral information was an essential part of a thorough assessment. (If needed, please refer to the glossary for definitions of MCV and GGT.)

As shown in this section, alcohol can be considered a great imitator. The same may be said of drug use. Knowing about the simple and more complex symptoms that can result from substance use can raise the clinician's index of suspicion. When physicians screen patients who have nonspecific complaints in emergency departments, 20% of the patients are misusing alcohol. What good will this knowledge do? If offered a brief alcohol counseling session, patients may be drinking less alcohol 6 months later and will have fewer emergency department visits (Crawford, 2004).

History Clues: Ask and Ask Again

Routine history taking should include questions about patients' habits of using caffeine, tobacco, alcohol, herbs, illicit drugs, and prescription as well as nonprescription medications. When patients report that they do not drink or that they do not drink any longer, it is a good idea to inquire as to why not. They may not drink because of a past alcohol problem or a family history of alcoholism. Or they may have given up alcohol very recently in response to a drinking incident, as illustrated in Case 2.

In this case, the clinician is aware that about three-fourths of the adults in the United States drink at least some alcohol. Religious affiliation and medical problems are common reasons people choose not to drink. However, abstinence may be due to problems that alcohol has caused in the patient or in family members. Useful information is sometimes gained when patients who do not drink are asked more about that decision, such as Ms. B in Case 2, who had struggled to quit because she had experienced negative consequences from drinking. Another good question to ask patients in the context of a substance use history is whether their significant others have problems with alcohol or drugs. This question may be an entry into the lifestyle of the couple.

Case 2

Ms. B was a 55-year-old divorced woman employed in clothing retail. She was undergoing an evaluation for depression. The psychiatrist asked about her use of alcohol. Ms. B said that she did not drink alcohol. The doctor then asked her if she had ever used alcohol. In answer to this question, Ms. B revealed that she had just given up drinking the previous week, in one of a number of recent attempts to stop drinking. She blamed her use of alcohol for the breakup of a 2-year relationship, because her boyfriend repeatedly complained about her negative attitude when she drank.

The National Institute on Alcohol Abuse and Alcoholism (NIAAA, 1995) advises physicians to ask all patients if they drink alcohol. If the patient's response is "yes," the NIAAA further advises clinicians to ask the follow-up questions in Table 4.1.

Table 4.1
Follow-up Questions for Alcohol Users

1. Has your family been concerned about your drinking?
2. Have you ever had a drinking problem?
3. Have you or anyone in your family ever had a drinking problem?
4. Has a doctor ever suggested that you stop drinking?
5. When did you last drink?
6. Do you feel a strong urge to drink?
7. Do you change your plans so that you can have a drink?
8. Are there times when you are unable to stop drinking once you have started?
9. Have you ever had a blackout?
10. Does it take more drinks than before to get high?

From NIAAA, 1995.

These suggested questions get at some of the common symptoms of alcohol dependence. The first four questions do not elicit defensiveness in most patients. For example, the first question, "Has your family been concerned about your drinking?", is seldom perceived as threatening because it focuses on other people. In answering that his wife worries about his drinking, a man might reason that it is she who has the flawed character because of a bias against the use of any alcohol. However, if loved ones have made their concerns known to the patient, it gives the interviewer information about the stress the patient's drinking has probably caused for those close to him or her. Perhaps surprisingly, patients often answer the second question accurately: "Have you ever had a drinking problem?" The words *have you ever had*, rather than the words *do you have*, allow the patient to look at the past, and the past is easier to discuss than the present. Question 3 on family history considers whether alcohol problems run in families. There may be a genetic vulnerability to alcoholism, such as that seen in men whose fathers are alcoholic and who are also at increased risk for alcohol dependence (Dick & Foroud, 2003). Or heavy drinking may have been a part of the family lifestyle. Question 4, "Has a doctor ever suggested that you stop drinking?", asks for a simple factual response. If a physician has told the patient to decrease or discontinue alcohol use, it is probably because there has been objective evidence of an alcohol-related health problem. If the patient failed to heed that advice, it may indicate an inability to abstain.

Questions 5–10 are more straightforward. Question 5 asks if the patient's last use of alcohol was within the past 24 hours; if yes, there is a high likelihood of an alcohol use disorder, especially if the patient feels that he or she has had a drinking problem in the past (Cyr & Wartman, 1988). Questions 6 and 7, "Do you feel a strong urge to drink?" and "Do you change your plans so that you can have a drink?", address the compulsion or preoccupation to drink. Positive responses indicate that the person thinks a great deal about drinking. Questions 8 and 9, "Are there times when you are unable to stop drinking once you have started?" and "Have you ever had a blackout?", address the issue of impaired control, which is one of the hallmarks of alcoholism and drug dependence. Blackouts are not the same as passing out, although drinking until one passes out is also a sign that one has lost control. A blackout is an amnestic episode caused by the consumption of too much alcohol. Blackouts can be quite frightening because people continue to function but do not remember what they have done. Unfortunately, a common example is a person driving home after a bout of drinking and not remembering how he or she got there.

The last question aims at information on tolerance. It can be difficult to determine whether a patient has become tolerant to alcohol, but question 10 is a solid attempt to do so: "Does it take more drinks than before to get high?" Tolerance is also an important symptom of drug dependence. Using slight modifications, the preceding questions can apply to drugs as well as they do to alcohol in the following areas: those related to family concerns, a past problem with drugs, family history, following a clinician's advice about discontinuing substances, the timing of one's last use, the presence of a strong urge to use, and losing control of one's use.

Some history-taking mistakes include (1) asking vague questions such as "Are you a normal drinker?"; (2) asking leading questions such as "You don't use marijuana, do you?"; (3) asking judgmental questions with an accusatory tone, such as "Are you an alcoholic?" (GAP, 1998). It is best to use an empathetic, nonjudgmental style that is based on concern about the patient's health. Such a style can be communicated through tone of voice. Weaving questions into the routine social or medication history is one way to help both patient and physician/clinician feel more comfortable about this line of questioning. This may be the same time questions about caffeine use, cigarette smoking, sleep hygiene, and sexual problems are asked.

It is medically important to quantify the amount of alcohol the drinker uses and the pattern of use. Although the diagnosis of alcohol abuse or dependence is determined by the individual's behavior when drinking rather than by the amount consumed, for many conditions there is a dose–response relationship between alcohol consumption and risk. The NIAAA recommends asking the following three questions:

1. How many days per week do you drink?
2. How many drinks do you have on a typical drinking day?
3. What is the maximum number of drinks you had on any given occasion during the last month?

NIAAA defines low-risk drinking as no more than two drinks per day for men and no more than one drink per day for women. Those older than 65 years should drink no more than one drink per day. Men who consume more than 14 drinks per week or 4 drinks per occasion and women who consume more than 7 drinks per week or 3 drinks per occasion are at risk for alcohol-related problems. Tables 4.2 and 4.3 summarize this information.

Screening Tools

Gathering a substance abuse history is difficult for many physicians and other clinicians. Some may consider it is too time consuming, embarrassing, or not pertinent to the patient's chief complaint. Some are poorly educated about substance use disorders and the response to treatment. However,

Table 4.2
Moderate Drinking Standards

	Men	Women	> 65 years
Drinks per day	0–2	0–1	0–1
Drinks per week	< 14	< 7	< 7
Drinks per occasion	1–4	1–3	1–2

From NIAAA, 1995.

Table 4.3
Definition of a Standard Drink

Type	Amount (ounces)
Liquor	1.5
Beer	12
Wine	5

From NIAAA, 2005.

there are others who firmly believe that substance abuse is their business but do not know how to address it. Here, predetermined questions can help. Because questions about quantity and frequency of alcohol use can make patients feel criticized, questionnaires typically focus on the consequences of the patient's use or on substance-using behaviors.

The CAGE questionnaire (Table 4.4; Mayfield et al., 1974) is an easy-to-use four-question screening tool most valuable for use with patients who have moderate to severe alcohol problems (Ewing, 1984). It has gained popularity because it is brief, can be included as part of the history, and it gives quick information about the likely severity of the patient's drinking. A score of 1 or 2 positive responses, occurring within the past year, indicates that the possibility of an alcohol problem needs to be explored. The patient has a very high likelihood of being alcohol dependent if there are three or four positive responses for the past year. This set of questions fits nicely into the history of patients' habits and guides the clinician toward a more complete assessment of a possible substance use disorder. An estimated 100 screening tests for substance abuse are in existence (Franklin & Francis, 1999). The CAGE has been a favorite since it was published more than 30 years ago. Its usefulness has not yet been surpassed.

Table 4.4
CAGE Screening Test for Alcoholism

Have you ever felt the need to **C**ut down on drinking?

Have you ever felt **A**nnoyed by criticism of your drinking?

Have you ever felt **G**uilty about your drinking?

Have you ever taken a morning **E**ye-opener?

Note: Two "yes" answers are considered a positive screen. One "yes" answer should raise a suspicion of alcohol abuse. Reprinted with permission from Mayfield et al., 1974.

The best screening tests to use with obstetrics patients who may be abusing substances are thought to be those that do not elicit guilt feelings. Some questionnaires have substituted inquiries about tolerance—the need for increasing amounts of alcohol over time—for questions that ask about guilt. One such screening test that was adapted from the CAGE is the T-ACE (*t*olerance, *a*nnoyed, *c*ut down, and *e*ye-opener). The only difference between the CAGE and the T-ACE is that the question about guilt is replaced by a simple question on tolerance: "How many drinks can you hold?" (Sokol, Martier, & Ager, 1989). The question about tolerance is thought to elicit less defensiveness than the question on guilt. Other examples of questions about tolerance include "How many drinks does it take to make you high?" and "Does it take more drinks than it used to take to get high?" A response that assumes tolerance in women is when more than two drinks are needed to feel the effects of alcohol (Secretary of Health and Human Services, 1997). The TWEAK (*t*olerance, *w*orry, *e*ye-opener, *a*mnesia, *k*ut) is another questionnaire for use in the obstetric population. Table 4.5 (Chan, Pristach, Welte, & Russell, 1993) includes a question on amnesia to indirectly ask about excessive use of alcohol per drinking episode.

Medical Clues

Medical symptoms that are red flags for alcohol-related toxicity include the typical suspects of liver disease and pancreatitis. Additionally, the medical review of symptoms may be positive for headaches or other forms of chronic pain, gastrointestinal complaints, memory and concentration concerns, depression and anxiety, sexual dysfunction, and insomnia.

Table 4.6 lists ailments that should alert the physician and other clinicians to the possibility of substance abuse. Fatty liver, cirrhosis, and pancreatitis

Table 4.5
TWEAK Screening Test for Alcoholism

1. How many drinks can you hold? (**T**olerance)

2. Does your spouse (or do your parents) ever **W**orry or complain about your drinking?

3. Have you ever had a drink first thing in the morning to steady your nerves or get rid of a hangover? (**E**ye-opener)

4. Have you ever awakened the morning after some drinking the night before and found that you could not remember a part of the evening before? (**A**mnesia)

5. Have you ever felt you ought to cut (**K**ut) down on your drinking?

Note: For positive answers to questions 1 and 2 score 2 points each, and for positive answers for questions 3, 4, and 5 score 1 point each. A score of 2 points or more is highly suggestive of an alcohol problem. Modified and reproduced with permission from Chan, Pristach, Welte, & Russell, 1993.

are known complications of alcoholism, whereas, hepatitis C is a common complication of intravenous drug abuse and unprotected sex. The risk of HIV is greatest in the IV drug user, though unprotected intercourse is a risk for anyone who is disinhibited from intoxication.

The medical examination is often normal in younger and healthier substance abuse patients. The medical examination of someone using illicit drugs is specific to the drug that is abused; yet there are often few telltale signs. There are the well-known needle tracks in IV drug users, and there may be

Table 4.6
Common Medical Problems Related to Substance Abuse

- Liver disease, including hepatitis C
- Pancreatitis
- Gastrointestinal distress
- Headaches
- Accidents/trauma (multiple emergency room visits)
- Insomnia
- Hypertension and stroke
- Depression and anxiety
- Sexual dysfunction
- HIV/AIDS

skin abscesses. Intranasal drug use may lead to irritated nasal mucosa. Marijuana can be irritating, causing pharyngitis or bronchitis in heavy smokers. In chronic alcohol or drug abuse, the patient may look older than the stated age, have poor dentition, or appear poorly nourished. In the chronic alcoholic, the physician may notice classic stigmata or facial flushing, acne rosacea, arcus senilis, spider angioma, palmar erythema, and bruising. The patient may be tremulous or show deteriorating self-care. Some patients sustain neurological sequelae such as stroke, neuropathies, brain damage with eventual dementia, or cerebellar dysfunction and gait abnormalities.

Excessive alcohol use is toxic to many organs. Abnormal laboratory values may be the reason the physician initially suspects an alcohol-related disorder. Elevations in the mean corpuscular volume, triglycerides, uric acid, and liver function tests are common. Of the laboratory tests that are abnormal, those reflecting liver damage are the most clinically useful. The most commonly used liver function tests include serum aminotransferases (two types, AST, ALT) and serum gamma-glutamyltransferase (GGT). Of these, the GGT is the most useful in detecting excessive alcohol use. The difficulty with most laboratory markers is their relatively low sensitivities, meaning many cases will be missed. GGT has a sensitivity of about 50% (Bean & Daniel, 1996), meaning that half of the patients with drinking problems are missed. Low specificity is also a problem, meaning that many patients with elevated GGT values will not abuse alcohol. Because the GGT is not very specific, other reasons for its elevation need to be eliminated. GGT is not part of a routine lab panel and must be ordered specifically when the physician wants it.

Carbohydrate-deficient transferrin (CDT), which is synthesized in the liver, is a biological marker that has been studied since 1976. Put simply, serum transferrin is a glycoprotein that has two binding sites for iron. Normally, carbohydrates attach to transferrin; however, heavy alcohol use disturbs the addition of carbohydrates. Consuming more than 60 grams (about four to five drinks) of alcohol daily for 2 weeks will increase CDT. During abstinence the CDT normalizes in 2–4 weeks (Allen & Anthenelli, 2003). CDT has an advantage of being less affected than GGT by other causes of liver disease; therefore, it is a more specific test for excessive drinking. CDT may also have greater sensitivity than GGT in some populations (Sillanauber, 1996). Its performance is reported to be better when it is combined with the MCV (mean corpuscular volume) or GGT. CDT appears most helpful in identifying heavy drinking in men over 35 and in those who are in recovery but have relapsed. Parameters of its usefulness in other populations continue to be studied. Because of expense and the limited capability of some laboratories, its routine use has been hindered. Some clinicians are able to use it routinely. A combination of abnormal laboratory findings that suggest organ toxicity related to alcohol should make the clinician even more suspicious of an alcohol use disorder.

The laboratory tests routinely used to detect drugs remain simple. Urine drug screens are the mainstay in identifying use or documenting recovery. Although hair analysis and sweat testing are available, they are limited to specific settings. The National Institute on Drug Abuse National Laboratory Certification Program requires that a laboratory be able to test for amphetamines, cannabinoids, cocaine, opioids, and phencyclidine (PCP). Such laboratories are capable of also testing for barbiturates, benzodiazepines, methadone, propoxyphene, methaqualone, and ethanol. Laboratories set up their "drug screen panel" but may test for additional substances, if requested. The interpretation of results depends on when the test was ordered in relation to the patient's last use of the drug. For instance, cocaine and its metabolites are detectable for only 2–4 days. On the other hand, a heavy cannabis user may have a positive test for up to 1 month after the last use. In high-stake situations positive results found through laboratory screening should be confirmed by more sophisticated and more expensive gas chromatography–mass spectrometry. Testing for ethylglucuronide (ETG) has become widely available as a qualitative urine test for ethyl alcohol. ETG is a byproduct of ethanol metabolism and a sensitive marker of even a small amount of alcohol ingestion. It may be present in the urine for 2–3 days after alcohol intake, which is longer than the presence of ethyl alcohol. Common abnormal laboratory findings are summarized in Table 4.7.

Table 4.7
Common Abnormal Laboratory Findings in Drug Abusers

- Mean corpuscular volume (MCV) > 95
- Elevated gamma-glutamyltransferase (GGT)
- Elevation of carbohydrate-deficient transferrin (CDT)
- Elevated triglycerides
- Positive breathalyzer
- Positive urine drug screen
- Positive urinary ETG

Emotional Clues

The mental health professional who is not a physician should also be alert to signals of substance abuse. Nonphysicians are likely to hear about headaches, insomnia, and depression. Alcohol is a common cause of chronic headaches. Hangovers immediately come to mind as well-known sources of headache, nausea, and malaise. Hangovers are believed to be an effect of dehydration and of acetaldehyde, the primary metabolic product of alcohol. Despite this being a centuries' old side effect of heavy drinking, it is a toxicity for which there is no reliable remedy. Alcohol is also a common trigger for migraines and vascular headaches. In addition, intermittent bouts of dehydration and hypoglycemia that result from binge drinking (when people fail to take in enough water and calories) are causative agents in alcohol-related headaches.

The relationship between insomnia and alcohol is complex. Although alcohol can cause insomnia, some drink to treat their insomnia. This is an explainable paradox. Alcohol is a sedative; however, it wears off after a few hours, causing minor withdrawal and subsequent wakefulness. A similar paradox occurs with depression and anxiety: Alcohol initially causes euphoria, but its later depressant effects predominate. Likewise, alcohol can feel relaxing until it wears off, leaving the person anxious. For some people, chronic drinking results in chronic depression and anxiety.

As Case 3 illustrates, the abuse of substances other than alcohol can cause symptoms not immediately attributed to intoxication.

In this case the patient is an older woman who is not viewed as a likely substance abuser. Her psychiatrist and primary care physician have a low index of

---

Case 3

Sixty-five-year-old Mrs. C was being seen in a psychiatric clinic for longstanding depression and anxiety. For a decade her primary care physician had treated her chronic daily headaches with Fiorinal, a combination of acetaminophen and barbiturate. Over the past year the patient had experienced a series of falls. After being hospitalized for a broken hip, she finally told her psychiatrist that, in addition to her prescription doses for Fiorinal, she had also been obtaining Fiorinal from a friend and was using much more than prescribed. Her frequent falling was due to episodic Fiorinal intoxication.

suspicion that substance abuse plays a role in the chronic nature of her problems. In patients with chronic or treatment-resistant depression, substance abuse should always be considered. As more information surfaced, it was apparent that the patient was medicating her emotions with sedative-containing headache medication. Finally, not enough attention was given to the patient's trauma history. It required a very serious fall for the patient to request help with her medication use. Had the physicians requested to speak to the patient's family about the chronic nature of her symptoms, they would have learned the family's suspicion that Mrs. C was taking too much medication.

Repeated trauma is a red flag for substance abuse of all types. Most types of violence are associated with substance use or abuse. Domestic violence, including date rape, often occurs in the context of alcohol or drug use. The same is true of homicides and suicides. Motor vehicle accidents seem to occur more frequently in the cannabis abuser because of a distorted sense of time. Hypertension and stroke are not only a problem for the older male alcoholic who is obese and sedentary; stroke can also occur with cocaine use. In most psychiatric disorders, screening for substance use should be routine.

The relationship of alcohol or drugs to psychiatric symptoms can be complex. Alcohol and drug dependence frequently coexist with psychiatric disorders to produce mood instability, anxiety, irritability, impulsivity, or psychosis. The following relationships are common ones.

1. Patients self-medicate a psychiatric disorder with substances. Mrs. C suffered from depression and anxiety. She initially took a sedative-containing medication only for headaches; however, she soon learned that the medication also helped her anxiety. Therefore, she began self-medicating her anxiety with the headache medication.
2. Psychiatric symptoms may develop because of the direct effect of alcohol or drugs. For instance, a patient who has three drinks every night sees a doctor with symptoms of insomnia and fatigue. As discussed earlier in the chapter, alcohol is a common cause of insomnia.
3. Problems that are the result of using drugs or alcohol lead to distress. Consider a patient who feels distraught when his wife starts divorce proceedings because he has bankrupted the family through his cocaine purchases.
4. Substance dependence and other psychiatric disorders may occur independently.

General life chaos is a red flag for substance abuse in the patient or in the patient's significant other. In addition to putting individuals at physical risk, substance abuse is commonly accompanied by disorder in the marriage, family, finances, legal history, or job. Chaos may take the form of frequent moves, an unstable work history, and "burning bridges" with friends and family. Relationships with significant others may prove difficult to maintain as drinking or drug use lead to loss of control. Finances may suffer, depending on the socioeconomic status of the patient. Legal issues often involve convictions for driving under the influence (DUI), disorderly conduct, or domestic violence. Jobs are preserved if at all possible; however, absenteeism is common. One should suspect substance abuse when a lifestyle is characterized by relationship, legal, occupational, or emotional instability.

The patient may not directly relate these difficulties to substance use because of denial or because of a willful decision to hide the problem. He or she may blame others for all the problems, refusing to accept that substance abuse is at the root of the trouble. The way in which the substance abuser can externalize his or her problems is both curious and frustrating. Case 4 is an example of this mental process. Here the patient blamed law enforcement for his legal problem, rather than accept responsibility for breaking the law.

In the mind of this patient, it was a case of bad luck that he was stopped for a minor vehicular offense, that the officer administered the breathalyzer test, and that it registered above the legal limit. Using the defense of rationalization, the patient externalized his legal problems by claiming bad luck and an unfair system. Others easily saw that his argument failed to take into consideration the well-established dangerousness of drinking alcohol while driving. Instead of taking responsibility for his actions, he defended his drinking by blaming others and focusing on a technicality.

Case 4

Mr. D was an unemployed divorced man in a treatment program for alcohol dependence. He was referred to the program because of a third DUI conviction. He said he was being unfairly treated because his most recent arrest was made after he was stopped for driving a car with a broken taillight. He argued that he should not have been charged with DUI because the broken taillight was the identified problem, and he was not stopped because of an offense directly related to intoxication.

Collateral Clues

The patient may not feel it is in his or her best interest to be frank in an interview that focuses on his or her substance use. Important points in the history may be left out, or the patient simply may not see drinking and its consequences in the way others do. Collateral information is therefore an essential part of the substance abuse evaluation. The most common sources of collateral information are family members and significant others. In addition, health care providers, social services workers, parole officers, lawyers, employers, and friends can help provide perspectives on the patient's substance use if the patient consents. In the cases of adolescents, school personnel and (in some situations) foster parents or guardians are essential informants. Obtaining this collateral information helps the doctor or clinician understand the extent of the problem and adds another tool for providing feedback to the patient. Sometimes family members consciously or unconsciously collude with the patient in keeping substance abuse hidden. This collusion may be prompted by a shared drinking problem, a desire to protect the patient, or similar denial about the patient's alcohol dependence and its consequences. Denial in a family member may serve the same function for the family member as it serves for the patient: to survive what seems like an insurmountable situation. The loved one's failure to recognize the problem and the accompanying resistance to change is referred to as *codependence* (Shaef, 1986).

A spouse who is codependent often has developed an exaggerated sense of responsibility, may have become isolated from others outside the family, and may have come to view abusive behavior and untruthful cover-ups as a normal way to live. In order for the marriage or family to survive, the spouse may have adopted some of the patient's beliefs. For instance, a wife may agree with her alcoholic husband that he drinks because he is under too much stress at work. She may even believe that if she were a better wife, he would be different. Though unhealthy and at worst deadly, this line of thinking preserves a way of life that has become familiar. Commonly, codependent family members enable the addictive behaviors of their family members. *Enabling* refers to actions that seem helpful but actually perpetuate the cycle of addiction. See Table 4.8 for examples of common enabling behavior.

Finally, examples of codependent behavior include taking care of the loved one when that person is ill or passed out from heavy drinking; calling the workplace on Monday morning to report that the patient is ill; and col-

Table 4.8
Common Examples of Enabling Behavior

- Assuming responsibilities that are the responsibility of the addicted person
- Making threats from which one later backs down
- Adjusting one's schedule in the hope of controlling the addict's use
- Canceling plans, vacations, etc. in order to take care of, or watch over, the addict
- Lying to children, relatives, friends
- Lecturing, nagging, or whining at the addicted family members

luding in other such cover-ups to avoid embarrassment for the entire family. Codependent members of the family may attribute the patient's problem almost entirely to a coexisting physical or mental illness, stress, personality characteristics, disillusionment, or phase of life, such as young adulthood or aging. At times the family's resistance may be consciously motivated by fear that the patient will lose employment or have to face legal consequences. Case 5 illustrates this bind.

In this scenario the patient and his spouse may have felt the need to protect their livelihood. This is a case that can be difficult to assess through his-

Case 5

Dr. D was referred for an evaluation of prescription drug use after someone from the hospital where he practiced contacted the State Medical Licensing Board. There was concern that on a number of occasions Dr. D had not been able to function at work because he was sluggish and did not seem to be thinking clearly. Dr. D reported taking the prescription narcotic Oxycontin three times daily, as prescribed by his doctor for chronic low back pain. He also admitted to a longstanding habit of drinking three glasses of wine with dinner every evening. Mrs. D said that her husband had no problem handling his pain medications and that he never drank irresponsibly. In fact, she had never seen him drunk. She reported that his back pain made him too ill to work on some occasions and his colleagues resented covering for him. Her hypothesis was that a colleague had turned him in out of revenge. She also doubted that people understood how serious back pain could be.

tory alone. Permission to seek other information through the patient's adult children, colleagues, physician, and pharmacist may be necessary to conduct a thorough evaluation. Discrepancies and inconsistencies in the pattern of use may give further clues about where the truth lies. Laboratory data for alcohol-related toxicity may help, along with a urine drug screen that can be quantified. Such a situation is particularly challenging because the family may purposely lead the care provider astray to protect the patient and the family's financial stability.

In most situations there is not an intentional collusion between the substance abuser and the family members. Education, therapy, or self-help groups such as Al-Anon are often very beneficial to family members. Most spouses and children of alcoholics or drug addicts want to be helpful in the patient's treatment. Typically, the family does provide important information about the patient's using behavior and the effect it has on the family's dynamics. Nonjudgmental questions may also be effective when talking to the significant other. Such questions focus on the substance abuser's behavior and the concern using may have caused. For example, good questions to ask collateral sources who have frequent contact with the patient include the following:

- "Does the patient's personality change while using?"
- "Has anyone been concerned or embarrassed about the use?"
- "Have you or others been uncomfortable about your safety in circumstances such as riding in a car when the patient has been driving after having drinks?"

Once recovery begins, a family often faces further adjustments. During active addiction, there is the reality that someone has to take care of business for the family. The substance-abusing member of a family is often unable to be a leader or partner in making decisions, and life has a way of going on despite the ill member. Sometimes this prior pattern creates an added dimension in the recovery process. For example, the spouse of the formerly addicted husband or wife may not easily relinquish control of some areas that he or she had to assume. Resentment about past behaviors can linger, with distance and uncertainty common accompaniments. Family members typically wonder, "Is it safe to have hope that recovery will continue or will we be let down once again?" The use of professional counseling, Alcoholics Anonymous (AA), Narcotics Anonymous (NA), and Al-Anon can assist a family with the struggles of readjustment that are common to early recovery.

The health care provider can play an important role in uncovering a substance abuse problem by knowing its many manifestations and which questions are most likely to elicit meaningful answers from the patient and significant others, by utilizing a questionnaires, and by following up on the disease over time.

Some physicians and other clinicians may not know how to interpret information about patients' illicit drug use. Does the use of any illicit substance constitute substance abuse on the basis of the substance's illegal status? The next chapter covers the diagnostic criteria for substance use disorders from the American Psychiatric Association's *Diagnostic and Statistical Manual of Mental Disorders* (IV-TR). According to those criteria, in adults the type of substance does not make a difference to diagnosis. Someone who occasionally uses an illegal drug is not necessarily abusing that substance, though he or she is taking a risk with the legal system. Even though the use of some drugs does not meet the accepted clinical threshold for abuse or dependence, some drugs are so highly addictive that it is prudent to discuss their risks with anyone who has tried them. Examples include heroin and crack cocaine. In these examples, it is not only the drug that is dangerous but also the route of administration. Heroin and cocaine are highly addictive. As well, intravenous use of drugs and smoking drugs are fast means of becoming addicted. Intravenous drugs directly enter the veins, are carried to the heart, and then distributed throughout the bloodstream. Inhaled drugs enter the lungs, where they have rapid access to the heart and the rest of the bloodstream. By contrast, there is more gradual absorption of intranasally and orally ingested drugs.

Mental Health Professionals as Detectives

The physician has the tools of the medical history, physical examination, and laboratory data to aid in the discovery of information that will help formulate the diagnosis and treatment plan. Although clinicians who are not medical doctors do not use those particular resources, they do have effective tools with which to identify and treat the problem. Likewise, family members can be resourceful investigators.

The mental health professional should conduct a thorough history that includes substance use history—that is, a current assessment of use, a past substance use history, and a family history. Inserting the CAGE questions into the history is a good way to introduce substance use questions. In terms of history clues, clinicians who are not doctors can also use the NIAAA recommended follow-up questions (see Table 4.1). If there is a current problem with substances, it is valuable to find out when the use of each particular substance began; if there was a period of time the substance was used every day, the approximate amount of substance the individual used, and the problems the use caused. It is also important to ask if the use was oral, nasal, or intravenous. There are several red flags to keep in mind. If a client is not getting better, one reason might be that he or she is abusing substances. In some cases, adding a urine drug screen and meeting with a significant other may prove enlightening. As noted previously, other red flags include the presence of domestic unrest or violence, unexplained trauma, multiple trips to the emergency department, or a motor vehicle accident. Clients with lives filled with general chaos are also at risk for substance abuse or may be steeped in chaos because they abuse substances.

It is easy to collude with the patient in his or her denial about using alcohol or drugs as a means of coping during stressful times. Saying nothing about this unhealthy tactic is a way of condoning it. Unfortunately, it can be difficult to confront patients who seem fragile or are irritable or protective of their use. However, these are patients who need help finding healthier ways of coping. If someone is already in recovery, any clinician is in a good position to periodically check in with him or her about how recovery is going. Find out the recovery program the individual is following; if there is none, find out why not. No therapist intends to enable detrimental behavior; however, substance abusers are practiced in the art of concealment. They are so good at camouflaging their addiction that they often fool themselves by minimizing the amount they use and the toll it takes. It is critical to remember that substance abuse is more prevalent in some psychiatric disorders; patients with antisocial personality disorder, borderline personality disorder, bipolar disorder, and schizophrenia are particularly vulnerable. In patients with one substance dependence, another is often present. Furthermore, patients with conditions such as pathological gambling and bulimia also seem prone to abuse alcohol and drugs.

Ideally, the clinician should refer the client if he or she does not have the expertise to handle the drug or alcohol problem. This need for referral is not always apparent at the outset, however. Clinicians can learn more about substance dependence problems through many resources. One resource that is free of charge is the National Institutes of Health, specifically the branches of the NIAAA and the National Institute on Drug Abuse (NIDA). These websites have much to offer. In addition, see Table 4.9 for suggestions mental health professionals can use to detect substance use disorders.

Table 4.9
Suggestions for Detection of Substance Use Disorders

- Add CAGE questions to evaluation.
- Consider substance use if treatment resistance is a problem.
- Talk to significant others if you have suspicions about a possible substance use problem.
- Watch for signs of violence, trauma, or chaotic lifestyles.
- Consider the psychiatric diagnosis of the client and its potential association with a substance use disorder.

Families and Friends as Detectives

The families and close friends of those who are dependent on alcohol and drugs often experience deep and lasting wounds. The most vulnerable are usually those in closest proximity to the substance abuser. Whereas adult parents, siblings, and friends are deeply saddened to see the self-destructive nature of addiction in a loved one, they generally have a choice about how much to be involved. If they choose, they have the capacity to go about their daily lives. However, the children and the spouse may not have such freedom, and they are sometimes irrevocably damaged. Movements such as Al-Anon and other self-help groups, such as Adult Children of Alcoholics, attest to the severe impact addiction can have on the family and the family's need for support.

The detective work for the family is often different from that of the clinician. For family, it is less often a question of what the problem is than of what to do about it. Of course, there are times when the family does not know what is wrong. In such situations there is a range of not knowing, from having no idea to praying it is not true. Either way, when it is apparent that something is amiss, it is nearly always appropriate to discuss those concerns with the individual. If there is trepidation about having such as discussion, talking it over with a professional is a recommended first step. Starting with a medical evaluation, for example, is a sound strategy. However, it is necessary to tell the physician about the family's behavioral concerns. If there is a past problem with substance use or with any mental health issue, the physician should know about it. If a psychiatrist is available, it is reasonable to start with a psychiatric evaluation, especially when the past history is suggestive of a behavioral problem.

Drug or alcohol problems are almost always signaled in some way. The age of the person is important in relation to the behavior of concern. In the adolescent, there may be a marked change in behavior. Although many teens exhibit periodic moodiness or irritability, parents often continue to recognize their son or daughter underneath the exaggerated affect. The parents also usually know the types of issues the child finds troublesome, such as rejection or failure. Changes in behavior that may indicate substance abuse include marked anger or irritability, sleeping a great deal, a global decline in grades, different friends and activities, breaking rules such as curfew, and cutting classes. The diagnosis may not be substance abuse; however, an adolescent who shows such signs and symptoms does need a professional evaluation. Because of the heightened risk for adolescents who abuse substances or who have a psychiatric illness, it is crucial to get assistance if there is any question about what may be going wrong with the teenager.

The questions noted in the previous tables can be asked by family members. In addition, consider the pattern of using drugs or alcohol. Has there been an increase in the quantity or frequency of use? Does the person use alcohol or drugs before or during school or work? Are there signs the person is losing control of his or her substance use? Examples of loss of control may be drinking before a social gathering at which alcohol will be served, drinking to the point of passing out, or experiencing loss of memory after drinking. Becoming obnoxious when using indicates overindulgence.

Another area of concern is whether the person has compromised his or her values in favor of substance use. For instance, a previously law-abiding person sells cocaine in order to finance a cocaine habit. Or perhaps the person's priorities have shifted, such as the individual who is too ill the day after "partying" to go to work (this is most likely to occur on a Monday). A problem or a beginning problem may be characterized by excessive use on a daily basis, using in inappropriate situations, or using to deal with stress. The following behaviors are often seen in alcoholic drinking:

- Impulsive drinking
- Larger than standard drink size
- Gulping drinks, especially the first drink
- Drinking alone
- Hiding bottles
- Tremors in the mornings
- Remembering the good times associated with drinking and having trouble recalling the problems

When it is clear that substance use is the problem, it is best to deal with it as soon as possible. Yet bad situations often linger. There are many reasons people stay stuck, and there are different points at which individuals decide to get help. One reason people are anxious about confronting a substance user regarding his or her use is that attempting to separate a substance abuser from his or her substance involves risk. The most common risk is that the family member doing the confronting may learn that, given a choice between the continued use of substances and remaining in a close relationship, drugs and alcohol are the priority. The more entrenched the problem, the greater that risk. On the other hand, when placed in such a position the addict may ultimately choose to remain with family. The dilemma for the addict can be expressed as: "The decision to give up the substance is made when the pain of not stopping is greater than the pain of stopping."

There are two issues for family members: The first is how to encourage the ill member of the family to get help, and the second involves getting help for themselves. The addict is most likely to be receptive to help during a crisis. Perhaps there is a legal problem; for instance, a charge of disorderly conduct while drinking with buddies, which was highly embarrassing. Or perhaps there is lost employment because of using on the job. Sometimes crises are precipitated, such as when a spouse threatens separation (though it is not recommended that a spouse make an idle threat). When the addict wants help, there are several avenues available:

- The individual's personal physician can provide a referral to an addiction specialist.
- The local mental health facility is also a good resource.
- In most communities AA or NA are available.
- For the individual with a serious addiction, the safest option is to get advice about a formal treatment program from a professional who specializes in addictions.
- An evaluation for psychiatric disorders is also important, because psychiatric comorbidity is common.

How can family members encourage a loved one to get help? The first step is to ask the person to get help. A discussion can be initiated by choosing a calm time and place. Avoid a time when either party has had alcohol or drugs. It is best to bring up concrete examples of the objections to the substance use. The next step (it is unlikely that the person will decide to give up after one discussion) depends on the way the message was received. Several discussions will probably be needed. Sometimes it is helpful to get other family members or a trusted member of the clergy involved. If the person is willing to see the family doctor, the neutrality of a medical setting can provide a good opportunity to intervene. Lastly, perhaps there is a friend or family member who will take the person to AA or NA.

When all offers of help are rejected, there may not be any further recourse in relation to the addict. A first step in getting assistance for *oneself*, however, is deciding not to live a secret life. When one of the parents in a household is dependent on drugs or alcohol, the family may take a paranoid stance as a means of maintaining the status quo. Secrecy is an awful burden, and one that perpetuates itself. To break through the pall of secrecy, tell trusted family, friends, or a religious leader about the situation. If the one-on-one format is threatening, try an anonymous group format: Self-help groups such as Al-Anon have helped many people deal with adult family members. Al-Anon is a 12-step program, free of charge, in which stories of family members can be uncanny in their similarity. Sometimes choosing individual sessions with a therapist can open the door to help; this option can be especially effective when the person comes from a substance-dependent family of origin and then marries an alcoholic or drug addict.

Determining whether a person abuses drugs or alcohol is worth the effort. Taking the next step to help the person get into a recovery program can be difficult. However, it may change or even save lives. Addiction is a serious, often chronic disease that has a relapsing nature. Treatment is effective, although monitoring progress over time is necessary in helping the individual stay in recovery.

5

Diagnosis

Highlights

• Diagnosis of a substance use disorder is an important medical process, not a matter of guesswork or labeling.

• Looking for substance-induced disorders may assist in diagnosing abuse or dependence.

• Mental health and medical practitioners can acquire relevant diagnostic information from collateral sources such as family, and in some instances from legal or employment sources.

• Determining whether or not abuse or dependence is present will, in some cases, be straightforward, but in other cases will require observation over an extended period of time.

• Co-occurring (dual diagnosis) disorders are very common, and the presence of a psychiatric disorder should alert the clinician to inquire about a substance use disorder (and vice-versa).

• A diagnosis should be presented with tact, optimism, and professionalism.

Diagnosis is critical to the practice of medicine as well as to the practice of therapy. Diagnosis shapes treatment planning, gives credence to the symptoms under consideration, and documents that thoroughness and thoughtfulness are shaping the clinical process.

Substance use disorders are represented by two diagnoses: abuse and dependence. (*Dependence* is used in place of the word *addiction*, which doesn't hold scientific standing today.) Information to make a diagnosis often requires information from collateral sources and may be obtained from family, legal records, employees, and by observing behavior and researching medical findings. As with other medical conditions, the diagnosis of a substance use disorder is based on specific criteria and is not a matter of "labeling" or "guesswork."

Before proceeding with diagnostic criteria for substance abuse and substance dependence, a brief word about substance-induced disorders is necessary. Substance-induced disorders are specific syndromes that may develop in a patient who is abusing or dependent on drugs or alcohol. There are eleven categories of substance-induced disorders:

1. Intoxication
2. Withdrawal
3. Intoxication delirium
4. Withdrawal delirium
5. Dementia
6. Amnestic disorder
7. Psychotic disorders
8. Mood disorders
9. Anxiety disorders
10. Sexual dysfunction
11. Sleep disorders

Intoxication is, perhaps, the most common such syndrome and can occur with all substances of abuse/dependence except nicotine (see Table 5.1). Some substance use disorders occur only with specific classes of agents; for example, a withdrawal delirium (commonly called "DTs," delirium tremens) is found only during withdrawal from alcohol, sedatives, hypnotics, or anxiolytics. Certain substance use disorders emerge only during intoxication (e.g., psychosis associated with use of amphetamines or cocaine), and others emerge only during a state of withdrawal (e.g., the delirium associated with alcohol, sedative, hypnotic, or anxiolytic withdrawal). Most substance-induced disorders are temporary and resolve when the offending drug is removed. Exceptions include dementia and amnestic disorders associated with alcohol.

Substance-induced disorders have separate diagnostic codes from abuse or dependence disorders, but obviously they co-occur with the substance-use

Table 5.1
Diagnoses Associated with Drugs

	Dependence	Abuse	Intoxication	Withdrawal	Intoxication Delirium	Withdrawal Delirium	Dementia	Amnestic Disorder	Psychotic Disorders	Mood Disorders	Anxiety Disorders	Sexual Dysfunction	Sleep Disorders
Alcohol	X	X	X	X	I	W	P	P	I/W	I/W	I/W	I	I/W
Amphetamines	X	X	X	X	I				I	I/W	I	I	I/W
Caffeine			X								I		I
Cannabis	X	X	X						I		I		
Cocaine	X	X	X	X	I				I	I/W	I/W	I	I/W
Hallucinogens	X	X	X		I				I*	I	I		
Inhalants	X	X	X		I		P		I	I	I		
Nicotine	X			X									
Opioids	X	X	X	X	I				I	I		I	I/W
Phencyclidine	X	X	X		I				I	I			
Sedatives, hypnotics, or anxiolytics	X	X	X	X	I	W	P	P	I/W	I/W	W	I	I/W
Polysubstance	X												
Other	X	X	X	X	I	W	P	P	I/W	I/W	I/W	I	I/W

From American Psychiatric Association, 1994.

* Also hallucinogen persisting perception disorder (flashbacks).

Note: X, I, W, I/W, or P indicates that the category is recognized in DSM-IV. In addition, I indicates that the specifier With Onset During Intoxication may be noted for the category (except for Intoxication Delirium). W indicates that the specifier With Onset During Withdrawal may be noted for the category (except for Withdrawal Delirium). And I/W indicates that either With Onset During Intoxication or With Onset During Withdrawal may be noted for the category. P indicates that the disorder is persisting.

disorder—that is, with abuse or dependence. Though a discussion of these 11 substance-induced disorders is beyond the scope of this text, the association between them and specific drugs is outlined in Table 5.1.

This chapter describes the criteria used in making a *substance use disorder* diagnosis. Awareness of a substance use disorder may occur by observing or documenting any of the above 11 substance-induced syndromes or by the steps of identification described in Chapter 3. It is obvious that the substance-induced disorder of intoxification does not necessarily imply the presence of abuse or dependence. The presence of withdrawal delirium *will* imply alcohol dependence.

Substance Abuse

DSM-IV criteria for substance abuse are summarized below:

1. Drug or alcohol use interferes with performance at work, school, or home. In other words, the role the person plays in society is compromised by alcohol or drugs. For example, a mother cannot be awakened when her daughter returns home from school because of sedative/hypnotic/anxiolytic use; a college student is "stoned" on cannabis and can't prepare for exams; an employee misses work on Mondays because of hangovers.
2. Drugs or alcohol are used in physically dangerous situations: for example, injecting drugs while working around dangerous equipment; driving while intoxicated.
3. Drug or alcohol use causes legal problems: for example, arrest for possession of a controlled substance; assault; public intoxication.
4. Drug or alcohol use interferes with personal or social relationships: for example, arguments with spouse; exclusion from social events because of previous intoxicated behavior.

Making a diagnosis of *abuse* is usually straightforward as long as the following points are taken into consideration:

1. If criteria for *dependence* are met, abuse is precluded.
2. The four criteria above—role failure, dangerous behavior, legal problems, and relationship problems—must be *recurrent* (i.e., have happened more than once).
3. The recurrence must occur within a *12-month period.*
4. Only *one* recurring episode is necessary for an abuse diagnosis.

Substance Dependence

Many patients do not progress beyond abuse, but for others, abuse is a step-pingstone toward dependence. As mentioned, in the DSM-IV *addiction* was replaced with the term *dependence*. Previously, *addiction* referred to frequent intoxication, strong craving, and a lifestyle that was increasingly oriented toward obtaining, using, and recovering from a drug's effects (Rinaldi, Steindler, Wilford, & Goodwin, 1988). The term *addiction* is now replaced by *dependence*. Alcohol, cocaine, or heroin dependence resemble "addiction," but anxiolytic/sedative/hypnotic, cannabis, or nicotine dependence may not.

The DSM-IV criteria for substance dependence are summarized below:

1. Tolerance: loss of effect of the drug with continued use or need to increase the amount of the drug to obtain the desired effect. If three drinks of alcohol are required to feel a "buzz" or six drinks to feel intoxicated, tolerance is probably established.
2. Withdrawal: a characteristic syndrome that develops when the drug is discontinued or the amount taken is lowered; or the symptoms of withdrawal are relieved by taking more of the drug or another substance that is closely related.
3. More of the drug is taken or used over longer periods of time than the user intended: This experience is what is meant by "loss of control." Most alcoholic patients can identify with the experience of only intending to have "a drink" but ending up drunk.
4. There have been unsuccessful efforts made or a desire expressed to cut down on the use of a substance. This criterion also reflects loss of control because, in spite of good intentions, the person cannot significantly control his or her use.
5. Time is increasingly taken up obtaining the substance (e.g., driving for miles to make a drug connection), using it (e.g., every hour is spent getting high on cannabis), or recovering from its effects (e.g., hangovers).
6. Interests or obligations—social, recreational, or occupational—are put aside in favor of substance use. This criterion describes the process whereby a substance gradually gains a higher priority in a person's life as other activities are neglected.
7. The substance is used in spite of known physical problems or psychological problems connected to its use; for example, alcohol use causes a flareup of pancreatic pain; methamphetamine ("speed") leads to irritability and arguments with spouse.

To qualify for a *dependence* diagnosis, *three* of these criteria must have been present at some time during the preceding year. Note that withdrawal or tolerance is not necessary for a substance dependence diagnosis.

Diagnostic Considerations in Adolescents

More often than not, adolescents do not display tolerance or withdrawal. Drug and alcohol use in adolescence is a shifting phenomenon—from drug to drug, depending on availability or fad. Therefore, tolerance to any one substance is uncommon and withdrawal syndromes absent or less pronounced than in adults. The diagnosis of polysubstance dependence is often applied. This term refers to a pattern of use involving at least three different substances, no one of which would fulfill criteria for DSM-IV dependence—but when considered together, dependence criteria may be met.

Adolescent use usually is sporadic in nature, rather than a daily pattern (marijuana use may be a noticeable exception). Binge drinking—the consumption of five or more drinks in a given setting—characterizes the more typical pattern of use in young people.

Adolescents, like adults, will minimize their use. When attempting to determine a substance use diagnosis in an adolescent, it is important to inquire about use by a parent, an older sibling, and by peers. All these have independent input on a young person's use, with peer and older brothers the most influential (Brook, Nomura, & Cohen, 1988).

Diagnostic Considerations in the Elderly

Older adults are unlikely to abuse or be dependent on illicit drugs. Sedative, hypnotic, or anxiolytics, as well as alcohol and prescription opiates, are the usual drugs of concern. The fact that alcohol use, in general, declines in the over-65 population does not preclude alcoholism in older individuals.

Falls, confusion, memory problems, tremor, and other symptoms may reflect side effects from appropriate use of medications or may be indicators of abuse or dependence. A careful assessment of the many medications that an older person may be using is essential. History from the family and reports of their observations are vital to making a diagnosis in older adults as well as in adolescents and young to middle-age adults. Chapter 8 further discusses substance use issues in older adults.

The "Gray" Zone

An abuse diagnosis is relatively straightforward: recurring legal or interpersonal problems; using drugs or alcohol in physically hazardous situations; or neglecting major functions at work, school, or home.

Making a dependence diagnosis can also be straightforward. Consider, for example, a 49-year-old man who presents at the emergency department with tremors, sweating, elevated vital signs, and the odor of alcohol on his breath. He has been drinking a fifth of Bourbon since his discharge 8 months ago after a bout of pancreatitis. Tolerance (fifth of gin per day), withdrawal symptoms (tremor, sweats), and continued drinking in spite of a known physical problem (pancreatitis) provide the three needed criteria.

Somewhat less obvious is the 46-year-old married woman who states "I can't stop myself." She drinks 20 ounces of wine between 6 and 10 P.M. nightly, experiences blackouts, and is unable to help her children with homework or drive them to places in the evening. Alcohol dependence is diagnosed in this case by her use of alcohol over longer periods of time than intended, by unsuccessful efforts to cut down, and by obligations put aside in favor of drinking.

Often it will not be certain if a substance dependence diagnosis is present. Many patients fall into a "gray zone" between abuse and dependence or between no substance use disorder and abuse. This ambiguity may occur because use is sporadic, resulting in one or two fulfilled criteria, but not more, within a 12-month period. The gray zone may also be encountered because it is difficult to determine if tolerance is present, particularly if withdrawal symptoms are absent. Has loss of control occurred? That is, has the individual tried to cut down unsuccessfully or wanted to cut down? It may be difficult for the patient or the physician to know if the quantity of use or length of time using has increased. Judgments regarding neglect of work, school, or recreational activities may be uncertain, as may determining whether known psychological problems have been exacerbated.

The first caveat for gray-zone cases is: *Don't rush the diagnosis*. Observe over time, gather more information, and firm up a relationship with the patient so that defensiveness and denial will be lessened. Schedule follow-up appointments and meetings with family members or others close to the patient.

Second, no harm will come if the physician *recommends abstinence from alcohol or other drugs*, even if dependence criteria are not certain.

Third, *a trial of controlled drinking* may enable the diagnosis to be made. For example, if the individual cannot limit him- or herself to one drink per day (women) or two drinks per day (men), continued use of alcohol may not be safe. Alternatively, a trial of the 3–3–10 rule could be started: No more than 3 drinks in a 24 hour period, 3 days a week with no alcohol, and no more than 10 drinks per week. Inability to hold to a controlled drinking regimen may help the individual appreciate that loss of control is occurring.

Presenting the Diagnosis to the Patient

A diagnosis can bring clarity to circumstances that were experienced as chaotic, confusing, or frightening. Further, a diagnosis can point to remedies and resolution. The stigma that many attribute to a substance use disorders makes presenting the diagnosis sensitive, however. An acronym—TOP, short for *tact*, *optimism*, and *professionalism*—outlines the process of presenting the diagnosis to the patient or family.

Tact: The physician or mental health professional explains that the findings indicate that "alcohol is having more control over your life than previously"; the "benefits of drinking have been outweighed by painful consequences"; "using pain medication is now interfering with areas of your life rather than eliminating the pain"; "your personal goals seem to be frustrated by using drugs," and so forth. The patient's experience with alcohol or drugs is mirrored for them as part of the foundation for a diagnosis of abuse or dependence. It is not necessary to include the word *alcoholic* or *addict*. It can be explained that a dependence has set in that is commonly referred to as alcoholism or alcohol (or drug) dependence. Further, it can be pointed out that the patient did not intend that this pattern would occur but, in fact, it does in many people—both men and women—of all ages.

Optimism: A clinician makes the diagnosis not as a sentence of shame or doom but as an opportunity for constructive change. The clarity of a diagnosis illuminates pathways to recovery. The patient and family feel that they have an ally in the clinician as they confront the steps needed to reverse drug or alcohol abuse or dependence. This alliance will be further reinforced by his or her capacity to assess treatment needs (Chapter 6).

Professionalism: The basis for the diagnosis is explained. Elevated liver enzymes, high blood pressure, mood changes, job problems, legal consequences, emotional symptoms, and any other consequences that fulfill diagnostic criteria are cited. That is, the physician draws on his or her training and experience to explain how medical findings are related to the substance use disorder—for example, the effect of alcohol on the liver, pancreas, or cardiovascular systems; and how the reward centers of the brain are targeted by drugs with abuse potential and stimulate the dopamine-rich mesolimbic pathways, triggering cravings; and how one's behavior progressively gives priority to obtaining and using the drug. Such explanations by the physician will help the patient appreciate that a process triggered by the effect of alcohol or drugs on the central nervous system has set up conditions that led to the complications in relationships, work, health, or legal areas. This effort by the physician or mental health professional will minimize shame and affirm the importance of dealing with a substance use disorder as a medical problem.

Co-Occurring Disorders (Dual Diagnosis)

The term *dual diagnosis* is used to describe the co-occurrence of psychiatric and substance use disorders. When this term was becoming popular, some practitioners in the addiction field objected to its use because, they argued, *dual* means *two*. Often multiple morbidities accompany substance abuse, especially medical and psychosocial problems. Nevertheless, the term has proven useful in maintaining awareness that addictions and other types of mental illnesses are often interrelated. The term seems embedded in the vernacular of addictive disorders and will probably remain.

Books on dual diagnosis are relatively recent. Despite the importance of the subject, studies on co-occurring disorders have been slow to accumulate. In truth, any mental illness can co-occur with addiction to any substance. However, some psychiatric disorders occur with such frequency that special attention to them is necessary to the comprehensive assessment and treatment of addicted patients. If the nonpsychiatric clinician were to become knowledgeable about only two psychiatric disorders that afflict addicted patients, the two conditions would be depressive disorders and anxiety disorders.

More is expected of clinicians who work directly with substance-abusing patients or in programs where special populations of patients are treated. In addition to depressive disorders and anxiety disorders, psychiatrists who see a general mix of patients need a working knowledge of other mental illnesses in which there is a high rate of substance abuse. Among the most common of these psychiatric disorders are bipolar disorder, schizophrenia, borderline personality disorder, and antisocial personality disorder.

The prevalence of psychiatric disorders is higher in patients with substance use disorders compared to individuals without substance use disorders, and those with drug or alcohol dependence will have a higher prevalence of psychiatric disorders than the general population (Hasin, Nunes, & Meydan, 2004).

Three sequences are possible: (1) A psychiatric disorder leads to a substance use disorder. For example, a bipolar patient finds that his or her irritability or disturbed sleep pattern is relieved by alcohol. Alcohol dependence develops and, once established, can be expected to continue even if the bipolar condition is stabilized with medications. Therefore, both disorders require clinical attention. (2) A substance use disorder leads to a psychiatric disorder. Chronic alcoholism or cocaine dependence, for example, may precede the development of a mood disorder. Even if the abused drug is discontinued, mood disturbance may continue and require specific treatment as well. An example is the not uncommon development of major depression after extensive use of LSD. (3) Each disorder develops independently. An example would be simple phobia (e.g., fear of elevators) and a co-occurring substance use disorder.

The designation of *primary* versus *secondary* refers to the time sequence of the development of the disorder. If, for example, a patient developed major depression in his or her 30s and was diagnosed with alcohol dependence at age 45, the depression diagnosis would be primary and the alcoholism secondary. Primary versus secondary does not designate importance or severity. The guiding principle is that both disorders, if present at the same time, must be treated. To overlook one will compromise the treatment of the other. Typically, the psychiatric disorder develops earlier than the substance use disorder (Kessler et al., 1994). An exception is that alcohol abuse/dependence in males precedes the onset of depression in about 75% of cases where both are present (Petrakis, Gonzales, Rosenheck, & Krystal, 2002).

Drug or alcohol abuse will often induce anxiety, depression, manic symptoms, hallucinations, or even delusions. Generally, such symptoms are considered substance-induced if they clear within 4 weeks of discontinuing the drug (American Psychiatric Association, 1994). If the psychiatric symptoms continue beyond 4 weeks, a psychiatric disorder independent of drugs or alcohol should be considered. Of course, even if the psychiatric symptoms are short-lived (i.e., less than 4 weeks duration), specific treatment of the symptoms may be necessary. The presence of delusions or hallucinations induced by cocaine, for example, are best addressed with antipsychotic medication; panic attacks may require brief use of benzodiazepines.

It is not always easy to determine if the patient who is abusing drugs or alcohol and experiencing psychiatric symptoms does, in fact, have two diagnoses. The following points will help determine whether dual diagnoses are present:

1. If the symptoms clear within 4 weeks of stopping drugs or alcohol, the symptoms were most likely substance-induced and not a separate psychiatric disorder.
2. If the patient's history reflects freedom from psychiatric symptoms during extended periods of abstinence from drugs or alcohol, the presence of a second psychiatric disorder is less likely.
3. If there is a family history of psychiatric disorders, the possibility of an independent psychiatric disorder rather than a substance-induced disorder is more likely.
4. If there is a clear history of the psychiatric disorder before the onset of a substance use disorder, the eventual co-occurrence of substance abuse/dependence with psychiatric symptoms would suggest the presence of two co-occurring disorders (dual diagnosis).

For many patients it is difficult to sort out historically which symptoms came first or if there were any drug-alcohol-free intervals. In such cases, treating both the substance use disorder and the psychiatric symptoms is warranted.

Comorbid Drugs and Alcohol

Although not usually referred to as a dual disorder, the combination of a drug use disorder and an alcohol use disorder is common. The National Comorbidity Study (Kessler et al., 1994) determined that 40% of individuals with alcohol abuse or dependence also have drug abuse or dependence. Concomitant use of alcohol and other drugs, for example, cocaine, has been found to increase the frequency of comorbid physical disorders such as viral hepatitis, sexually transmitted diseases, electrocardiographic abnormalities, and hepatic dysfunction (Salloum et al., 2004). In a 2000 survey, it was found that binge-drinking teenagers abuse drugs in two-thirds of cases, whereas only 5% of teenagers who don't drink abuse drugs (U.S. Dept. of Health and Human Services, 2002).

Smoking rates among alcoholics are 90%, with 70% smoking at least one pack of cigarettes per day (Kipniss & Miller, 2003).

Comorbid Mood Disorders

DEPRESSION

One-year prevalence rates for major depression are about 5%, but individuals with substance use disorders have major depression at a rate four times greater (Cacciola, Alterman, McKay, & Rutherford, 2001). The relationship between depression and substance abuse is complex. The question of which came first, the chicken or the egg? has been asked and answered: Yes, depression can be the chicken; yes, depression can be the egg. The simple explanation is that an individual may use substances in an attempt to alleviate depressed feelings. Conversely, some substances such as alcohol have depressant properties, which lead to feelings of depression. Based on the frequency of its occurrence, most practitioners will see cases of depression many times during their careers, with and without addictive disorders.

If all types of depression are considered, the lifetime prevalence may be as great as 20–25% of the population. If we consider the lifetime prevalence of major depressive disorder alone, it is a substantial 12% of the U.S. population (Sadock & Sadock, 2005). It is well known that depression afflicts women more often than men. Women are almost twice as likely to have a major depressive episode at some time in their lives. However, the reasons behind this gender difference are not understood.

It is useful to think about the presence of both physical and cognitive symptoms when exploring the possibility of a depressive disorder, especially when more sensitive diagnostic tools are not within easy grasp. Common physical symptoms of depression, often classified as vegetative symptoms, are reductions in appetite, energy, libido, and sleep. The DSM-IV-TR (American Psychiatric Association, 2000) is a definitive diagnostic resource. In addition to the physical symptoms of depression, the DSM-IV-TR emphasizes cognitive features: reduced interest in pleasurable activities, poor concentration, excessive guilt feelings, and suicidal ideas.

Several conditions are associated with major depression, and alcohol dependence is one of the most common. Major depression occurs nearly four times more often in patients who have alcohol dependence than in the general population (Modesto-Lowe, Pierucci-Lagna, & Kranzler, 2004). There may be a strong gender difference in the timing of its onset in people with alcoholism. In most males, alcoholism seems to occur prior to the onset of depression; in most women, depression precedes the onset of alcoholism (Helzer & Pryzbeck, 1988).

BIPOLAR DISORDER

Bipolar disorder is diagnosed more frequently today than in past decades. The recognition of varying patterns of mood instability accounts for the increased rate of bipolar diagnoses. Bipolar I disorder is the classic form of what was previously called manic–depressive disorder. Bipolar II disorder refers to a condition that is predominately characterized by depression, with interspersed periods of hypomania (rather than a full-blown manic episode). Some patients have a mixture of depressive and manic symptoms at the same time, and others experience rapid cycling (at least four shifts from manic symptoms to depression, and vice versa, in a 12-month period).

Bipolar patients have a co-occurring substance use disorder in 60% of cases (Regier et al., 1990). This form of dual disorder often leads to a rapid cycling, earlier onset of bipolar symptoms and frequent hospitalization.

Depressive episodes dominate the longitudinal course and treatment usually requires utilization of mood stabilizers (e.g., lithium, divalproex, carbamazepine) as well as antidepressants, and possibly second-generation antipsychotics (Judd & Akiskal, 2003). Medication compliance is often an issue; psychotherapy can be helpful in improving compliance. Typically, the bipolar patient is best referred for specialty psychiatric treatment.

Comorbid Anxiety Disorders

Individuals with anxiety disorders are at increased risk to develop a substance use disorder. One large study reported the risk of a substance use disorder to be 2.5 times greater for persons with anxiety disorders (Kessler et al., 1996). Substance use, as well as withdrawal from drugs or alcohol, can produce anxiety symptoms. To determine whether or not the patient's anxiety symptoms are a result of use or of withdrawal, a sufficient period of observation off the drug is necessary. A rule of thumb is 4 weeks, although withdrawing from long-acting substances such as methadone or some benzodiazepines would require a longer time of observation.

Anxiety disorders may precede substance abuse problems, or extensive use of drugs or alcohol may unmask a vulnerability for anxiety (Brady, 2004). The overlap between substance abuse and anxiety disorder occurs broadly and is found for panic disorders, generalized anxiety disorders, social anxiety disorder, posttraumatic stress disorder, and obsessive–compulsive disorder.

The treatment of patients with both substance use and anxiety disorders can be complicated, especially around the issue of whether or not to use benzodiazepines. Ordinarily, benzodiazepines are a mainstay in the treatment of anxiety, but their potential for abuse or dependence must be given extra consideration in the patient with a history of substance abuse. For this reason, increasingly, selective serotonin reuptake inhibitors (SSRIs) are a frontline approach to anxiety disorder. Essentially, this issue is best addressed on a case-by-case basis, taking into account the patient's history of substance use, alternative treatments, and symptom severity (Ciraulo & Nace, 2000).

Comorbid Schizophrenia

The lifetime prevalence of schizophrenia is close to 1%. However, 47% of schizophrenics will have an alcohol or drug use disorder, with at least one-third developing alcohol abuse or dependence. Tobacco dependence is extremely high in the schizophrenic population as well as in alcoholic patients (Drake & Mueser, 2002). Alcohol or other drugs may temporarily relieve symptoms of schizophrenia as well as relieve side effects of antipsychotic medications.

Comorbid Personality Disorders

Personality disorders are apparent by late adolescence or the young adult years and persist over time. The presence of substance use disorders in this population is about 50% (Grant, Hassin, Chou, Stinson, & Dawson, 2004). The "Cluster B" personality disorders have the highest rates of alcohol or drug abuse/dependence (Nace, Davis, & Gaspari, 1991). Cluster B includes borderline, antisocial, narcissistic, and histrionic personality disorders, all of which have dramatic, erratic, or impulsive features.

Co-occurring disorders should be the expectation of the clinician and not considered an exception. Some major principles in the treatment of co-occurring disorders are summarized below.

- Whether presenting symptoms indicate a substance use disorder or an anxiety, mood, or psychotic disorder, consider and screen for the possibility of a dual disorder.
- Do not consider one disorder an "excuse" for the other; for example, "He drinks because he's been so depressed." There may be linkage between the disorders, but both will need specific treatment.
- Acuity determines which disorder is treated first. A suicidal or psychotic patient will need to be psychiatrically stabilized before the substance

78

use disorder can be addressed. A patient in substance withdrawal will need to be withdrawn safely before a co-occurring psychiatric disorder is treated.

- Relapses are more common in patients with dual diagnosis. Establishing trust, communicating understanding, and promoting learning are more therapeutic than criticism or confrontation.
- Even in the face of relapse, any necessary psychotropic medications should be continued rather than withheld until the patient is "motivated" or continuously abstinent.

To conclude, the clinician who appreciates that the co-occurrence of psychiatric disorders with substance use disorders is common (and not the exception) will be better prepared to diagnose and plan treatment for this population. To overlook or neglect one of the disorders results in extended morbidity and increased medical and social costs (Drake et al., 1998).

Treatment Options

Highlights

• Addiction treatment occurs in outpatient, residential, and hospital settings, depending on the intensity of care the patient is likely to need.

• There are a number of options available for patients with substance use disorders. It is the clinician's responsibility to let the patient know which option best fits his or her needs.

• Motivational interviewing is a style of interacting with the patient that is based on an empathic and nonjudgmental approach.

• Physicians and mental health professionals have issues that limit their ability to effectively help addicted patients. These issues can be overcome with information and education.

Health care providers who diagnose substance use disorders and then guide patients toward treatment need to know the various recovery programs available and the way in which patients are matched to an appropriate treatment setting. Identifying the type of program that will best fit the needs of a particular patient can be confusing. It was once common for patients to enter a "one size fits all" 28-day residential treatment program. Now there are several options from which to choose. The range of settings that provide substance abuse treatment has expanded since the late 1980s. A driving force for change was the pressure for cost containment. Although the move toward more individualization in treatment plans makes sense, the downside is that individualization has sometimes meant limited resources for the treatment of some patients' addictions.

Intensity of Care

With the initial changeover from a fee-for-service model to a managed care model, there was general confusion for both patients and for health care providers. Payers developed their own payment structures for the treatment services they would approve for particular patients. It seemed to many physicians and mental health professionals that they were no longer in charge of recommending the services patients looked to them to propose. Programs adapted to this change in a number of ways. One way of coping with the curtailing of payment was to expand the options of care to include less intensive services, such as a range of outpatient programs.

The American Society of Addiction Medicine (ASAM) developed patient placement criteria that have been widely accepted. These criteria are based on an assessment of the patient's medical and life situations that would effect treatment and recovery. These guidelines are useful as providers think through a particular situation and communicate their rationale with payers. ASAM has been at the forefront of these efforts and has provided updated editions of placement criteria to keep up with developments in the field (American Society of Addiction Medicine, 1996). Table 6.1 lists the domains that are often considered in assessing the intensity of care needed by a patient.

Setting and staffing are two variables that define the level of care a treatment program provides. The aim is to treat the patient in the least intensive

Table 6.1
Domains Considered in Assessing Intensity of Care

- Detoxification needs
- Medical comorbidity
- Psychiatric comorbidity
- Potential for relapse
- Recovery environment

From American Society of Addiction Medicine, 1996.

program that meets his or her needs. An ideal scenario would be to find the optimal treatment effort that produces an optimal treatment result. Unfortunately, the science of recovery is not so precise.

Most patients are treated in an outpatient setting, the least intensive level of care. There are a several types of outpatient programs, defined by the programming they provide. Typically, a patient who is treated as an outpatient has withdrawal symptoms that are easily managed. When comorbidity is present, it is not acute. Patients appropriate for this level of care are believed to be capable of maintaining sobriety for the duration of treatment. Also, there is a reasonable home environment for the patient during "off" hours.

A more intensive level of care is the residential program. One might think of residential care as the level of care between outpatient treatment and hospitalization. In essence, residential treatment occurs in facilities where the patient stays overnight in a sober community and is treated for addiction. Patients may need residential care if their potential for relapse is high, or if their living environment is not conducive to maintaining sobriety. The recovery environment is closely tied to the potential for relapse. It is easy to imagine the homeless addict needing a more supportive living environment. However, the affluent suburban alcoholic who lives with an undermining alcoholic spouse may also need more support for maintaining abstinence. For both addicts, recovery may be elusive unless they move into a place where sobriety is a top priority.

Very few patients require inpatient hospitalization, which is the most intensive level of care. Hospitalization provides 24-hour medical staffing for patients who are medically or psychiatrically unsafe. Among types of patients who may require hospitalization is a heavy drinker who had difficulty controlling the DTs during a previous treatment for alcoholism. Another is an older adult with unstable angina who is to be detoxified from a high dose of sedatives. Still another is the imminently suicidal patient who needs addiction treatment.

There are patients who do poorly in each level of care described. Some patients' brains require more time to recover than a particular program is designed to provide or a payer authorizes. Such patients may need to live in a substance-free environment for several months. We might consider the methamphetamine or cocaine or heroin addict as needing significant brain recovery time; however, the need for such time to fully recover may include patients who are dependent on alcohol or nearly any other drug, if the addiction to that drug is severe.

Next we consider three case vignettes. Case 1 exemplifies a patient situation for which an outpatient treatment program was recommended; in Case 2 a residential treatment program was recommended, and in Case 3 a medically sophisticated psychiatric inpatient facility was recommended.

In Case 1 the patient had a serious medical condition but did not require inpatient care. The risk of imminent relapse was assessed as minimal, considering the strong support of the spouse, the patient's motivation for transplant, and his recent record of abstinence. An outpatient program was therefore an appropriate treatment setting.

In Case 2 any treatment that required the patient to live at home would likely fail. There she would have to confront the substance use around her in a daily basis. Triggers or cues might come in the form of her brother's use, seeing drug paraphernalia, or inhabiting the rooms in which she had frequently gotten high. Emotional triggers might include her mother's drinking, their conflicts, and undermining comments from mother and brother. This patient needed a sober, supportive environment in which to begin recovery and learn effective coping strategies.

In Case 3 the patient is at risk for a difficult and complicated withdrawal because of the length of time she has taken sedatives and the amount she has taken during the past 2 years. If the patient has used a single pharmacy and

---

Case 1 (Outpatient)

Mr. A was a 56-year-old man referred for addiction treatment prior to liver transplant. He had used alcohol excessively for at least 30 years. Mr. A had never gone to AA or to an addiction treatment program. He was not expected to have withdrawal symptoms, did not require around-the-clock medical or psychiatric supervision, and was motivated by his need for the transplant. Despite his diseased liver, he was not convinced that drinking was the cause of his health problems. His spouse was very supportive of the treatment. It would have been medically risky for Mr. A to drink alcohol, and he had maintained abstinence during the previous 3 months. The goal of treatment was for Mr. A to accept his dependence on alcohol, to personalize the consequences of his drinking, and to become involved in a firm recovery plan. The addiction psychiatrist recommended that Mr. A enter an outpatient addiction treatment program.

Case 2 (Residential)

Ms. B was a 20-year-old woman who sought help for cocaine dependence. She had used cocaine for 2 years. She had begun using occasionally with friends, then her use had increased steadily. Ms. B sought help because she had recently tried crack cocaine, which frightened her. She lived with her brother, who abused cocaine, and with her mother, who was alcohol dependent. Ms. B had made unsuccessful attempts to stop using cocaine by attending NA.

No detoxification, medical, or psychiatric problems were anticipated. However, the home environment placed her recovery in jeopardy. It was recommended that Ms. B enter a residential program. Following treatment she decided to live in a halfway house—a lower-intensity residential placement—which allowed her to solidify her recovery without the burden of living in an environment where substances were abused.

---

has not obtained her medication from other sources, the pharmacist can give useful information about the amount she has used. This patient's heart disease makes the withdrawal symptoms of hypertension and an increased heart rate risky for her. She needs a medically-oriented setting in which detoxification can proceed safely. Once withdrawal is completed and the pa-

---

Case 3 (Hospitalization)

Mrs. C, a 73-year-old widow of 2 years, had taken a variety of sedatives for anxiety and insomnia since the birth of her third child 40 years ago. She smoked one and a half packs of cigarettes per day. Mrs. C had suffered a myocardial infarction at age 68 and had unstable angina.

After her husband died, she steadily increased the amount of sedatives she used. When her children became concerned that she was using too much medication, they arranged for her to be evaluated. A thorough medication history revealed that Mrs. C was using a combination of lorazepam, temazepam, and butalbital as needed for anxiety, insomnia, and tension headaches. She was not certain as to the specific doses she took on any given day.

---

tient has started the process of recovery, she may be ready for treatment in a less intensive setting.

In summary, outpatient treatment is appropriate for patients who have the ability to maintain abstinence during the treatment program and who are not expected to have problems with detoxification or medical or psychiatric issues. Residential treatment is appropriate for patients who are likely to have difficulty maintaining sobriety but who do not need 24-hour medical management. Inpatient treatment provides the services of a hospital and is recommended when around-the-clock medical or psychiatric care is needed.

Self-Help Groups

AA and other self-help groups play an important role in recovery. Higher levels of AA attendance during and following professional treatment are consistently associated with better outcomes (Emrick et al., 1993). Some AA groups are open, meaning anyone can attend, whereas some are closed to the general public. Attendance at an open AA meeting can be enlightening for clinicians who refer patients there.

Despite the proven effectiveness of AA, there are also concerns. Quality of the groups varies depending on each group's leaders and members; there is no quality assurance for the programs; and abstinence is not a requirement for attendance, which may seem hypocritical to those entering recovery. Some AA groups have discouraged members from taking prescribed medications such as antidepressants and antipsychotics, even though they are not addictive.

AA slogans can be useful, such as "One day at a time," whereas others can be discouraging, such as "One drink away from a drunk." For instance, when someone "slips" or "relapses" that individual may feel like a hopeless failure. Furthermore, "One drink away from a drunk" (GAP, 1998) is not true for all recovering addicts; many people have a misstep along the way without relapsing into full-blown uncontrollable use. However, it is a slogan that may be useful for the very brittle alcoholic because it warns that one drink could ruin his or her recovery.

Some patients may reject AA because of bad experiences with it or because they do not wish to focus on spirituality. Although AA is the prototypic self-help group, there are other similar groups. For instance, Recovery, Inc. does not emphasize God or a higher power. Narcotics Anonymous (NA) and Cocaine Anonymous (CA) may be better choices for individuals who have problems with illicit drug use. Professionals' groups aimed at those in specific occupations, such as attorneys or physicians can be ideal for some.

Resistance to AA may represent a legitimate patient concern or a resistance to recovery, but it can be difficult to make that discernment. It is important that patients know that those who are recovering with the help of AA have a better prognosis, and that it is common for recovering individuals to try more than one group before finding one suited to their needs. They should also know that alternative resources exist.

One of the keys to helping patients succeed in their recovery program is to look at substance dependence as a chronic neuropsychiatric condition in which the brain has been repeatedly assaulted. The condition is often chronic and relapsing; however, the brain can improve and recover through abstinence. Treatment and continuing recovery can change the life of the addicted person and those with whom he or she comes in contact.

The Option to Refer to Available Treatment Modalities

A physician or mental health clinician may not want to directly participate in the treatment of a substance use disorder. Time and required experience may not be available. Therefore, knowledge of treatment options and referral sources can do much to assist the recovery process. This section outlines such referral options.

Inpatient Treatment or Rehabilitation Programs

The managed care era has severely restricted the use of inpatient and residential treatment. Patients with the acute problems described above often gain approval for this level of care. Nevertheless, the restricted use of inpatient and residential treatment is unfortunate because many patients will only benefit fully from treatment in an intensive setting that concentrates on their denial and other pathological defenses, their relapse triggers, and their coping strategies. If a patient has not responded to brief hospitalizations for detoxification or outpatient programs, placement in an inpatient or residential setting may be indicated.

What can physicians do when intensive options would prove most beneficial? First, physicians and clinicians need to inform patients of these options when they believe they are indicated on the basis of acuity or to maximize recovery potential. If third-party resources are not available, personal and family resources can be considered.

Second, physicians and clinicians should recommend programs in which they have confidence. Knowledge of local and national programs is essential. Phone numbers, websites, and hard-copy information (e.g., brochures) on these programs should be on file in their offices and made available to prospective patients. The best programs can conduct an evaluation of medical and psychiatric needs. The patient's acceptance of making this commitment to treatment may be enhanced if the practitioner places a phone call to the admissions office or medical director, briefing him or her on the patient's condition and needs, and inquiring as to bed availability, length of stay, and family participation.

Finally, physicians and clinicians will find it helpful to ask the patient to call them once he or she has settled into such a program so that they can learn of the patient's experience at that treatment center and assist in planning follow-up care.

Day Hospital or Intensive Outpatient Program

There are several types of outpatient programs. Day hospital, also known as partial hospitalization, refers to a structured program of group psychotherapy, educational lectures, and individual counseling that takes place 6–8 hours per day 5–6 days per week. An intensive outpatient program (IOP) is similar, except that it is typically held during evening hours for 3–4 hours. Attending day hospital is like going to a job; IOP is held after work hours for patients who have returned to work.

Patients discharged from a brief hospitalization for detoxification usually enter one of these programs, or if initial hospitalization was not necessary, they may use these modalities as the initial treatment experience.

Inpatient and residential treatment programs, day hospital, and IOP all educate patients about the disease of addiction, signs of relapse, how to cope with cravings, family dynamics, stress and anger management, and 12-step programs. Patients begin attending AA or NA meetings while in treatment. Families are invited to specific sessions. Individual and group counseling is available to help each patient overcome pathological defenses and to gain hope for the future. A psychiatric assessment should be conducted prior to or during treatment to assess for psychiatric comorbidity and to make available appropriate pharmacological and psychotherapeutic approaches.

Consultation with, or Referral to, an Addiction Specialist

Some physicians specialize in addictive disorders. Psychiatrists who are members of the American Academy of Addiction Psychiatry (AAAP) are examples; these physicians are usually certified by the American Board of Medical Specialties. Physicians who are members of ASAM also specialize in addictions. The latter organization is open to physicians of all specialties. Some of these physicians have a special interest in addictions because they are in recovery themselves. Personal experience of recovery from addiction can be a valuable therapeutic asset, but is not a satisfactory credential in itself. Further training and exploration of personal dynamics and limitations are necessary to equip such physicians to advise and treat patients with substance use disorders with optimal competence.

Addiction specialists may assist primary care physicians through consultation, by helping to design treatment and intervention plans, by providing information (e.g., on treatment centers), or by managing the addiction treatment on either an inpatient or outpatient basis.

Twelve-Step Programs

AA and its sister organizations, NA and CA, are critical resources for substance-abusing patients. Several patients in one's practice are likely to attend meetings. Physicians and clinicians may want to ask their recovering patients if they are involved in AA and how they (i.e., the physicians and clinicians) can help other patients get involved. AA and NA members are willing to meet newcomers (e.g., following an appointment at the clinician's office) and accompany them to a meeting or share their experiences in AA or NA. It is useful to keep an updated schedule of AA, NA, and CA meetings in one's office to hand out to patients in need.

As noted previously, attending an open AA meeting can be highly instructive for physicians and clinicians. By attending a meeting the process and format will be better understood and easier to explain to patients. NA meetings are for those with drug problems of any kind; CA meetings are for those whose primary problem is cocaine, and the attendees are usually younger. Some older drug-dependent patients are more comfortable at AA meetings. Sometimes an AA group prefers only members with alcoholism, not those with drug problems. However, since the only criteria for joining AA is to have a desire not to drink, the drug-dependent (nonalcoholic) patient may still "fit in" because avoidance of alcohol, as well as the "drug of choice," would be expected for recovery to be successful.

Twelve-step programs encourage each participant to obtain a sponsor, that is, a more experienced member with long-term sobriety who will guide the newcomer and help him or her understand and work the steps of the program. The most common format for a 12-step meeting is a "speaker meeting" in which a member recalls his or her story—what it was like, what had to be done, and how it is now. Other formats include discussion meetings and step study meetings. AA, NA, and CA members warmly welcome newcomers, are non-judgmental, and share their "strength, hope, and experience." They appreciate physicians and clinicians who show interest in, and support, their efforts.

The Option to Work with the Patient Toward Recovery

Many mental health clinicians and physicians will work directly with their patients during the recovery process. Their work may be in lieu of using the resources discussed earlier, or may be in addition to using these resources. The methods below discuss effective communication and relationship approaches, describe processes of change, and review problems common to clinicians that arise in work with substance abusing patients.

Motivational Interviewing

Thus far we have emphasized the prevalence of substance use disorders and the consequences associated with them. We have discussed how to identify and diagnose substance abuse and dependence, ways in which the intensity of treatment services are determined, and the array of available treatment options. Using motivational interviewing, the clinician can work with the patient in a way that is empathic and nonjudgmental. This approach can help patients decide to change their substance use habits because the clinician's advice is given with respect for the patient—and respect may be in short supply for the person with an addiction problem.

At this junction in treatment we make a major shift—a shift from the cognitive and observational to the empathic and personal. This is the point when the clinician communicates an empathic and genuine sense of concern for the patient. Before outlining the empirically established techniques of motivational interviewing (Miller & Rollnick, 1991), it should be obvious that the clinician's success in identifying, diagnosing, and referring substance-abusing patients will be contingent on his or her communicating to the patient and family his or her interest, concern, patience, seriousness, empathy, and respect.

Motivational interviewing incorporates, and is founded on, such attributes. A traditional approach to substance-abusing patients has been to assume that they are unable to recognize or acknowledge their problem and therefore incapable of making rational decisions to address it. An authoritarian and often threatening approach was taken in order to break through denial and proscribe treatment goals and plans. In contrast, motivational interviewing is really a style more than a set of specific techniques. It recognizes that *motivation for change is a fluid and changing state, not a fixed trait*. External influences can either increase or decrease motivation for behavioral change.

The sequences or stages of change identified by DiClemente and colleagues (1991) are illustrated in Figure 6.1. Clinicians can identify where any given patient is in this sequence and approach or "motivate" him or her accordingly.

Precontemplation is the stage in which patients may not recognize drug or alcohol use as a problem. These patients may be identified by laboratory results or physical findings. The initial approach with patients at this stage is not to recommend treatment options, but to increase their perception of the risks of their current behavior and to move them toward *contemplation.* In the stage of contemplation, patients are nudged toward further changes by helping them fully acknowledge the consequences of their addiction. Simultaneously, they must be reassured that they can change this behavior with help—and that the clinician will be part of that help. *Determination* indicates that a decision is made, but this stage can be transitory. Patients need help to decide on the appropriate level of treatment and to access that treatment with minimal delay. Once treatment is initiated, the *action* stage has been reached. This stage is generally considered to last 6 months and may include the range of needs from inpatient detoxification through intensive outpatient

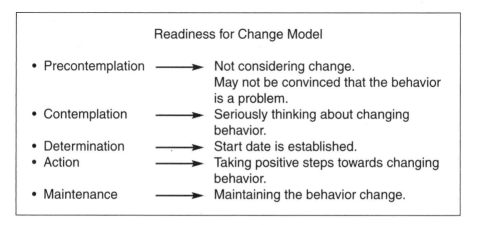

Figure 6.1 Sequence of behavior change. (DiClemente et al., 1991.)

programs. The *maintenance* phase usually includes gaining an ability to prevent relapse and utilization of 12-step programs or psychotherapy. Should relapse occur, work with the patient to reinitiate *determination* and take *action*. Relapse should be seen as part of the disease of addiction and from which the patient can learn to strengthen his or her recovery (e.g., working more closely with a sponsor, avoiding environmental triggers).

The style of motivational interviewing informs the process of change and involves the strategies listed in Table 6.2. *Giving advice* is critical because the physician, in particular, is uniquely placed to help the patient understand the impact of alcohol or drug abuse on brain functioning and other organ systems. *Overcoming barriers* refers to solving logistical problems such as child care needs for a mother or practice coverage for an impaired physician. Barriers may also include resistance to treatment on the part of a spouse or other family member, in which case assessment for the presence of a "co-addict" is indicated. A co-addict may fear loss of his or her role as caretaker or fear abandonment if the patient recovers.

Providing a choice of treatment options often helps remove the barriers. Allowing, indeed encouraging, the patient to think through the best option for him- or herself usually results in increased commitment to the treatment process. The clinician, of course, should counsel the patient on the optimal approach, based on the variables reviewed earlier in this chapter.

Throughout this process of behavioral change (which may take place rapidly during an office visit or slowly over weeks or months), the clinician assists the patient in reflecting on the *desirability of change* and the undesirability of not facing the problem. This reflection is fostered by *empathic*

Table 6.2
Motivational Interviewing Strategies

Giving advice

Overcoming barriers

Desirability of change

Practicing empathy

Providing feedback

Clarifying goals

Active helping

From Miller & Rollnick, 1991.

responding; that is, appreciating and, if indicated, acknowledging (1) the patient's fear of change, (2) his or her attachment to the effect of alcohol or drugs, (3) his or her doubts about whether change is necessary (or possible), and (4) his or her shame over the addiction predicament.

Giving feedback to the patient about progress in the addiction area or in other areas such as smoking cessation, sustained work record, or commitment to family strengthens motivation. Feeding back to the patient his or her expressed concerns about alcohol or drug use or his or her fear of job or marital consequences is useful as well.

Clarifying goals expected outcome are essential—for example, prevention of liver damage, financial stability, improved marriage, and regaining self-respect. Goals should be "owned" by the patient and not imposed by others. The clinician, however, is in an excellent position to point out feasible goals.

Active helping on the part of the clinician communicates sincere interest and concern. For example, the clinician might call a treatment program or a consultant while the patient is in the office, or call the patient the next day to see if he or she has made any progress in arranging admission to a treatment program, has gotten to an AA meeting, or if any further barriers have arisen.

Motivational interviewing with the patient, as he or she goes through the stages of change, is a process that may develop rapidly over hours to days, as in Case 4, or may take months before desirable results occur, as in Case 5.

Case 4 (Rapid Development)

Jack, 39 years old, married and self-employed, came to the office with his older brother. Jack's wife was angry and disgusted with him when she discovered that his cocaine abuse was leading to use of pornographic materials. Jack had lost weight, was depressed, and didn't want to lose his marriage. He had moved from precontemplation *to* contemplation *days before the appointment. In the office, feedback, empathy, information on the health risks of cocaine use, and the removal of financial barriers for treatment (e.g., checking his insurance coverage) led to* determination *on Jack's part to change and to take ac-* tion *by entering a rehabilitation program 2 days later.* Maintenance *was achieved through the use of AA, antidepressant medications, and individual psychotherapy.*

Case 5 (Slow Development)

Mark, a college athlete, returned home midsemester acknowledging that he was depressed. He said his problem was that he had chosen the wrong university where he could not identify with many of the students and which was in the wrong climate. Concern about his alcohol, cocaine, and marijuana use, as expressed by his coach, teammates, and parents, was brusquely disregarded. Mark agreed to antidepressant therapy but continued to "party" over the next 2 months. One night he had a serious paranoid reaction to cocaine use and requested help from his parents. By virtue of that drug-induced experience, he had moved from precontemplation to contemplation. An appointment with the family led to determination on Mark's part to change, but he was ambivalent and his motivation fluctuated day by day. When, after several more weeks, it seemed likely he would not be allowed to return to scholarship status without treatment for substance abuse, Mark took action and entered a rehabilitation program. His goal of playing college athletics has sustained him during this stage of action and into the early phases of maintenance.

Clinicians' Issues: Countertransference and Pessimism

We know that patients "transfer" feelings that they have experienced toward earlier important figures in their lives (typically parents) to clinicians. Respect for such feelings and the responsibility not to take advantage of them is a fiduciary responsibility of all health care workers. The feelings provoked in clinicians by patients can be considered broadly to constitute "countertransference." Clinical maturity is marked by a clinician's mindfulness of his or her own emotional reactions and attitudes (Novack et al., 1997). Patients with substance use disorders typically provoke negative countertransference reactions. Clinicians might reexperience painful feelings that were engendered decades ago by an alcoholic member in their own families, or they may be angered and frustrated by a patient's denial. Aspects of the chemically dependent patient's behavior may be experienced as appalling or disgusting. Unlike many disease states, substance abuse does not typically evoke compassion or sympathy. However, by acknowledging these feelings to themselves and stepping past their negative reactions, clinicians can engage constructively the addicted patients they encounter. Experience with addicted patients soon teaches clinicians that these individuals are suffering and that their defensiveness is a cover-up for confusion, shame, or hopelessness (Khantzian, 1997). Clinicians who are willing to negotiate their own as well as their patients' emotional states plant the seeds for collaboration and constructive clinician–patient relationships.

Pessimism among clinicians about treating alcohol- or drug-abusing patients is common. The origins of pessimism often are found in early clinical experiences treating alcoholism in a busy emergency room or witnessing the destructive effects of drugs in acutely ill medical patients. Sometimes the roots go deeper into a clinician's family experience. Uncertainty about how to proceed with a substance-abusing patient after acute medical issues have been addressed is another potential source of pessimism. Hopefully, material in this book will help clinicians overcome uncertainty and doubt.

If a clinician has access only to the short-term view of patients with substance use disorders, a pessimistic attitude can be expected. If, however, the clinician is able to work with or follow patients over an extended period of time—not just during acute crises—optimism often has a chance to replace the reflex-like pessimistic attitude. In fact, substance-abusing patients are as compliant with treatment as most other patients with chronic illnesses— for example, as those with asthma, diabetes, or hypertension. Staying focused on data that demonstrates good outcomes (McLellan et al., 2000) and that counters expectations of poor compliance will help clinicians not succumb to early training experiences or stereotypes. As resources and clinical experience overcome defeatist attitudes, clinicians are able to communicate effectively their positive expectations for this group of patients.

Tables 6.3–6.7 provide professionals with ideas and data that they can incorporate into their work with patients.

One reason to talk to patients about their excessive alcohol use is to help them realistically assess their drinking habits. Being aware of the information about U.S. drinking patterns can help clinicians to compare a patient's drinking to the drinking of other Americans. This knowledge, in turn, can help patients better understand their own drinking habits.

Approximately 30% of adults in the U.S. can be described as "at risk" drinkers who may benefit from advice about their use of alcohol. Most patients in this category are imbibing more than what is considered healthy. A smaller number are dependent on alcohol and should stop

Table 6.3
Practical Ways to Begin the Work with Patients

- Incorporate the CAGE questions into your history taking.
- Listen for "red flags" in the history, such as:
  1. Blackouts
  2. Chaos in several life areas
  3. ER visits
  4. Gastrointestinal complaints
  5. Insomnia
- Ask about the amount of alcohol the patient uses and the types of drugs, amount, and frequency as part of your inquiry into patient habits:
  1. How many drinks per day?
  2. How many drinks per week?
  3. What was the maximum number of drinks per occasion in the past month?
  4. Which drugs have you used in the past months?
  5. How do you use them (route of administration)? How often? How much? What quantity (e.g., how much money is spent per week or day on drugs)?
- Assess the information obtained. Asking similar questions to the patient more than once may be necessary to overcome resistance, embarrassment, or fear of being judged.

drinking altogether, which will probably require some type of treatment. In the National Institute of Alcohol Abuse and Alcoholism's booklet, *Helping Patients Who Drink Too Much* (NIAAA, 2005), two parameters are suggested that allow for a comparison of one person's drinking to the drinking of other U.S. adults.

Table 6.4
Screening Parameters

Consider your initial screen as positive and gather more information if:

- A man consumes > 14 drinks/week or > 4 drinks/occasion.
- A woman consumes > 7 drinks/week or > 3 drinks/occasion.
- CAGE score is > 1.
- Drugs are currently being used. Explain to patient that for health reasons it is important to learn more about the effects of alcohol or drugs on their life, and proceed with the steps in Table 6.5.

Table 6.5
How to Obtain More Information

- Request laboratory tests: GGT, MCV, other liver function tests, and consider ordering/requesting triglycerides and CDT.
- Ask for permission to speak to the spouse or significant other.
- Find out if alcohol or drugs have caused problems in an important life area:
  1. Medical
  2. Legal
  3. Occupational
  4. Marital/family
  5. Financial

The parameters are: (1) the number of drinks a person has consumed on any given day during the past year, which should not exceed 4 standard drinks for men or 3 for women, and (2) the number of drinks the person has in a typical week, which should not exceed 14 standard drinks for men or 7 for women. These are the maximum daily and weekly limits.

Table 6.6
Therapeutic Considerations

How to approach the patient with a drug or alcohol problem:

- Counsel the patient using a fact-based, nonjudgmental approach.
- Consider conducting sessions in the presence of the significant other.
- Show evidence of laboratory abnormalities and organ damage that is the result of drugs or drinking more than the body can safely handle.
- Compare the patient's alcohol use to U.S. drinking norms to provide a realistic perspective on his or her drinking.
- Provide information about the NIAAA recommendation for low-risk drinking: for men, no more than two drinks per day; for women and those over 65, no more than one drink per day.
- Educate the patient about the risks of using common drugs (e.g., cannabis, cocaine, methamphetamines, etc.).
- Educate the patient that the tendency to drink excessively and abuse drugs often runs in families.
- Provide educational literature.
- If the patient is unable to follow low-risk drinking guidelines or discontinue drug use, he or she may need help in achieving complete abstinence.

Table 6.7
Recommendations for Cases of Alcohol or Drug Dependence

- Suggest referral to a specialist or a specific treatment program, or if the patient is not ready . . .

- Recommend a period of abstinence and follow-up (consider the possibility of a withdrawal syndrome; warn the patient and family about what might happen).

- Advise attendance at AA or NA.

- Schedule periodic 10-minute follow-up appointments to monitor the substance use.

- Explore whether or not the significant other is interested in Al-Anon or Nar-Anon.

Ten percent of American adults exceed both maximum limits. Within this group are the drinkers who are most likely to have a diagnosable substance use disorder. Some people whose lives revolve around the use of alcohol believe almost everyone drinks in the same way. Confronting this rationalization with facts can start to reorient the individual toward a more realistic perspective of his or her drinking. It may be helpful for these patients to hear that most people in the U.S. never exceed these limits (72%), and many of these individuals either abstain or average one drink per month.

To determine whether a patient drinks at low risk, is somewhere in the middle range, or imbibes heavily, the clinician must ask key questions: If the patient drinks, has he had more than four drinks (three for women) on any given day during the past year? How many drinks are consumed during a typical week? Individuals who exceed both the maximum daily and weekly limits consume as much or more than 90% of Americans, a perspective that the patient may not have considered previously.

Following up these questions with a discussion about the physical ramifications of heavy drinking may in turn lead to a discussion of other problems associated with excessive alcohol use. The clinician can introduce the subject of changing one's drinking patterns, and find out the patient's feelings about this. Table 6.7 offers some additional ideas for intervention.

This chapter has addressed some of the options available to clinicians who want to work with people who have problems related to substance use. This work may take the form of counseling, motivational interviewing, self-help groups, or more formal interventions.

Part III
Special Topics

Substance Abuse in Adolescents

It is a myth that adolescence *must* be a turbulent time. However, teenagers are in a stage of life marked by considerable physical, emotional, and cognitive maturation. The adolescent is in the process of becoming comfortable with his or her changing body, developing personal values, searching for independence, and negotiating a social position. In sum, it is a time of preparation for the tasks of adult love and work. Today's adolescents are exposed to adult experiences earlier than their predecessors. Teenagers are over-scheduled and overstimulated. Stresses that adolescents commonly face include drugs, easy sex, constant cellular phone and beeper communication, an enormous amount of information available on the Internet, and an array of options and choices that, with their inexperience, may lead to very poor choices. Further, there seems to be less parental availability and therefore less authoritative guidance than in previous generations. Nearly 50% of teenagers live in single-parent households, leading to the potential for decreased structure in home life and less capacity to be directed by authority figures (Dias, 2002). Whether the household has one or two parents, poor parental monitoring, low bonding, lack of daily structure and rules, and high family conflict increase the risk of adolescent drug abuse (van den Bree & Pickworth, 2005).

Offer and Offer (1975) described three patterns of adolescent development: continuous, surgent, and tumultuous growth. In their paradigm only 21% of teens experienced tumultuous growth. The lives of these teens were characterized by more family conflict and less stable backgrounds, and they showed greater self-doubt. Those who experienced continuous growth were considered healthiest, and those in the surgent group were described as "late bloomers" who experienced more moments of depression and anxiety than the continuous group. Likewise, Pataki estimated psychological maladjustments in 20% of adolescents (Kaplan & Sadock, 2005).

Environmental and developmental factors are difficult to untangle when considering their impact on drug or alcohol use in adolescence. Being an unwanted baby or experiencing major illness in early childhood may be associated with future alcohol, cigarette, and marijuana use (Brook, Gordon, Brook, & Brook, 1988). A study of the mother–adolescent relationship found that the more satisfaction the mother expressed for the adolescent child and the more time spent with him or her, the less use of substances. Unrelated to whether the child used drugs or alcohol was the style of the mother's communication, whether the mother was "child centered," and the degree of maternal affection (Brook, Nomura, & Cohen, 1988).

One of the most difficult issues for adolescents to negotiate is gaining independence from the family even as they harbor a wish for continued dependence. Parents are often conflicted about this stage of development. Most adolescents gradually gain independence in socially acceptable, age-appropriate ways. They begin to demand more privacy; the peer group increases in importance, as the influence of the parents is overtly rejected; and through this struggle they may experiment with sexuality, test rules, adopt unconventional fashion trends, and experiment with substance use (Shapiro & Hertzig, 1999). It may help parents to know that much of what their teenager is experiencing is normal. Nonetheless, it remains the job of the adults to provide guidance through establishing rules, setting limits, and consistently responding to misbehavior.

Why Shouldn't Teens Drink or Use Drugs?

One reason for teens not to use substances is that drinking and illicit drug use is, well, illegal. However, there are other important reasons to take adolescent substance use seriously. Commonly cited dangers include date rape and motor vehicle accidents. Research has shown that teens are more likely to have sex and are less likely to use condoms when they have been drinking. A leading cause of teen morbidity and mortality is accidents. Many accidents that involve driving, drowning, burns, and falls involve alcohol (Kaminer & Bukstein, 2005).

Of the accidents related to alcohol, it is drinking and driving that frequently result in multiple tragedies. Victims who happen to be in the way of the intoxicated driver, or passengers along for the ride, may suffer or die, as may the driver. Of the nearly 8,000 drivers ages 15–20 who were killed in fatal crashes in 1995, 20% had used alcohol. Among all fatalities related to drinking and driving, passengers are more likely to die than drivers (NIAAA, 2000).

Drinking in college is sometimes deadly when students drink far too much, far too fast. College binge drinking has been, and remains, a serious health problem on our nation's campuses. Binge drinking is defined as five or more drinks in a row for men and four or more in women, at least once in the previous 2 weeks. Frequent binge drinking is defined by three or more binge drinking episodes within a 2-week period. Binge drinking in high school predicts binge drinking in college. Alcohol-related problems are very common in students who binge drink. The most frequent alcohol-related problem is missing classes, followed by "doing something I regret," and getting behind in schoolwork. Unplanned sexual activities, unprotected sex, property damage, getting hurt or injured, and driving after drinking were additional commonly found alcohol-related problems in young binge drinkers (Wechsler et al., 2000). Engaging in other risky behaviors increased the likelihood of binge drinking in Wechsler et al.'s study. Examples included having several sex partners in the month before the survey, smoking cigarettes, or using marijuana. Living in a fraternity or off campus was associated with binge drinking compared to living in a dormitory. Students who valued parties and strongly valued athletics were more likely to binge; students who rated religion as important in their lives were much less likely to binge drink.

Secondary effects of college binge drinking include sexual assault (i.e., date rape), property damage, and injuries caused by those who are drunk (Wechsler et al., 2000). Efforts to curb this problem have largely been unsuccessful, and information on the adverse effects of alcohol is largely ignored. Positive student role models and enforcement of college policies regarding the presence or use of alcohol are critical.

Early alcohol use is often seen as part of a broader syndrome of problematic adolescent behavior that includes other drug use, earlier sexual activity, conduct that deviates from social norms (including aggressive behavior). These youngsters often sustain their risky lifestyle by establishing or joining a like-minded peer group (NIAAA, 2000). Table 7.1 lists characteristics of children at highest risk for alcohol-related problems.

Psychiatric disorders may accompany substance abuse in this age group. Conduct disorders head the list. The term *conduct disorder* refers to repeti-

Table 7.1
Risk Factors for Alcohol Abuse in Teens

- Using alcohol or other drugs before the age of 15
- Having a parent who is a problem drinker or an alcoholic
- Having close friends who use alcohol or other drugs
- Showing aggressive, antisocial, or hard-to-control behavior from an early age
- Experiencing childhood abuse or other major traumas
- Having current behavioral problems or failing at school
- Having parents who are not supportive, do not communicate openly, and do not keep track of their child's behavior or whereabouts
- Experiencing ongoing hostility or rejection from parents or harsh, inconsistent discipline.

tive and persistent patterns of behaviors that may involve aggression to people or animals, property destruction, theft, lying, and violation of rules (e.g., truancy and running away from home). Conduct disorder can begin before age 10 (childhood-onset type) or after age 10 (adolescent-onset type). There has been a lot of interest in the relationship between attention-deficit/hyperactivity disorder (ADHD) and substance abuse; adolescents with both ADHD and conduct disorder pose the greatest risk for substance abuse. When undiagnosed, boys with ADHD had at least one substance use disorder in 75% of cases; treated ADHD boys had a substance use disorder in 25% of cases, compared to 18% of boys without ADHD (Biederman et al., 1999). Increased rates of substance abuse or dependence are also found in adolescents with mood or anxiety disorders, with a co-occurring rate of at least 25% (Burke et al., 1994). Adolescents with eating disorders report substance abuse in at least 25% of cases (Cavanaugh & Henneberger, 1996).

Smoking cigarettes before age 13 should also be seen as a marker for future substance abuse or psychiatric problems. One study found that depressive disorders were four times more likely, conduct disorder 13 times more likely, and cannabis abuse 24 times more likely in adolescent cigarette smokers than their nonsmoking peers (Upadhyaya et al., 2003).

It is critical to look for substance abuse in young patients with psychiatric disorders and to look for psychiatric problems in substance-abusing adolescents. Adolescents often find it difficult to describe their feelings, or they may be reluctant to admit to depression, mood instability, or anxiety. If the clinician builds a trusting relationship with the teenager, a more complete history can be expected and the role of alcohol or drugs in producing psychiatric symptoms can be better assessed. Similarly, the presence of depression or anxiety may precede alcohol or drug abuse. Both sets of symptoms—the psychiatric and the substance use—will need attention. As in adults, psychiatric disorders usually worsen when accompanied by substance abuse. The issue of dual diagnosis, or comorbid disorders, is addressed in Chapter 5.

Is It a Common Problem in Adolescents?

Alcohol and drug use are common during adolescence, as confirmed by the University of Michigan's Monitoring the Future survey of U.S. high school students' use of substances during the past quarter century (Monitoring the Future, 2003). In 2002 the survey found that by age 18, 78% of U.S. youth had used alcohol, and about 50% had used alcohol during the past month.

More startling was that 28% of high school seniors and 22% of 10th graders were classified as binge drinkers, meaning they had ingested five drinks on at least one occasion within the past 2 weeks. Addiction is four times as likely to develop in youth if drinking begins before 15 years of age, compared to those who begin drinking at age 21 (Grant & Dawson, 1997). It is critical that parents and health care providers strive to delay the onset of initial drinking in youth, because the risk for lifetime alcohol dependence will decrease by 8–14% for each year of the delay (Garofalo et al., 1998). Also alarming is the fact that in spite of the smoking rate in the United States having decreased among adults, it has remained steady for teenagers. The average age of smoking initiation is 10.7 years for boys and 11.4 for girls. Again, attention to delaying the onset of smoking is a critical goal for health care providers and parents, because youth who are nonsmokers at age 19 are less likely to start smoking in their 20s. The Monitoring the Future study found that 54% of those surveyed had used illicit drugs by age 18. The most commonly abused illicit drug is marijuana. One in five 12th graders, and nearly as many 10th graders, reported using marijuana during the previous month.

The primary care physician and the mental health clinician are in an excellent position to observe many possible signs that could suggest drug use. For example, an increased appetite for sweet foods commonly occurs with marijuana. Odors of alcohol, marijuana, or other substances, particularly volatile hydrocarbons, may be apparent in the teenager's clothes or on the breath. Reflux symptoms or symptoms of gastritis may be reflective of alcohol abuse, and alcohol abuse is common in bulimic patients. Constipation may be related to opiate abuse, and dilated or constricted pupils are potential signs of substance abuse. Nosebleeds, nasal perforations, and "allergy" symptoms may occur with cocaine and inhalants. Changes in behavior are usually easily elicited from parents and include symptoms of anxiety, paranoia, and possibly complete or partial amnesia during states of intoxication, particularly with alcohol and sedative types of "date-rape" drugs. Complaints of chest pain, rapid heartbeat, or even arrhythmias may occur with stimulants such as cocaine and amphetamines. Needle tracks (i.e., darkened streaks at the site of injection on the skin) will occur with intravenous drug use as well as with intramuscular or subcutaneous steroid use. Inhalant abuse such as can be obtained from freon in aerosol containers or gasoline may produce red, runny eyes, chemical burns, and possibly sores around the mouth, paint stains on the face or clothes, or an unusual chemical odor in the breath.

Is there a "normal" range of teenage alcohol or drug use? Given that 50% of teenagers in secondary school have used marijuana (Johnston, O'Malley, & Bachman, 2003) and 50% of high school seniors have drunk alcoholic beverages in the past 30 days, from a statistical perspective use in adolescence is "normal." However, as noted, use in adolescence can lead to additional serious problems. Delaying use of alcohol and drugs as long as possible should be a parental mandate. Further, early use (before age 16) is associated with factors that could be addressed by parents and schools in the interest of prevention: for example, peer involvement with substance use, unhappiness in school, delinquency, and lack of participation in religious activities (van den Bree & Pickworth, 2005).

Parents need to know that "experimentation" with alcohol or drugs is common in adolescence. This reality does not mean that parents should be blasé or indifferent to such use. Rather, parents should take a "generational stand" against such use, recognizing that their position will be tested. Sanctions should be put into place when parental values are violated. Such sanctions should be proportionate to the situation and realistically enforceable.

How do parents know if their teenager's drinking or drug use is a part of normal adolescent experimentation or is symptomatic of a problem? One crucial question is whether or not the adolescent is experiencing consequences related to the use of substances but continues to use despite the difficulties. Some common problems that signal trouble for using teens are listed in Table 7.2.

Law enforcement agencies provide good advice for parents as well. For example, law enforcement officers strongly recommend that parents realize that they can legally search their children's rooms and that signs such as empty beer, wine, or liquor bottles, cigarette rolling papers, spray paint cans, or pills or substances that they cannot explain should be investigated by

Table 7.2
Common Warning Signs of Teenage Drinking or Drug Use

- Decline in grades
- Change in friends
- Change in activities
- Moodiness or irritability
- Heightened family conflicts
- Behavioral or legal problems

them. Furthermore, drug-testing kits can be purchased at any pharmacy. Another point that may be of assistance in evaluating the potential an adolescent has for developing drug or alcohol use is to consider whom does he or she emulate the most. Is it the parents, or is it rock stars, movie stars, or athletes? Celebrities are notorious models of poor behavior involving alcohol and drug abuse. Of course, it is important for parents to know the names of their children's friends, where they live, and to meet their parents. Developing relationships with children's friends and parents can provide a very useful source of information (Dallas Fraternal Order of Police, 2004).

Warning signs of drug and alcohol use within the family and home include aggressive behavior toward younger siblings, escalating conflicts with parents, repeated breaking of family rules, and escalating verbal or physical aggression. Further, a decrease in respect for self or others and frequent curfew violations or staying out all night are all red flags. Similarly, time loss that cannot be explained and a declining interest in family, social activities, or hobbies are common. Isolation in the adolescent's bedroom and stealing (or missing money) can be expected with an emerging pattern of drug abuse, as can vague explanations of whereabouts, manufactured excuses, lying, as well as a decline in hygiene and orderliness. Defiant behavior, unwillingness to participate in family responsibilities, returning home with signs of intoxicated behavior, or wearing items symbolic of a drug culture should alert the family to an emerging problem. In school there may be a drop in performance as well as irregular attendance. Interest in sports or other curricular activities may lessen and avoidance of old friends and an attempt to make new friends who may be older or have a poor reputation should be suspect. Being secretive with parents about friends and activities should be considered a red flag for further investigation of the teen's activities.

Some of the areas commonly affected by substance abuse may be explored by remembering the mnemonic HEADS (Goldenring & Cohen, 1988):

H   home
E   education
A   activities (also note: affect, ambition, anger)
D   drugs
S   sex

Relationships often deteriorate in the home when a teen is abusing drugs or alcohol. Difficult adolescents become even more difficult when substances fuel problems in relationships with parents and siblings. School truancy often increases as grades decrease. However, school failure may not occur in teens of high intelligence, who may continue to bring home good grades despite a developing problem, while friends, interests, attitudes, and motivation change.

More specific screens are available for quick use to gain additional insight. One that holds promise is CRAFFT (Knight et al., 1999; see Table 7.3). Two or more positive responses indicate that substance abuse is present and may be serious.

The best questions to screen for substance abuse are those designed to elicit the least amount of defensiveness. The CRAFFT questionnaire focuses on behavior; it does not ask for answers that involve quantity such as, "How much? How often?" Questions that are quantitative often sound accusing or judgmental. At some point quantitative data are needed, but not at the beginning of an interview.

Common Drugs Are Commonly Used

Monitoring the Future (2005) surveys the percentage of high school seniors who have used specific substances in the preceding month. In the 2005 survey, 47% of high school seniors reported alcohol use; 23% had used cigarettes and therefore risk developing a chronic addiction to tobacco that extends into adulthood. Substances most used by our society as a whole—alcohol and tobacco—pose the greatest risk to the majority of youth in the United States.

Because it is illegal, marijuana can serve as a "gateway" or steppingstone to other illicit drugs (Kandel, 2003). The use of marijuana has significant

Table 7.3
CRAFFT Questions

C: Have you ever ridden in a CAR driven by someone (including yourself) who was "high" or had been using alcohol or drugs?

R: Do you ever use alcohol or drugs to RELAX, feel better about yourself, or fit in?

A: Do you ever use alcohol or drugs while you are by yourself, ALONE?

F: Do your FAMILY or FRIENDS ever tell you that you should cut down on your drinking or drug use?

F: Do you ever FORGET things you did while using alcohol or drugs?

T: Have you gotten into TROUBLE while you were using alcohol or drugs?

From Knight et al., 1999.

adverse consequences for an adolescent. Brook, Gordon, Brook, & Brook (1988) studied high school students in 9th and 10th grades and again in 12th grade. They found that regular use of marijuana led to lower achievement and more deviant behavior on the part of the users, and greater rebelliousness. Further, the adolescent's relationship with his or her parents deteriorated and the association with drug-using friends increased. More recently, adolescent substance use has been associated with chronic problems in similar life areas (Kaminer & Bukstein, 2005).

Other drugs deserving of attention include the inhalants, anabolic steroids, and the "club drugs." Inhalants are identifiable by one main characteristic: They are rarely, if ever, taken by any means other than inhalation. Typically, volatile solvents such as paint thinners, glues, or aerosols are used. Inhalants are of special importance because they are the first drugs that some young children try, due to availability. Their intoxicating effects are similar to alcohol.

Anabolic steroids have been used over the past several decades to boost athletic performance. Some reports indicate their use is on the rise among high school athletes (Middleman, Faulkner, & Woods, 1995). Use of steroids may damage the hepatic, cardiovascular, and endocrine systems, as well as cause aggressive behavior. Use among boys is greater than among girls, though there is concern that use in girls is growing. Monitoring the Future (2003) reported that 1.4% of 12th graders had used steroids within the past 30 days.

The term *club drugs* refers to those drugs that young people use at all night parties. These drugs do not come from any single class of drugs and may change as trends change. Those most recognized by name are (1) ecstasy or MDMA (methylenedioxymethamphetamine), a drug that has both stimulant and hallucinogenic properties, with potentially long-term neurotoxic effects; (2) methamphetamine, a stimulant toxic to the dopamine system that can be manufactured using over-the-counter stimulants; (3) rohypnol, a tasteless and odorless benzodiazepine known to produce anterograde amnesia, which are properties making it well known for its use in sexual assaults; (4) gamma-hydroxybutyrate (GHB), a make-it-at-home sedative that has also been implicated in date rape.

Treatment Options

Modern psychiatric treatment attempts to integrate the biological, psychological (including developmental), and social variables that influence the emergence of a disorder. This biopsychosocial model is well applied to substance use disorders in adolescents. Although genetic factors involved in substance use disorders remain elusive, familial association is well established, especially with alcohol dependence. Genetic heterogeniety is assumed to be operating in the transmission of substance use disorders across generations. Twin studies have found that about 40% of monozygotic pairs and 22% of dizygotic pairs are concordant for alcoholism. This finding indicates that about 40% of the variance is genetic and 60% is environmental (Plomin, Owen, & McGuffin, 1994). Other studies have determined the heritability of stimulant or opiate use, which was found to range from 0.11 to 0.45 heritability. Similarly, heritability for smoking initiation ranges from 0.46 to 0.84, depending on the study (Enoch & Goldman, 1999).

Differences between the children of alcoholics and control groups have been found across a wide variety of variables, including a decreased response to alcohol (i.e., having less sense of being intoxicated, less body sway after drinking, and a greater endocrine response). In addition, fewer alpha waves on encephalography have been found in both male alcoholics and their sons, a deficit that is presumably corrected by consuming alcohol. This finding suggests that alcohol has a particularly beneficial and calming effect for these vulnerable individuals (Liepman et al., 2002).

Cloninger (1987) proposed two types of alcoholism presented in Table 7.4. This subtyping helps to separate different etiological risk factors and perhaps different treatment needs. Essentially, the youth-onset (Type B) form of alcoholism is apparent before age 21 and involves males predominately. The personality traits of such individuals are characterized by high risk-taking and thrill-seeking behaviors. These individuals are low on harm-avoidant behaviors, and low on a need for social rewards to influence behavior. They tend to be polydrug users, availing themselves of any and all substances. There is often antisocial behavior resulting in delinquency and crime. In childhood there are increased findings of oppositional disorder, ADHD, conduct disorder, or learning problems. This youth-onset type of alcohol and drug abuser is generally considered more difficult to treat and has a higher heritability factor (a higher heritability factor indicates a greater genetic influence relative to environmental factors) than the Type A (adult-onset) group. In the latter alcohol dependence usually doesn't emerge until age twenty-one or later, and males and females are equally represented. These individuals have different personality traits and do not tend to be risk takers or thrill seekers. They are much more harm avoidant and much more dependent on others' opinions of them (i.e., responsive to social rewards). Alcohol or other

Table 7.4
Youth- and Adult-Onset Types of Alcoholism

Dimension	Type A (Adult Onset)	Type B (Youth Onset)
Age of onset	>21	<21
Gender	Male = Female	Male > Female
Temperament: danger	Harm avoidant	Risk taker
Temperament: reward	Social reward dependent	Thrill seeker
Drug preference	Alcohol, sedatives	Any and all
Legal involvement	Drunk driving offenses	Delinquency, crime
Adult behavior	Passive, compliant	Antisocial
Childhood behavior	Compliant, teacher's pet	Oppositional defiant, ADHD, conduct disorder, learning problems
Treatment difficulty	Less	More
Genetic heritability	0.2	0.8

Modified with permission from Cloninger, 1987.

sedatives tend to be the primary drug of choice, and their legal problems are usually confined to drunk driving offenses. Typically they are compliant and passive and do not have learning disabilities or psychiatric disorders. Their treatment potential is considerably greater than those in Type B, and the heritability of this form of alcoholism is substantially less than the youth-onset form.

Treatment options are limited for many adolescents. However, studies show that substance abuse treatment is effective in changing behavior. Promising outcomes have been reported for family-based interventions, cognitive–behavioral therapy, motivational enhancement techniques, and 12-step facilitation (Kaminer, 2001). Each of these treatments can be effective, even though each is built around a different premise. Family therapy, for example, works to identify and change dysfunctional family patterns. Young and middle teens are especially vulnerable to acting out family stresses in ways such as using substances. Cognitive–behavioral therapy strengthens the individual's ability to cope with high-risk situations that may precipitate relapse; role-playing and the development of skills to handle tempting situations are used to reinforce the individual's resources. Motivational enhancement therapy aims to help the adolescent identify his or her problem and resolve to change the self-defeating behavior. Twelve-step approaches view substance abuse as a spiritual and medical disease and are based on AA's principle of total abstinence. Although this form of treatment is traditionally associated with adults, it can be useful for adolescents as well. The abstract thinking involved in utilizing concepts such as a higher power and powerlessness may pose some challenges for young adolescents. However, supportive peer groups are likely to be quite helpful to individuals in this age group.

What Level of Treatment Is Necessary?

Inpatient or outpatient? One-to-one counseling or a formal, organized program? These questions are often difficult to answer, and resources—insurance or other financial arrangements—may be the determining factor. That said, an intense outpatient program (IOP) combined with one-to-one counseling may be optimal for the teen who has a supportive family structure that includes accountability. Frequent urine drug and alcohol screens should be conducted by the IOP or, if necessary, by the family. The teen should be cooperative, prosocial (i.e., not delinquent), and free of any major psychiatric disorders.

Teens rarely need hospitalization for detoxification. However, if compliance is an issue, admission to a residential program where 24-hour observation is possible may be necessary. Such programs provide an intense treatment experience and typically indoctrinate patients into 12-step programs.

Adolescents with signs of suicidal behavior, serious depression or anxiety, or psychotic symptoms should be admitted to a psychiatric facility for observation, diagnosis, and treatment. Substance abuse treatment can proceed after psychiatric assessment and stabilization.

Family counseling and family participation in Al-Anon are essential when dealing with an adolescent substance use disorder. If family members can change some of their possibly dysfunctional or enabling behaviors, the adolescent will be confronted with a "changed system" and will be freer to make changes him- or herself (Azrin et al., 1994).

Not only do adolescent treatment programs reduce drug abuse, they produce other improvements as well. The National Institute of Drug Abuse (NIDA) supported a large-scale study of treatment outcomes in 1,100 adolescents who participated in a variety of residential, inpatient, and outpatient programs (Hser et al., 2001). Drug and alcohol use declined significantly in those involved in recovery programs. Additionally, school attendance and academic performance improved, and criminal activity declined. Adolescents reported fewer thoughts of suicide, less hostility, and higher self-esteem.

Patients who completed their programs tended to do better than those who dropped out early.

What Parents Can Do

Prevention is key. Even though adolescence is a time for teens to experiment with various levels of freedom, parents are advised to (1) keep track of their teens' activities, (2) have household policies about substance use along with known consequences for breaking rules, and (3) set a good example regarding their own alcohol use. Parents of high-risk teens are especially advised to pay close attention. Clinicians are in an excellent position to advise parents to educate themselves about adolescent substance abuse before it starts.

The NIAAA (2000) publication "Make a Difference: Talk to Your Child about Alcohol" has some excellent tips for parents about ways to strengthen their relationship with their teen through improved communication. It suggests the following parent behaviors:

- Encourage conversations through active listening and showing interest in subjects that interest the child.
- Ask open-ended questions rather than those that require only a "yes" or "no" response.
- Control emotions and think before speaking, showing respect for the child's viewpoint.

Either the clinician or parent can engage in brainstorming with the adolescent about how to say "no" to alcohol or drugs. Some ideas, from mildest to strongest, are listed in Table 7.5.

Table 7.5

Six Ways to Say No

1. No, thanks.
2. I don't feel like it—do you have any soda?
3. Alcohol's *not* my thing.
4. Are you talking to me? *Forget* it!
5. Why do you keep pressuring me when I've said *no*?
6. *BACK-OFF!*

From NIAAA, 2000.

In addition to helping the teen learn how to say "no," parents can raise topics (perhaps during a sit-down dinner, free of television or telephone interruptions) such as their children's dreams for the future.

- Does the future look happy, and hopeful to you? (If not, why not?)
- Who do you most admire—at school, in the community, and beyond (e.g., politicians, celebrities, athletes)?
- Who or what gives you support, courage, or comfort when times are tough?
- Is participation in religious observances or activities enjoyable for you?
- What are your personal decisions about substance use or abuse?
- Do you believe substance abuse affects families, friends, or health?
- Are you concerned about any of your friends' or their parents' or brothers' or sisters' use of drugs or alcohol?
- Are you concerned about our use of alcohol or drugs?
- Are you concerned about your use or whether you can saw "no" to use?

Parents will need to sort out their positions on teen behaviors and provide a united front. Adolescents benefit from clear statements of family values. Parents should not be discouraged if their views are belittled, scoffed at, or otherwise disparaged. A consistent family philosophy is likely to be internalized by adolescents and, even if tested or rejected for a time, offers a return to a safe island in a culture of confusing choices.

Substance Abuse in Older Adults

Highlights

• The number of people over age 65 that abuse substances is expected to double by midcentury.

• Clinicians are encouraged to identify substance abuse and dependence in geriatric patients.

• Doctors who prescribe sedatives and opiates need to closely monitor the use of these medications in older patients.

• Common medical and psychiatric problems may worsen with the use and misuse of alcohol and psychoactive medications.

• Suggest a program sensitive to the issues of aging when addiction treatment is needed.

This chapter is about adults over age 65 who abuse substances. The excessive use of alcohol and prescription medication complicates the lives of some older adults. Illicit drug use is much less common in this population as compared to younger groups. Some organ systems are particularly vulnerable to the toxicity of alcohol and deteriorate more quickly when exposed to chronic drinking. Late-onset drinking or prescription drug abuse is also a problem because intoxication impairs equilibrium (which may already be taxed), clouds thinking, and may alter emotional reactions.

Alcohol, sedatives, and opiates are the substances that older adults most frequently abuse. The U.S. government expects the number of people abusing substances in later life to double by midcentury. There is general agreement that the "Baby Boomer" cohort will soon make up a large proportion of those over the age of 65. Baby Boomer lore includes the liberal use of illicit substances and the greater use of alcohol than their parents. Although we do not know what drugs these older adults will abuse in the future, alcohol will likely remain near the top of the list. Less certain is the way in which prescription drugs will be misused. In 25 years will sedatives be misused, as they sometimes are now? Will the demand for opiate analgesics increase in a patient population that is living longer? Will medical marijuana be legalized, and might this have ramifications in a cohort that grew up with access to cannabis?

It is predicted that European Americans will continue to comprise the majority of the elderly population for many years. This is noteworthy because European American men are the group most likely to continue using alcohol into late life (Secretary of Health and Human Services, 2000): The prototypic person who continues to use alcohol into old age is the European American male with chronic alcoholism. He is easy to identify provided he demonstrates the typical "stigmata" of long-term alcohol abuse.

Alcohol abuse is more difficult to identify in women and may not have been diagnosed when they were younger (Tinsley, 2004). Many women currently in the older age group were stay-at-home mothers, so their use of alcohol was less apparent than it might have been had they worked outside the home. Stigma has been greater for female alcoholics and has probably played a role in reinforcing the tendency to hide their drinking for as long as possible. Another cause of difficulty is the fact that society, including clinicians, does not expect women to be problem drinkers. In that realm, it is still a man's world.

Older women are more often associated with prescription drug abuse, especially benzodiazepines. The extent to which older women misuse benzodiazepines in this decade is not well delineated; however, they comprised the group that most often received long-term treatment with benzodiazepines (Farnsworth, 1990), and some became dependent on these medications. Physicians continue to prescribe benzodiazepines to older adults, though perhaps to a lesser extent (Blazer et al., 2004). As of 2006, young men with polysubstance dependence probably use the most sedatives. Even so, sedatives and opiates are medications that both men and women abuse in later life.

Often substance abuse, including alcohol consumption, declines with age. Some older adults who enjoyed social drinking earlier in life decide that they feel better without any alcohol. Increasing fatigue, headaches, disequilibrium, and other ill effects make the decision to stop using alcohol, sedatives, or opiates an easy one. These individuals do not have substance dependence, and they stop using without distress. However, older adults do not comprise a homogeneous group; there is a great deal of variation. For starters, gender differences are significant. Whereas some older men increase their use of alcohol, women often decrease their consumption (Secretary of Health and Human Services, 2000). An important point is that those who consume even small amounts of alcohol or drugs may still experience ill effects, especially when frail or medically ill.

Some patients are dependent on substances and cannot easily quit. Still others use more substances when life changes produce overwhelming emotions. Aging is a time of many psychosocial changes, with predominant themes of loss and loneliness. Emotional and physical pain may be reasons for escape through the use of mind-numbing medications or alcohol. Paradoxically, the psychological, emotional, and somatic distress of aging often intensifies with intoxication. Whatever medical compromise exists, substance abuse is likely to make it worse, further dampening the person's quality of life.

Organ Systems That Falter in Older Adults

Alcoholism can serve as a prototype for substance dependence for persons over the age of 65. Alcohol is the most widely used and abused substance, aside from nicotine, and the list of medical illnesses associated with chronic alcohol use is lengthy. These illnesses are more challenging for older adults because of the frailty that comes with advancing age. The following organs are among those that weaken with age and are prone to the toxic effects of chronic alcoholism: liver, peripheral nervous system, and brain.

Liver

Chronic, heavy use of alcohol can induce both reversible and irreversible liver changes (Secretary of Health and Human Services, 2000). The changes that are usually reversible with abstinence are a "fatty liver," seen after binge drinking, and the more serious problem of alcoholic hepatitis, which is an inflammation of the liver. The most devastating form of alcohol-induced liver disease is cirrhosis. The cirrhotic liver becomes hard and fibrous, with its function seriously compromised. In the later stages of liver disease, hepatic encephalopathy and prolonged bleeding times portend a poor prognosis, especially in the elderly patient who has little physical reserve.

Not all heavy drinkers develop irreversible alcohol-induced liver disease. It is not clear why some people are more vulnerable to these effects; however, malnutrition may be a factor (Mendenhall, Roselle, & Moritz, 1995). It is important that elderly alcoholic patients maintain proper nutrition, although older patients experience a number of obstacles to healthy eating: Food preparation may be unhealthy, finances may be limited, and alcohol may be their preferred source of calories.

The liver, like other organs, changes during the aging process. Hepatocytes (i.e., liver cells) regenerate slowly, and blood flow to the liver decreases. Therefore, in later life, clearance and elimination of many medications decelerate (Blazer et al., 2004). The decreased efficiency in metabolizing drugs is an important reason for the reduced dosing recommendations of many medications that are prescribed to older patients. Elderly patients with liver disease are at considerable risk for medication toxicity.

Peripheral Nervous System

Many diseases are associated with peripheral neuropathy in older adults. Chronic alcoholism is one such disease. The peripheral neuropathy that occurs in alcoholism is a toxic polyneuropathy, resulting in both sensory and motor disturbances. The skin on the legs is characteristically thin and shiny. The patient commonly complains of paresthesias, numbness, weakness, and impaired mobility. Paresthesias can be very painful and typically involve the feet. An inadequate intake of B vitamins is believed to be one factor that makes individuals vulnerable to an alcoholic polyneuropathy, and vitamin B supplementation is often an aspect of treatment (Rakel & Bope, 2005).

The process of aging taxes mobility due to weakened muscles and diminished range of motion. Adults in later life may have additional diseases that compromise mobility, such as osteoarthritis or Parkinson's disease. On top of any of these burdens, alcoholic polyneuropathy can exact a tremendous toll. As deterioration from aging and disease adds up, the likelihood of falling increases. Falling becomes even more of a risk with intoxication.

Brain

Dementia is not a normal condition of late life; mild memory impairment is much more common. In fact, most people experience some mild memory loss with age. Also unwelcome is the diminished learning efficiency that occurs in most people during later life. However, these changes seldom concern anyone except the person experiencing them. They are mild changes of normal aging that are benign and nonprogressive.

Alzheimer's disease is the most common type of dementia. It is a progressive and terminal illness. The dementias affect approximately 3% of the population (American Psychiatric Association, 2000). In addition to Alzheimer's disease, other dementias—such as vascular dementia, normal pressure hydrocephalus, and Lewy body disease—are a part of the differential diagnosis of dementia. Alcoholic dementia may be the second leading cause of dementia after Alzheimer's disease (Eckardt, 1986).

MRI imaging studies of older alcoholics show cortical atrophy of gray and white matter, particularly of prefrontal gray matter (Pfefferbaum, 1997). There is evidence that the frontal lobes are especially vulnerable to the toxic effects of alcohol, and that impaired executive functioning constitutes the core cognitive disorder in older alcoholics. Patients with executive dysfunction cannot reliably control impulses, regulate emotions, solve problems, or maintain concentration. In alcoholic dementia, as in all types of dementia, memory and learning are seriously impaired. Not all studies agree about the specific areas of greatest damage. Regardless of the specific areas of impairment, however, the severity of alcohol-related changes in brain and cognition are more pronounced in older alcoholics (Kaplan, 2004).

The brain is extremely sensitive to the neurotoxic effects of alcohol. As in other diseases related to alcohol, genetics and nutrition are suspected to influence vulnerability. The effects of medication, trauma, premorbid brain function, and the presence of other dementias may help explain individual susceptibilities. Patients with alcoholic dementia have a serious condition. With abstinence, the condition may slow or show small improvements. With bouts of intoxication, the situation becomes more precarious.

Geriatric Syndromes

The term *geriatric syndromes* refers to a set of symptoms with a high prevalence in older adults (Olde Rikkert et al., 2003). Some of these conditions worsen when complicated by the excessive use of alcohol or prescription drugs. Three such examples are polypharmacy, falls, and alcoholic dementia.

Polypharmacy is the use of multiple therapeutic agents, specifically prescription and over-the-counter medications. Older patients are heavy consumers of medicine—prescribed, over-the counter, and herbal agents. Even without the effects of substance abuse, polypharmacy poses risks that increase with the number of medications and the less efficient metabolism that accompanies older age. The added effects of substance abuse bring greater dangers. Indeed, polypharmacy can go seriously wrong in the elderly patient who abuses substances, leading to greater cumulative side effects and toxicities. Obvious ill effects include sedation, ataxia, and other symptoms that are caused by exceeding therapeutic drug levels.

In addition, medication nonadherence (or noncompliance) is a problem for the individuals who are frequently intoxicated. Patients may forget to take the medication, may not understand the instructions, or may take the wrong dose. If finances are limited, there may be a conscious decision to buy alcohol or food instead of medication. Case 1 describes a man with longstanding alcohol dependence, a serious psychiatric disorder, and an unusual form of medication nonadherence.

This is an example of a patient who prioritized drinking over taking the medication he needed for optimal control of his bipolar disorder. His choice to discontinue lithium intermittently may have represented denial about his alcoholism or about his mental illness. He rationalized his behavior by telling himself that he was, at least in part, following doctor's orders.

Case 1

Mr. A, a 66-year-old man, was hospitalized for a severe episode of mania. The patient had abused alcohol during most of his adult life and had a history of multiple hospitalizations for bipolar disorder. At the time of admission his lithium level was only 0.2 mEq/L, when it should have been close to 1.0 mEq/L. When the patient's condition had stabilized, the treating psychiatrist asked him if he had been taking his medication. The patient answered that he had. The psychiatrist told Mr. A that on admission his lithium level was very low. Then Mr. A clarified that because he was told not to mix medications and alcohol, he had not taken lithium when he was drinking.

Falls in older adults occur frequently enough to be classified as a geriatric syndrome. The scenario in which an elderly person falls, sustains a hip fracture, and is immobilized is common and in some cases disabling. After a serious fall, the fear of falling can lead to anxiety leaving the home, which may then lead to a loss of independence. Many medical illnesses can disturb a patient's gait or equilibrium and contribute to falling; alcoholic polyneuropathy is one such problem that was discussed above. Dehydration, medication side effects, musculoskeletal disease, poor eyesight, and nervous system diseases all carry risks of falling that increase dramatically with intoxication.

Alcoholic dementia is a common form of dementia. The clinician who is unfamiliar with the patient's drinking history is at a disadvantage in making a diagnosis of alcoholic dementia, however. In any patient evaluated for cognitive decline, it is necessary to ask the patient *and* family about his or her alcohol history.

In addition, a person with dementia who continues to abuse substances is likely to shorten the length of time he or she can live independently. Alcoholics who drink throughout adult life sometimes alienate family, losing important emotional and financial resources. Case 2 describes a man with alcoholic dementia who was no longer able to care for himself.

Both physicians and other clinicians can recognize cases of substance abuse by keeping in mind the ways in which substances can impact older adults. The physician can rely on the medical and psychiatric history, physical examination, laboratory data, and collateral data, as discussed in Chapter 4. Others can be alert to changes in older adults that may indicate an

---

Case 2

Mr. B, a 76-year-old divorced man who lived alone, was referred for an evaluation of cognitive decline. The patient had abused alcohol for most of his adult life and was estranged from his three children. A social worker accompanied Mr. B to his appointment and provided most of the history. Mr. B's poor memory had made it impossible for him to take his medications reliably. He had also started wandering at night, and neighbors had seen him foraging for food in garbage cans outside his apartment building.

excessive use of substances. Depression may be a sign, as may declining nutrition, alertness, enjoyment, interactions with peers, and changes in sleep.

Mental health professionals are typically experts in dealing with families, and most are keen listeners. They often take time to gather collateral data that helps understand the patient's personality, including his or her strengths and weaknesses. This knowledge can help predict particular life changes that may be difficult for the patient to handle. In the vignette above, it was the social worker who sorted through family relationships, information from neighbors, interviewed the patient, took the patient to medical appointments, and assisted in locating more appropriate housing.

Coping with Changes in Later Life

Erikson defined the primary task of later life as the successful resolution of the conflict of ego integrity versus despair (Erikson, 1987). Achieving integrity implies that the individual accepts his or her unique life and the important people in it. Rather than focus on what might have been, the person feels pride in his or her accomplishments. Other factors that seem to help a person manage the hardships of aging include the presence of a social network, mature coping skills, adequate finances, and physical well-being. Health in these areas protects from maladaptive responses to stress, such as substance abuse. Nonetheless, the ability to withstand change often diminishes as cognitive and physical reserve declines.

It is unusual for a lifelong teetotaler to begin abusing alcohol in the sixth or seventh decade of life. However, the social drinker may increase his or her alcohol use following a stressful life event or a change in life circumstance. One such time when social drinking may change to alcohol abuse, or when prescribed medication becomes abused, is after retirement when there is loss of lifestyle. Case 3 illustrates one such situation.

Later life is a time of change. A life that has been full and happy may later be perceived as lonely and shallow. Changes that are particularly painful include losing a spouse, developing physical limitations, retiring from a job that was highly valued, moving away from the family home, and diminishing finances. Reliance on alcohol or medications may serve as a psychic balm. Older people may use escapism as a way of dealing with painful situations. Although it may be true that Mr. and Mrs. C initially drank as an enjoyable activity, their drinking quickly became a liability.

Patients are not the only ones who must cope with the changes of aging. Children and grandchildren also feel the passage of time, along with shifts

---

Case 3

Mr. and Mrs. C were referred for an evaluation of their alcohol use. They had been happily married for 40 years. Throughout adult life, Mr. C had steadily worked as a carpenter and Mrs. C had been a housewife. The couple's adult children were concerned that their parents' use of alcohol became excessive after Mr. C retired. Mr. and Mrs. C said that they enjoyed drinking now that they had fewer responsibilities, and they resented their children's interference. The couple's children had noticed the following symptoms of alcohol abuse in both of their parents: slurred speech, argumentativeness, drinking instead of eating dinner, and walking with an unsteady gait. In addition, Mrs. C had fallen, requiring stitches on her forehead.

---

in roles. As in the vignette about Mr. and Mrs. C, who did not appreciate what they saw as interference from their children, not all attempts to intercede are met with good cheer. Yet many families are left with the tasks of looking out for the well-being of their aging parents.

Family members may wonder how much drinking (or use of sedative medications) is too much for an elderly person, and the answer to this question must be individualized. There are two ways to consider this issue. The first is whether the function of the older person is compromised because he or she uses alcohol or other sedating drugs. The second is whether there is a substance use disorder that makes discontinuing the use of drugs or alcohol difficult. Both may be the case. In situations where the patient is not able to use alcohol or drugs responsibly or to abstain if that is the recommendation, a formal treatment program is necessary.

When the older adult has used substances for many years, the family is usually well versed in recognizing the signs and symptoms of addiction. When alcohol or medication abuse is a new development, there are clues. (When family members live in a different part of the country, frequent telephone calls may be the only way to stay in touch.) Family members can be advised to listen for slurred or rambling speech and atypical quarrelsomeness. Other clues are cognitive impairment and minor traffic accidents or other forms of trauma. Detecting alcohol abuse is probably easier than detecting the excessive use of medications that are authorized (i.e., prescribed).

It is important for a family member to accompany the older person to medical and psychiatric appointments. Even younger patients have trouble recalling everything that the clinician says during an appointment. Asking questions the elder may forget to ask about medication interactions and side effects can be a preventive step. Being aware of the potential for habituation to medications is also helpful—although this area can be tricky. There can be an overemphasis on the addictive potential of drugs, as seen in a reluctance to use opioid analgesics. Providing guidelines about dosage and approximate duration of use can put this issue into perspective for family members, who can then keep a graph of medications and doses over time. They can ask their loved ones if they are using only the medications their physician prescribed. Family members should be made aware of medication side effects and addictive potential, which is information readily available from the physician, pharmacists, and the Internet. Lastly, family members should be encouraged to contact the physician with any concerns.

Abuse of Prescription Medications in Later Life

The degree to which benzodiazepines are abused in later life is an area of debate. There may be a decline in sedative prescriptions as antidepressants have become easier to prescribe and are efficacious in treating depression and some anxiety disorders. However, sedatives remain an important component in the treatment of many psychiatric illnesses. Adults who began taking benzodiazepines for the treatment of anxiety and depression often continue to take them in later life. When additional stresses occur, clinicians may be inclined to prescribe more medication. This practice is often reasonable in the short term. However, a cycle may develop in which the patient uses the medication to escape, then requires more medication to fulfill this need. The clinician may agree to increase the dose if he or she has no other support to offer or if the patient refuses other types of help.

Some patients are prone to abuse medications. Having a psychiatric disorder increases the risk of taking prescription medications and therefore of abusing them. Female gender has been reported as a risk factor for developing sedative/hypnotic abuse (Finlayson, 1994). There are several reasons for sedative use in older women. In general, women have more depression and anxiety than men and may take sedatives as part of their treatment regimen. Also, elderly women see clinicians more often. Then there is the fact that women outlive men. Widowed women experience many changes. Case 4 is an example of benzodiazepine abuse developing in this context.

Case 4

Mrs. D's primary care doctor referred her to an addiction treatment service. She had taken alprazolam 0.5 mg twice daily for several years, and it had been very helpful for treatment of her anxiety. She was maintained on a stable dose until her husband died unexpectedly 2 years prior to the referral. Following the death of Mrs. D's husband, the doctor increased the alprazolam dose. The doctor also suggested an additional dose at bedtime when the patient had trouble sleeping. Without the doctor's knowledge, Mrs. D also obtained sedatives from a well-meaning neighbor. When Mrs. D had a minor traffic accident, it alerted her son to the fact that she was taking too much medication. When the doctor attempted to reduce the alprazolam, Mrs. D became anxious, tearful, and could not sleep.

Case 4 illustrates several important points. The benzodiazepine was used at a stable dose for several years to treat the target symptom of anxiety. The increase in dose following the husband's death would have been a reasonable short-term option, had the physician monitored his patient's use of the drug. Elderly patients sometimes share medications, as this example illustrates. Limited finances or the belief that nothing should ever be wasted may account for this practice. The patient undermined her care by failing to tell her doctor about obtaining extra medication from her friend. Sedatives are commonly used in the elderly, but they pose dangers. Mrs. D was lucky in having only a minor accident. In another scenario she might have had a more serious motor vehicle accident or a different traumatic event, such as a fall. When a patient has developed physiological tolerance to high doses of benzodiazepines, dose reductions can be difficult and even dangerous, and inpatient detoxification may be necessary.

Many of the same safeguards apply to prescribing opioids for chronic, non-progressive pain as apply to using sedatives for anxiety states (see Table 8.1). The physician and patient should discuss these prescribing parameters prior to the initiation of treatment with sedatives and opioids. There needs to be an understanding between the clinician and the patient that the patient will use only one pharmacy and will obtain these medications from only one clinician, even though the patient may be seeing more than one prescriber. This

Table 8.1
Suggestions for Prescribing Sedatives and Opioids

• Discuss prescribing parameters before starting treatment.

• Discuss potential side effects with patient and family.

• The patient should agree to use one prescriber and one pharmacy.

• The clinician needs to keep accurate records of prescriptions.

• Increases in medication during symptom flares should be time limited.

• Patients should bring bottles of all medicines to appointments.

understanding includes an agreement not to borrow medication from friends or relatives unless first discussing it, and not to modify medication doses without prior discussion.

The clinician needs accurate records of prescriptions in order to track the patient's use and to be certain the dosage remains stable. Increases during symptom flares should be time limited. Both benzodiazepines and opioid painkillers are used to treat target symptoms, but they can also alleviate emotional pain. Ideally, involving a family member in discussions about medications that have relaxation effects is a good idea so that he or she can watch for signs of oversedation and unsteadiness. Concern about the inadequate use of pain medication in controlling progressive cancer pain and postoperative pain is appropriate; addiction is not a problem in these situations.

Like social drinkers who abuse alcohol during times of stress, patients who take sedatives and opiates can abuse these medications during difficult times—and like most people who abuse substances, older adults do so in an attempt to feel better. The clinician wants to help the patient; however, in doing so he or she may make the mistake of overprescribing.

Treatment of Substance Abuse in Later Life

The elderly person with an addiction in later life, usually comes to the attention of a health care professional because someone has intervened. Like the younger person who abuses substances, the older person may be reluctant to change. However, the patient with a new substance abuse problem will probably be easier to talk to about sobriety than someone with a chronic problem. The motivation of the patient who began abusing a substance in response to a stressor is more easily understood, and therefore the patient may be more willing (i.e., feel less shame) to talk about the problem. In both instances of recent and chronic abuse, shame is probably a significant factor, although in chronic substance abuse the denial system has had years to become entrenched. The patient with the longstanding problem may feel that he or she "has heard it all before."

The chronic pain patient who is addicted to opiates is well served from a medical assessment if there remains doubt about the etiology of the pain problem. Sometimes the evaluation of the pain's etiology has been conducted in a piecemeal fashion, and the information must be collated for the patient and family. There may not be a clear physiological etiology for the pain. In that case, the physician should explain that because sedatives and opiates are habit forming, it will take increasingly higher doses to ameliorate the pain. The possible side effects of these medications, including constipation, disequilibrium, sedation, and cognitive impairment, should be clearly ennumerated. In brief, the message should accurately convey that continually escalating the medication doses can sacrifice the person's independence. For chronic, nonmalignant pain, small and stable doses of opiates may be fine. However, this is a very different situation from that in which the patient is clearly abusing opiate pain medications in order to enter a euphoric state of intoxication.

Beginning a discussion about alcohol or prescription drug abuse can be difficult. However, it is essential. Elderly alcoholics are seldom aware of how aging intensifies the damage of alcohol on the body (Gambert, 1992), and this may be a good place to start the discussion. The physician can talk about the facts regarding how substances harm the body. Even more effective are more personalized specifics about "how your body has been harmed." The patient may not realize that some of his or her medical problems are worse due to substance abuse. Because most older adults are worried about disability, it may be effective to ask about related symptoms that are linked to substance abuse, such as accidents, falls, poor memory or concentration, fatigue, and changes in sleep habits. These are symptoms that will worsen with abuse of any psychoactive substance.

The results of laboratory data showing the toxic effects of alcohol, such as an elevated gamma-glutamyltransferase or an elevated mean corpuscular volume in someone with alcohol dependence, present stark evidence to reluctant patients. Showing the X-ray of a broken bone after a person has fallen or data from neuropsychiatric testing can convey the same principle. Unfortunately, in some cases even solid data will not be convincing enough; for others, cognitive impairment may limit their grasp of the information.

Family intervention is sometimes a useful tool. Family members can be helpful in persuading their older loved one that sobriety is necessary. In the case of the chronic alcoholic, some family members may still collude in protecting their loved one; however, the family is often a powerful ally. The difficulty in some families is that adult children have also become addicts. They may not want to face a parent's addiction because, as that son or daughter may view it, he or she may be interrogated next. Many families need encouragement to confront a patriarch or matriarch about longstanding alcoholism or addiction to prescription drugs. A family can make a powerful impact by confronting the person with specific instances when intoxication led to a humiliating, dangerous, or hurtful situation. This type of interaction is known as an intervention.

If the patient and family decide to pursue formal treatment, there are several considerations. As noted in Chapter 6, the aim is to provide treatment in the least intensive program that is reasonable, given the patient's symptoms. Most addicted patients are treated in an outpatient setting, and this holds true for older patients; however, there are some additional considerations. As with younger adults, it is important to anticipate the need for detoxification. Mild withdrawal is usually safely handled in an outpatient setting; however, older adults are likely to have problems if unstable heart disease is present. In sedative and alcohol withdrawal, the heart must be strong enough to withstand the stress that comes with a rise in blood pressure and pulse rate.

A few patients require 24-hour medical staffing during detoxification. At risk are those dependent on high doses of sedatives or on alcohol, especially when there is a history of DT or withdrawal seizures. Any risk in a healthy adult is compounded in elderly patient who is frail or otherwise medically compromised. Opioid withdrawal poses much less risk, though it can be uncomfortable. If a detoxifying agent is needed for alcohol or benzodiazepine withdrawal, a short-acting medication such as lorazepam is often a better choice in the elderly than one that is long-acting, such as chlordiazepoxide. This is especially true for the patient who has liver disease. The use of a short-acting agent can minimize the risks of falls and cognitive clouding; it is safe as long as the patient receives adequate coverage for withdrawal symptoms.

Another treatment issue for the older patient is the relative lack of cognitive resiliency. The brain may take longer to recover, and some patients may fail to grasp their problems. For instance, they may not be able to think abstractly enough to apply the steps of AA to their personal lives. The recovery environment for the older patient will be determined by the need for supervision. The same is true for the decision about where the patient is to live after treatment.

Some treatment programs treat all patients in the same milieu. A caveat for older people is that they sometimes feel out of place with a younger generation of substance abusers. This type of disconnection is particularly true for the prescription drug abuser in late life who finds little in common with the marijuana-smoking or cocaine-dealing addict. Even though one opiate is pharmacologically similar to another, the older chronic pain patient can seldom take the similarity to the next step and identify with the heroin addict. If possible, programs need separate groups, assignments, and video programming.

One area of concern is whether or not the elderly addict can continue to live independently. A residential care facility may be the only option available for those who can no longer live alone or who cannot stop abusing substances. The advantages can be multiple: supervision, socialization, meals, hygiene, medication oversight, closer health monitoring, and less access to alcohol.

Late life can be a time of continued psychological growth and appreciation for life. A colleague with a wrongheaded view of addiction once said, "Alcohol is all the old person has left, so let's not take that away too." The nonaddict sometimes needs reminding that addiction is not fun. It is true that some people who eventually become addicted began using in order to have a good time, or some used alcohol or drugs initially to dull psychic pain. However, as the use of substances progressed and sober times became more difficult to predict, using became an enormous burden. Addiction is not a happy or enviable condition. The elderly are like most other people who have become habitual users; they want to return to a clearheaded life.

9
Smoking

Highlights
• Smoking prevalence remains high in the U.S. despite the well-known adverse health effects.
• Physicians and mental health practitioners are urged to attend to smoking behaviors in their patients.
• Strategies to initiate smoking cessation include using each clinical encounter to review readiness to quit.
• Brief interventions with follow-up contact are often successful.
• Common obstacles to cessation—depression, weight gain, loss of stimulation—can be overcome by individualizing treatment plans.

In the past half-century tens of millions of people have quit smoking. The 1964 Surgeon General's report (U.S. Department of Health, Education, and Welfare, 1964) initiated a cascade of subsequent medical reports documenting the harmful effects of smoking tobacco, with its 4,000 or so active chemicals (Chiba & Masironi, 1992) and its capability of inducing nicotine dependence. As of today, smoking prevalence in men has decreased by 50% compared to its peak in the 1960s but has decreased by only 25% in women during this same period. Regrettably, it is estimated that more than 3,000 adolescents become chain smokers every day (Gilpin, Chol, Berry, & Pierce, 1999).

At least 40,000 books and articles on tobacco and health and 22 Surgeon General's reports have been available and widely disseminated (Satcher & Erikson, 1994), yet nearly 50 million Americans smoke, and smoking increased during the 1990s among high school students (Johnston, O'Malley, & Bachman, 2003).

Physicians are continually urged to advise smokers to quit (Richards, 1992; Tomar, Husten, & Manley, 1996) and are, of course, well aware of the extensive medical consequences of smoking, as is the general public. (See Table 9.1 for a summary of medical complications.) Secondhand smoke causes thousands of deaths yearly, or serious illness in nonsmokers such as relatives and children of smokers (Office of Health and Environmental Assessment, 1992).

Why Smoke?

Most smokers begin using in adolescence. Today, 15% of middle schoolers and 34% of high school students smoke (Centers for Disease Control and Prevention, 2001). The reasons are multiple:

1. Fit in with a peer group
2. Rebellion
3. Macho/sexy image
4. Modeling an adult smoker in the family
5. Weight control
6. Tension relief

Whatever the reason(s) for initiating cigarette use, nicotine is reinforcing through its impact on dopaminergic pathways projecting from the ventral tegmental area to the cerebral cortex and limbic system (Pontieri, Tanda, & Orzi, 1996). In addition to stimulating dopaminergic pathways, nicotine results in increased circulating norepinephrine, epinephrine, vasopressin, beta-endorphin, ACTH, and cortisol. As a result, the smoker experiences decreased tension as well as improved

1. Attention
2. Learning
3. Reaction time
4. Problem solving

Table 9.1
Some Medical Consequences of Smoking

Skeletal (Hollenback et al., 1993; Krall & Dawson-Hughes, 1991)

- Accelerated osteoporosis
- Decreased bone mass density
- Impaired bone blood flow
- Delayed bone healing (e.g., as in fractures and spinal fusions)

Respiratory (Boyle & Maisonneuve, 1995; Mullen et al., 1986)

- Lung cancer (typically adenocarcinoma)
  - 80–90% of lung cancers are linked to smoking
- Chronic obstructive pulmonary disease (COPD)
- Chronic bronchitis
- Emphysema

Reproductive (Walsh et al., 1997; Wisborg et al., 1999)

- Reduced fertility
- Lower birth weight
- Increased risk of spontaneous abortion
- Increased risk of ectopic pregnancy

Cardiovascular (Rigotti & Pasternak, 1996; Robbins et al., 1994)

- Coronary artery disease (increased coronary vascular resistance; decreased coronary flow velocity; increased platelet thrombus formation; increased triglyceride level)
- Stroke
- Peripheral vascular disease
- Aortic aneurysm

Urological (Mikhailidis et al., 1998)

- Bladder cancer
- Prostate cancer
- Renal cancer

5. Mood
6. Skeletal muscle relaxation

The ritual of smoking is also enjoyable; that is, the smell of tobacco, the stimulation of the pharynx and bronchi, the visualization of smoke, the social settings associated with "lighting up." The wide array of the effects of nicotine, although not as dramatic or powerful as other addicting substances, is pervasive and increasingly compelling for the smoker.

Who Becomes Dependent?

The criteria for substance use dependence are presented in Chapter 5. Specific instruments for assessing nicotine dependence are described later in this chapter. Ninety-five percent of nicotine dependence is to cigarette smoking (Grant et al., 2004b); 25% of Americans smoke (at least one cigarette in the past year) and one-half of these (12.8%) are nicotine dependent. Nicotine dependence in the past 12 months was found in 14.1% of males and 11.5% of women (Grant et al., 2004b).

Only about 5% of dependent smokers became dependent in the same year in which daily smoking began. The highest rate of nicotine dependence occurs in the first 16 years from the year of onset of daily smoking. In a study of nicotine dependence in the United States it was determined that a lifetime prevalence of daily smoking (defined as smoking daily for a month or more) was 49.5%, and the lifetime prevalence of nicotine dependence was 24.1% (Preslau et al., 2001).

A comparison of the percentages of adults using tobacco and other substances of abuse, the rates of dependence on these substances, and the related risks for dependence are presented in Table 9.3 (Anthony, Warner, & Kessler, 1994). Tobacco poses the highest risk for dependence. This increased risk is due to tobacco being legal, widely available, and non-intoxicating (thus avoiding adverse reactions).

In a 15-year follow-up study in Finland it was found that 26% of daily smokers and 46% of occasional smokers at age 15 had quit by the age of 28. The cessation rate was higher among females, the married, and those employed, and rates of cessation were lower if the individual had friends or family who smoked. Cessation was also lower in those who consumed higher amounts of alcohol and who had less leisure-time physical activity. The conclusion was that one-third of all teenage smokers stopped smoking before the age of 28 (Paavola, Vartiainen, & Puska, 2001).

Who is likely to become dependent? Compelling evidence indicates that early smoking initiation and subsequent dependence are more likely to occur in people who suffered adverse childhood experiences, have a psychiatric disorder, or have another substance use disorder.

Anda et al. (1999) outlined types of adverse childhood experiences:

- Childhood abuse, which has these categories:
  - Emotional abuse
  - Physical abuse
  - Sexual abuse
- Household exposure to:
  - Battered mothers
  - Substance abuse
  - Mental illness
  - Parental separation or divorce
  - Incarcerated household member

The prevalence of smoking by 14 years of age was 25% for those with a history of sexual abuse and 9% for those not sexually abused. Any adverse childhood experience at least doubled the odds for becoming an early smoker and, similarly, increased the odds by nearly twofold that the individual would be a smoker in his or her 50s (Anda et al., 1999).

The presence of a psychiatric disorder is much more likely in nicotine-dependent persons. Major depression is 3 times more common in dependent smokers compared to nonsmokers, and panic disorder is 4 times more common.

Similarly, alcohol dependence is 6 times more common in smokers and drug dependence nearly 16 times more common in smokers than in the nonsmoking population.

Individuals with a psychiatric disorder plus nicotine dependence make up 7% of the U.S. population but consume over 34% of the cigarettes (Grant, 2004a). Although most smokers do not have a psychiatric disorder or other substance use disorders, the prevalence of psychiatric disorders in smokers is much higher than in the nonsmoking population.

Over 75% of alcohol- and drug-dependent patients smoke cigarettes in early recovery, and they tend to be heavy, nicotine-dependent smokers (Kalman et al., 2005).

Patients with depressive disorders can be expected to be smokers in nearly 60% of cases, and bipolar patients in 70% of cases (Hughes et al., 1986). Anxiety disorder patients show a wide range of smoking behavior, with obsessive–compulsive disorder the lowest (Kalman et al., 2005), and panic disorder and posttraumatic stress disorder the highest (approximately 56% of each; Lasser et al., 2000; Baker-Morissette et al., 2004). Schizophrenic patients smoke in at least 80% of cases (Lasser et al., 2000). And finally, data indicated that current smoking increases suicidal behavior in young adults (Preslau et al., 2001).

The "take home" message for physicians and mental health professionals is simple: If you have a patient who smokes, screen for other substance use disorders as well as other psychiatric disorders. Similarly, when working with a patient with a substance use disorder or with any psychiatric disorder, inquire about his or her use of cigarettes. Table 9.2 shows the risk of dependence for commonly used drugs.

Table 9.2
Substance Use and Risk of Dependence

	Ever Used (%)	Dependence (%)	Risk (%)
Tobacco	75.6	24.1	31.9
Coccaine	16.2	2.7	16.7
Heroin	1.5	0.4	23.1
Alcohol	91.5	14.1	15.4
Cannabis	46.3	4.2	9.1

Reproduced with permission of Anthony et al., 1994.

Screening for Nicotine Dependence

Patients readily admit to smoking, and administration of the Fagerstrom Tolerance Questionnaire (FTQ) can provide an estimate of the severity of dependence (Fagerstrom & Schneider, 1989; see Table 9.3). The stages of change cycle (DiClemente et al., 1991) discussed in Chapter 6 provides the clinician with a guide by which to gauge the person's readiness to change and a "map" for monitoring the patient through the stages of behavior change. Mental health professionals as well as physicians have an obligation to inquire about, screen for, and assess smoking behavior and to encourage each patient who smokes to take the steps outlined in this chapter.

Almost all people who smoke will admit that they do to their physicians. How much a person smokes will determine the degree of dependence. The large majority of smokers smoke 10–40 cigarettes per day (Fagerstrom & Schneider, 1989).

Table 9.3
Fagerstrom Tolerance Questionnaire

Questions	Answers	Points
How soon after you wake up in the morning do you smoke your first cigarette?	Within 30 min. After 30 min.	1 0
Do you find it difficult to refrain from smoking in places where it is forbidden	Yes No	1 0
Which cigarette would you hate most to give up?	The first one in the morning Any other	1 0
How many cigarettes a day do you smoke?	15 or less 16–25 26 or more	0 1 2
Do you smoke more frequently during the first part of the day after awakening than during the rest of the day?	Yes No	1 0
Do you smoke when you are so ill that you are in bed most of the day?	Yes No	1 0
What is the nicotine level of your usual brand of cigarette?	0.9 mg or less 1.0–1.2 mg 1.3 mg or more	0 1 2
Do you inhale?	Never Sometimes Always	0 1 2

The FTQ has a scoring range of 0–11 points, with a score of 0 assumed indicative of minimum nicotine dependence and a score of 11 indicative of maximum nicotine dependence. The mean score is usually in the range of 5–7 points, with a standard deviation of 2 for smokers asking for treatment. From Fagerstrom & Schneider, 1989; reprinted with permission.

Biochemical markers of smoking are available. Nicotine has a half-life of 1–3 hours and is therefore relatively difficult to detect in blood samples. However, its major metabolite, cotinine, has a half-life of 10–14 hours and is excreted mainly in the urine. Both urine or salivary samples can be analyzed for cotinine. Hair samples can be used to detect nicotine or cotinine and have been obtained on maternal and infant hair specimens as a means of evaluating smoking behavior during pregnancy (Eliopoulos et al., 1994).

Biochemical markers are rarely necessary in the clinical setting. However, an assessment of dependence can be a first step toward addressing tobacco cessation. As noted, the FTQ (Fagerstrom & Schneider, 1989) provides a simple, validated means for dependence assessment (Table 9.3). Scores on the FTQ correlate with cotinine levels (Hall & Killeen, 1985).

Factors Favoring Quitting

In a study by Hymowitz et al. (1997), a quitter was defined as someone who, at his or her final contact in 1993, reported not smoking any cigarettes for the preceding 6 months or longer. Of those initially interviewed by telephone (13,415 smokers) and followed between 1988 and 1993, 67.2% had made a serious attempt to quit and 35.6% were successful. The strongest predictor of inability to quit was time to first cigarette of the day; that is, if it was less than 10 minutes after waking in the morning, only 17.9% quit; if it was greater than 61 minutes, 35.9% quit. Also, number of cigarettes smoked daily was a factor. Those smoking more than 25 per day had a quit rate of 18.7%, and those who had smoked less than 5 a day had a 46% quit rate; 5–14 cigarettes per day had a 32.4% quit rate, and 15–24 cigarettes per day had a 22.7% quit rate. Also, favoring quitting were male sex, older age, greater household income, and less consumption of alcohol. For example, daily drinkers had a quit rate of 20.9%, whereas those who had less than one drink a month had a quit rate of 25.6%. Smokers who had previously made at least two quit attempts were subsequently successful in 27.7% of cases, compared to those with a history of one previous quit attempt (24.4% cessation rate). Also, number of other household smokers helped; 25.5% quit if there was no other smoker in the house, compared to 22.1%. Premium cigarette smokers had a higher quit rate than discount or generic cigarette smokers. Race and education had relatively little predictive value. The most prevalent reason, in terms of rank ordering, for making a serious quit attempt was concern for current or future health. The reason given the least was smoking restrictions at work.

Five A's of Brief Intervention

Each patient encounter is an opportunity to move the person away from a destructive habit. Consistent but simple steps on the practitioner's part will maximize the possibility of smoking cessation (Hughes et al., 1999). These steps include the "Five A's" of brief intervention (Fiore et al., 1995; Fiore et al., 1996):

$$Ask \rightarrow Advise \rightarrow Assess \rightarrow Assist \rightarrow Arrange$$

Ask

Ask if the patient smokes or uses any other tobacco product. A "tobacco user" sticker can be placed on the charts of smokers as a reminder for the clinician to explore willingness to quit or to assess any progress toward quitting. Some patients will become defensive and not want to be "hassled" about tobacco use. The response, "I understand, but I want to let you know that help is available if you change your mind" is usually agreeable. Other patients will welcome the nudge to implement a cessation plan and will work with the practitioner. Most patients will fall somewhere in between; that is, they acknowledge that they should quit, that they want to quit ("someday"), and that they will think more about it.

For those who are willing to continue the dialogue, the next step is:

Advise

Perhaps the initial advisory effort should focus on helping the patient overcome the tendency to postpone quitting: "There is never a perfect or even a convenient time to quit"; "The time to do it is now, before you get sick (or sicker) from cigarettes." The patient isn't alone in this process. The doctor can assure the patient the he/she and the staff will guide, prescribe, encourage and support the effort at quitting. The patient can be asked what he or she thinks would most help him or her. Many will say, "I have to do it myself." The doctor can counsel with "I can help by working with you on a treatment plan." (Specific stages are outlined later in the chapter.) In addition, the doctor should encourage the patient to take action by emphasizing quality-of-life issues: "This is the most important thing you could do to stay healthy and to (see your grandchildren grow up; be able to work more vigorously; enjoy your retirement for many years)"; "The time and effort will be the best health investment you can make."

Assess

As the clinician "asks" and "advises," the process of assessment is occurring. Is this patient willing to act on the advice? What further information should the clinician provide, or what additional motivational probes can be offered? The clinician is trying to move the patient from contemplating quitting to taking action and quitting with the help of a treatment plan. If the patient agrees to quit, setting a quit date is the next step. Throughout, the clinician remains *empathetic* (to the fear of failure, to the fear of giving up a substance that has become part of the fabric of life, to fear of weight gain, depression, or other personal doubts); *respects the autonomy of the patient* (choices are available as to treatment approaches and quit dates); and *reinforces self-efficacy* (recalls with the patient other struggles he or she has overcome or other health behaviors acquired (e.g., exercise, weight loss, work skills).

If the patient refuses to take action, the clinician can simply remark that he or she will be available if the patient changes his or her mind. Tossing in a few more facts about the benefits of quitting or recalling a patient who quit and reflecting on his or her improved health as well as his pride in being a nonsmoker can also be useful.

If the patient says he or she will quit but won't pin down a quit date or consider treatment options, the physician can schedule a follow-up visit within 1–2 weeks, perhaps, to review blood work or adjust medication doses, and, in addition, to refocus on the benefit of quitting and setting a quit date. The mental health practitioner can stay alert to any openings in future conversations during regular sessions.

If the patient agrees that this is the time to quit, the process moves to the next stage:

Assist

This stage includes specific treatments to be prescribed or arranged (these treatment options are reviewed later in this chapter). Less formal is the counseling in preparation for quitting (Fiore et al., 2000). Patients are encouraged to:

1. Tell family and friends what they intend to do.
2. Ask for their support and understanding.
3. Set a quit date within 2 weeks.
4. Get rid of smoking paraphernalia—ashtrays, matches, lighters, tobacco products.
5. Clean clothes and vehicle to remove odor of smoking.
6. Anticipate the inconvenience of not smoking—that is, not having what they want when they want it.

7. Plan to drink extra amounts of water.
8. Start or add a mild exercise routine each day.
9. Avoid situations, when possible, where there is smoking.
10. Begin to envision themselves as "nonsmokers" making this new status an important part of their identity.

Arrange

Support, encouragement, and accountability will help the patient quit. Follow-up appointments provide these factors and should be scheduled promptly after the quit date is set. For example, at least four follow-up sessions in the first month (10 minutes each) should be scheduled with the doctor or nurse. The first appointment should occur within the first week of quitting. Some of these appointments can take place by telephone or face to face, but at least half of these should occur in person.

At these sessions the physician (1) reviews any relapses and encourages the patient to learn from the experience; (2) adjusts dosages (e.g., 4 mg nicotine gum may be more effective than 2 mg); (3) overcomes discouragement or resistance to further effort by pointing out that relapse and cravings are common but do not lessen the chances of success if the person keeps trying; and (4) helps to identify "triggers" for smoking and how to avoid them or minimize their impact. The physician's interest and encouragement will do much to bolster cessation efforts.

A dose–response relationship exists between counseling intensity and success of smoking cessation. According to the U.S. Department of Health and Human Services Clinical Practice Guidelines on "Treating Tobacco Use and Dependence" (Fiore et al., 2000), individuals should be offered four sessions about 10 minutes each. In addition, pharmacotherapy should be offered such as buproprion or nicotine replacement therapies.

Specific Treatments

How do clinicians decide which treatment(s) to use? Our preference is to use the full array of treatments simultaneously—nicotine replacement, medication, and psychosocial support. The "lighter smoker" or less dependent smoker (less than one pack/day) may not need nicotine replacement. Some smokers deny craving and may not need buproprion; others will object to taking a pill or wearing a patch to help them resist smoking. Many will think it unnecessary to have ongoing counseling or other professional supportive efforts. Therefore, offer each patient all the possibilities and utilize what he or she will accept. Maintain contact by appointment, telephone, or e-mail for continuing assessment, encouragement, and coaching on additional treatment or switching treatment, as necessary. If treatment "fails," start over again. Previous failures do not preclude success with the next effort.

Nicotine Replacement Therapy

There are several forms of nicotine replacement therapy (NRT), all based on the same premise: withdrawal symptoms will be minimized or eliminated, making stopping easier (see Table 9.4).

- *Nicotine patch.* The patch is the preferred initial NRT because compliance is high and less clinician time is necessary in training patients how to use it. Smokers of less than 15 cigarettes per day can start at the 14 or 10 mg patch. The patch should be applied immediately upon awakening in a relatively hairless area between the neck and the waist. An advantage of the 16-hour versus the 24-hour patch has not been demonstrated (Fiore et al., 2000). Patches should be used between 6 and 12 weeks.
- *Nicotine gum.* Nicotine gum, 4 mg, is recommended for smokers of more than 20 cigarettes per day, those who smoke within 30 minutes of awakening, and those who have a history of nicotine withdrawal symptoms. Otherwise, the 2 mg dose is recommended. The gum should be used for 1–3 months, chewing a piece every 1–3 hours. Most patients use less gum than this and have poorer results (more "slips" and greater withdrawal symptoms). The gum should be chewed slowly until a taste emerges, then "parked" against the inside cheek to facilitate nicotine absorption. The "parking" should be sustained for about 30 minutes or until no more taste is detected. Coffee, soft drinks, fruit juice—that is, acidic beverages—interfere with the buccal absorption of nicotine. Only water should be ingested during the 15 minutes before or during chewing.
- *Nicotine lozenge.* Lozenges come in 2 and 4 mg doses. As an alternative to gum, the lozenge may be more socially acceptable and does not adhere to dental work. Heavy users of lozenges may experience nausea, hiccups, or dyspepsia. One lozenge may be used every 1–2 hours while awake.
- *Nicotine nasal spray.* Each bottle contains about 100 doses (0.5 mg nicotine); 1–2 doses per hour, or a maximum of 40 doses per day, are the recommended upper limits of use. Minimum usage is eight doses per day (4 mg of nicotine). Each application induces 0.5 mg of nicotine per nostril, with the

Table 9.4
Available Forms of Nicotine Replacement Therapy

Patch

- Seven strengths: 5, 7, 10, 14, 15, 21, and 22 mg
- 16- or 24-hour release
- Recommended for 6 to 12 weeks

Gum

- 2 and 4 mg doses
- Recommended for up to 12 weeks

Lozenge

- 2 and 4 mg doses
- 1 lozenge to be used very 1–2 hours while awake
- Recommended for up to 12 weeks

Nasal spray

- 0.5 mg per spray
- 1–2 doses every hour
- Not to exceed 40 doses per day
- Can be used for 3–6 months

Inhaler

- 4 mg per cartridge
- 1 cartridge to be used every 1 to 2 hours while awake
- 6–16 cartridges per day
- Can be used up to 6 months

Based on Schroader, 2005; reprinted with permission.

head tilted slightly back. Sniffing, inhaling, or swallowing should be avoided during application to minimize irritating effects. Duration of use is 3–6 months.

- *Nicotine inhaler.* If use of the patch or gum has failed, the nicotine inhaler, which contains a cartridge of 4 mg of nicotine, can be tried. Each cartridge contains eight puffs or inhalations, and 6–16 cartridges per day may be necessary. Duration of use is in the 3- to 6-month range. As with the gum, acidic beverages should be avoided.

Medications

Various pharmacologic approaches have been tried to aid smoking cessation. Buproprion and nortriptyline are the two most successful, thus far.

- *Buproprion.* The only first-line pharmacological treatment for smoking is buproprion (Wellbutrin, Zyban), a sustained-release agent that has at least three mechanisms of action (Slemmer, Martin, & Damaj, 2000):

  1. Blockade of norepinephrine reuptake
  2. Blockade of dopamine reuptake
  3. Antagonism of high-affinity nicotinic acetylcholine receptors

The drug is begun 7 days before the quit date at a dose of 150 mg and increased to 150 mg bid after 4 days. Unlike NRT, cessation of smoking is not a requirement for use of buproprion. Usually, cravings and urges to smoke begin to subside by the quit date. Duration of treatment should be at least 12 weeks. Buproprion is contraindicated in patients with bulimia and anorexia nervosa, because an increased rate of seizures was reported in a group of patients (Ascher et al., 1995).

- *Nortriptyline.* This tricyclic antidepressant is a second-line agent and may be useful in smokers with comorbid depression or anxiety disorders. Side effects are common, however, especially dry mouth, blurred vision, urinary retention, tremors, and dizziness. The starting dose is 25 mg per day, increasing by 25 mg every 4 days to 100 mg. Duration of treatment is typically 12 weeks but can be extended.
- *Other medications.* Clonidine, naltrexone, buspirone, SSRI antidepressants, monoamine oxidase inhibitors, and mecamylamine have been tried but have no clear efficacy. A patient who has not succeeded with NRT or buproprion may be considered for these third-line agents.

Psychosocial Approaches

Psychosocial treatments are multimodal approaches using behavioral and cognitive strategies designed to lessen cravings, sustain commitment to smoking cessation, and prepare the smoker for triggers (i.e., stimuli that prompt a desire to resume smoking). The skills to avoid or control triggers and the ability to recognize moods or thoughts that draw the person back to smoking are taught and explored.

Behavioral coping skills include how to recognize and avoid triggers; how to get away from a high-risk situation (e.g., how to refuse a cigarette); and how to manage time that previously was used for smoking. Daily exercise (e.g., taking a walk each morning and after work), drinking more water than usual, and having a low-calorie snack in place of a cigarette are useful behaviors.

Cognitive skills include recognizing automatic thoughts such as "This is too hard," "I always fail," "I'll get fat," or "I'll be depressed" as unfounded, irrational, or unnecessary. Demoralizing internal messages need to be countered with the person's appreciation of his or her resources to initiate and sustain nonsmoking status.

Patients can be encouraged to (1) recall the stigma and cost (both health and financial) of smoking and to (2) begin identifying as nonsmokers to help bolster themselves. The clinician can give a "pep talk," such as the one that follows:

Deliberately recall the cost, pain, shame, embarrassment, and frustration that smoking causes whenever you experience craving, euphoric recall, rationalization, or discouragement. The urge to smoke will be dampened by simultaneously remembering why you are quitting. Don't be blindsided by a feeling that you will inevitability relapse. These negative thoughts are temporary; they pass with time. Counter the negative thoughts by deliberately and consciously recalling the downsides of smoking—for example, cancer, heart disease, having a bad habit, breaking promises to quit, disappointment, and so on. Then deliberately and consciously appreciate that you will—within a few minutes or hours, or by tomorrow—be much relieved that you didn't smoke that cigarette and now have another 24 hours of recovery.

"Identify yourself as a nonsmoker. Make *nonsmoker* part of who you are, just as you are a woman [man, mother, father, etc.]. Imagine yourself as a nonsmoker. You weren't born on this earth to engage in behaviors or habits that rob or cheat you of health and personal fulfillment. Think through your personal values and make them goals (not merely wishes, desires, or needs). Some of these values may not be especially profound—such as a clean-smelling home and car or a more youthful complexion. Nevertheless, they are in the service of your health. You may discover other values that are deeper and more enduring: a commitment to the concept that your body (and therefore your health) is an incredible creation that behooves you to manage to the best of your ability.

Integrating an experience of drug dependence and establishing an identity as a "recovering person" are powerful cognitive strategies that require mental effort but become self-reinforcing as each 24-hour period passes without a cigarette.

Psychosocial treatments are usually carried out in a clinic or clinician's office. Unfortunately, dedicated psychosocial treatment for smoking cessation is very underutilized in spite of enormous empirical support for its efficacy (Baille et al., 1994).

Roadblocks to Successful Cessation

Mental health practitioners and physicians will be a step ahead if they can address issues that might discourage patients from attempting cessation. The three most common issues are discussed below and, when put into perspective, can be overcome. These issues—fear of depression, weight gain, and loss of stimulation—are ofen more threatening to patients than withdrawal symptoms. Clinicians' knowledge and support vis-à-vis these issues will boost a patient's chances of quitting.

The Issue of Depression

A 40-year longitudinal study found in the 1952 and 1970 samples that associations between smoking and depression were small and nonsignificant (Murphy et al., 2003). By 1992, however, smokers were three times as likely to be depressed as nonsmokers. Smoking was not found to lead to depression; rather, those who were depressed were more inclined to use tobacco. A self-medication hypothesis is a plausible explanation for the increased rate of smoking in people with depression. Alternatively, depressed smokers may be inclined to take health risks because they feel life is not worthwhile (Murphy et al., 2003).

Major depressive disorder has been found in some studies to hamper smoking cessation (Glassman, 1993). Patients with repeated episodes of major depression have the most difficulty quitting, but the success rates can improve with attention given to the depression. Brown and colleagues (2001) found that abstinent rates at 1 year for smokers with a history of depression were 25% if given "standard" cessation cognitive–behavioral therapy, but increased to 33% if the therapy focused on both smoking cessation and depression. Although the above percentages were not significantly different from each other, a statistically significant improvement in cessation at 1 year did occur for patients who had had repeated episodes of major depression and for heavy smokers when the depression was specifically addressed.

Depressed smokers may have lower cessation rates than nondepressed smokers, but these differences can be narrowed by NRT. Depressed smokers who were given placebo gum ceased smoking at a 90-day follow-up in only 12.5% of cases, but depressed smokers given nicotine gum achieved an abstinence rate of 29.5% at 90 days, which was close to the 37% abstinence rate in nondepressed smokers using nicotine gum (Kinnunen et al., 1996).

A study from Germany found that at 36 months' follow-up, both depressed and nondepressed smokers had quit in 15% of cases; depression did not predict maintenance or cessation of smoking for either men or women (John et al., 2004). Similar results were found in a U.S. study (Breslau et al., 1998).

We know that depression (as well as other psychiatric disorders) increases the risk of smoking (Grant, 2004a). Adverse childhood experiences (e.g., emotional, physical, or sexual abuse; battered, divorced, or incarcerated parents; or mental illness or substance abuse in a parent) increase the risk of early smoking (by 14 years of age) and heavy smoking (Anda et al., 1999). Nevertheless, depressed smokers should be encouraged to quit. With proper treatment of both depression and nicotine dependence, these smokers can succeed in quitting just as well as other smokers.

Should a person attempt to quit smoking as he or she initiates recovery from alcohol or other drugs? Recent studies have shown that smoking cessation can be integrated into treatment for psychiatric and substance use disorders (McFall et al., 2005; Rustin, 1998; Stuyt, Order-Connors, & Ziedonis, 2003; Ziedonis & William, 2003). We no longer have to accept the rationalization that a patient can only quit one drug at a time. The health of recovering people will obviously be improved by smoking cessation, and, in fact, there are data that demonstrate improved alcohol and drug recovery rates as well (Hurt et al., 1994; Stuyt, 1997).

The Issue of Weight Gain

Fear of weight gain is common and deters many, especially women, from trying to quit smoking (French & Jefffrey, 1995). The average smoker weighs 4–7 pounds less than nonsmokers and gains about 4–7 pounds after quitting (Klesges et al., 1989).

In addition to mild weight gain, smoking cessation leads to a lower heart rate, decreased metabolic rate, lower cortisol and catecholamine levels, and sleep EEG changes (Hughes & Hatsukami, 1992).

The small gain in weight is not likely in women who are already trying to lose weight. The tradeoff of weight gain for smoking cessation obviously is highly favorable from a health viewpoint. Many are able to lose the added weight over the course of the first year of cessation. Most of the weight is gained in the first 3 months of cessation; increased physical exercise and healthy food choices should be encouraged. Dieting is not recommended as a person attempts to quit (Hall et al., 1992) because relapse may be more likely. Nicotine gum appears to minimize weight gain and is recommended until abstinence from smoking is fully established (Perkins, 1994).

The Issue of Reduced Stimulation

Some smokers miss the stimulation of nicotine, and attention and concentration may seem off for a while. These cognitive issues can be expected to resolve. Patients need to remain heartened by their decision to improve their overall health and longevity. Alternative strategies for relaxation are readily available through exercise and a decision to expand one's behavioral repertoire (e.g., develop hobbies, join social groups, participate in volunteer activities).

Conclusion

Quitting smoking is not more difficult than abstaining from alcohol or other drugs. Over the decades most smokers have quit without specific forms of treatment. We now have effective counseling strategies, NRT, and medications to aid the cessation process. The initially high "failure" rate noted in smoking cessation attempts does not mean that the next attempt will not be successful. Unfortunately, the incentive to quit smoking often develops only after a serious medical consequence such as heart attack. Physicians and clinicians can accelerate the motivation for smoking cessation by providing encouragement and information and by implementing the cessation strategies outlined in this chapter.

Pharmacological Treatment

Highlights

• With an understanding of substance use disorders, physicians should be able to prescribe the medications discussed in this chapter.

• Clinicians who treat substance abuse patients need access to psychosocial therapies and higher levels of care.

• Medications used to manage addiction act in one of the following ways: as maintenance on a cross-tolerant medication, as an aversive agent, to block the drug "high," or to prevent craving.

• Widely used medications for the management of alcoholism include disulfiram, naltrexone, and acamprosate.

• Medications used for the management of opioid dependence are methadone, naltrexone, and buprenorphine.

Addiction treatment can intervene at the neurobiological level. Attacking substance abuse and dependence through pharmacotherapy is compatible with the biopsychosocial method of treatment in modern psychiatry. In past decades, addiction treatment focused on psychosocial variables primarily through use of 12-step programs, counseling, and education. The aim was to mobilize the individual's resources to abstain and redirect his or her life.

Psychosocial treatment often provides inspiration, improved morale, and a sense of hope. These efforts, as described earlier in this text, continue to be appropriate and essential today.

Role of Pharmacology

Despite the effectiveness of psychosocial interventions, pharmacology increasingly plays a role in the treatment of substance use disorders. One reason for this role involves the intractable nature of some addictions. The degree to which a substance "takes hold" of an individual varies, and the motivation to abstain varies. There are multiple factors that influence abstinence and response to treatment. The first four categories of medications presented in Table 10.1 are used to help patients maintain abstinence.

Table 10.1
Classes of Pharmacotherapies Used for Addiction Treatment

1. Maintenance treatment with a cross-tolerant agent
   A. Methadone or buprenorphine treatment for opioid dependence
   B. Nicotine patches or gum for nicotine dependence

2. Agents to block the drug high
   A. Naltrexone for opioid and alcohol dependence

3. Aversive therapy
   A. Disulfiram treatment of alcoholism

4. Agents used to suppress craving
   A. Naltrexone in alcohol dependence
   B. Acamprosate in alcohol dependence
   C. Buproprion in nicotine dependence

5. Agents that block signs and symptoms of withdrawal
   A. Clonidine in opioid withdrawal
   B. Benzodiazepines in alcohol withdrawal

6. Pharmacotherapy of comorbid psychiatric disorders
   A. Antidepressants and mood stabilizers in mood disorders
   B. Neuroleptics in psychotic disorders

Adapted from NIDA, 1997.

Maintenance treatment with a cross-tolerant agent is one type of pharmacological strategy. The term *cross-tolerant* simply means that two or more drugs are in the same family, and that they behave in similar ways. Nicotine provides an easy illustration. Although cigarettes are made up of other chemicals, with regard to the nicotine it is the delivery system that makes the difference between cigarettes and the nicotine patch. A person can replace cigarettes with the nicotine patch or gum, which mimics the intoxication or ameliorate withdrawal symptoms.

Agents that block the drug high prevent the drug from causing intoxication. Naltrexone blocks the opioid receptor so that another opioid, for instance, heroin, cannot exert its usual effect on the user. Aversive therapy is a treatment that causes unpleasant symptoms if the user takes the drug against which the aversive agent acts. The classic example is disulfiram (Antabuse) for the treatment of alcoholism. If a person ingests alcohol while disulfiram is in the body, he or she will become ill with symptoms that vary in intensity from nausea and flushing to hypertensive crisis. Agents used to suppress craving are exciting in their potential to remove the desire to take the drug in those patients who respond to the medication. Acamprosate (Campral) is a relatively new agent used in cases of alcohol dependence.

Physicians interested in treating substance abuse patients can use all the medications found in this book, with a few cautions. Some patients are sicker than they first appear, and the problems of intoxication are well known. However, the risk of a poor outcome increases when comorbid psychiatric disorders are present, unless both conditions are treated. Clinicians are wise to ask the patient if he or she is depressed, if there are other psychiatric disorders, suicidal ideation, or past suicide attempts. If the physician is not a psychiatrist, it is almost always prudent to ask a psychiatrist to collaborate on the case.

Clinicians who decide to treat patients who have substance use disorders need to know about local treatment programs and have some information within easy reach: brochures on AA, NA (or other recovery groups), and Al-Anon. It is necessary to conceptualize substance use disorders as chronic and relapsing and to ask the patient to return at intervals appropriate to his or her condition. Include a close family member, if at all possible.

Table 10.2 lists some key points for prescribing medications for patients with substance abuse or dependence. The following paragraphs elaborate on these points.

1. Patients in AA may hear some attendees criticize the use of medications, though this probably happens much less frequently than in the past.

Table 10.2
Medication Prescribing Points for Substance Abuse Patients

1. The use of medication does not conflict with AA or NA.
2. Medications are not a substitute for comprehensive rehabilitation.
3. Most medications used to treat addictions are not addictive.
4. There is no fixed duration of treatment.
5. Psychiatrists usually treat comorbid psychiatric disorders.

Society has become more sophisticated about psychiatric disorders and the importance of treating them. Use of medications listed in Table 10.1 will be acceptable to most. However, it is possible for patients to experience criticism, so it is important for them to understand that the use of medication does not conflict with the principles of AA, NA, or any other 12-Step approach. Nor do medications conflict with the use of psychotherapy or other rehabilitation modalities. Medication and psychosocial rehabilitation attack addiction at different levels of brain functioning.

2. Medications are not a substitute for 12-step participation or formal rehabilitation programs. Taking a pill only requires a few seconds of time per day; more effort than these brief seconds is necessary to overcome an addiction. Physicians and other clinicians must be vigilant on this point, especially early in treatment. It is at this time that patients may feel good about their decision to stop using alcohol or drugs; yet it is a critical time for relapse. The patient may be convinced that the problem is solved, but there is still much work to do in order to maintain sobriety.

3. The medications prescribed for the treatment of substance use disorders are not addicting, except for methadone and buprenorphine, which are opiates that substitute for pathological patterns of opiate use. Dependence on methadone and buprenorphine will be acquired by virtue of this substitution process. This benign dependence allows the individual to gain social stability and psychological equilibrium. Methadone is a medicalized addiction that replaces the chaotic use that is associated with criminality and HIV. Eventually, a slow withdrawal from methadone or buprenorphine should be attempted. Patients for whom treatment has been successful may be afraid to stop a medication that has helped. As always, it is preferable to discontinue the medication during a period of general stability and low stress, and to make very gradual reductions. Unless there is toxicity or disturbing side effects, there is no hurry to stop these medications.

There may be questions about psychological dependence on these medications in patients who easily become addicted. For these medications and the others listed, there must be consideration of medication risks versus benefits. Reliance on these medications is most likely to occur with the cross-tolerant agents that are actually addictive.

Patients who take medications that block them from feeling a high from their precious drug of choice do not like taking the medicine. Anti-craving medications are not inherently desirable! This is why naltrexone is seldom successful in patients who use illicit opioids. It is too easy to forego the naltrexone and buy heroin on the street. The patients who do better on naltrexone are professionals who are closely monitored. Some patients with severe alcoholism want to continue disulfiram when it is the only treatment that has worked for them. More often, patients want to discontinue the medication before they should—an urge that may be part of their denial about the severity of the alcohol or drug dependence.

4. How long does the patient need to take addiction-specific medication? There is no fixed duration or limit on the use of these medications. We typically recommend at least 1 year, but many patients will use the medication for longer periods; and, of course, some for shorter periods of time. If the patient is participating successfully in AA, NA, or CA, remaining abstinent, and not experiencing cravings or continuing temptations to use, stopping the medication can be considered. Some will return to the medication if relapse occurs or if they feel vulnerable to relapse.

5. Pharmacotherapy of comorbid psychiatric disorders (e.g., depression, bipolar disorders, anxiety disorders, schizophrenia) is usually managed by a psychiatrist. In most instances it is not necessary to stop these medications if the person is relapsing. This is, of course, a judgment call and is best handled on a case-by-case basis. Typically a return to the use of addicting substances should not provoke the physician to withhold medications that might be effective in curbing other psychopathological processes.

With these caveats in mind, we turn to specific agents that have proven or possible efficacy in treating addictive conditions.

Pharmacological Treatment of Alcoholism

Three medications are widely used to treat alcohol dependence: disulfiram, naltrexone, and acamprosate. (Refer to the Appendix for alcohol withdrawal protocols.)

Disulfiram

Disulfiram (Antabuse) has been available in the United States since 1948. It is typically administered in a 250 mg tablet and is taken every day. A 500 mg tablet is available as well and may be necessary if an individual discovers that he or she can ingest alcohol at the lower dosage without a significant reaction. About 12 hours after disulfiram is ingested, its full effect can be expected. It acts as a deterrent to drinking because of the ethanol–disulfiram reaction. This reaction results from the fact that disulfiram blocks the enzyme aldehyde dehydrogenase. The ethyl alcohol molecule is metabolized to acetaldehyde by alcohol dehydrogenase and then is, under normal circumstances, converted to acetic acid by acetaldehyde dehydrogenase. However, when acetaldehyde dehydrogenase is blocked, acetaldehyde levels increase by 5–10 times normal and produce a toxic reaction. Table 10.3 lists common symptoms of this reaction.

The intensity of the ethanol–disulfiram reaction is proportionate to the amount of alcohol ingested. The person begins to experience symptoms within minutes and usually stops drinking alcohol. The reaction typically lasts 30–60 minutes. A severe reaction can be treated with ephedrine (for hypotension) and the administration of oxygen and intravenous antihistamines. Ascorbic acid intravenously in a 1 g dose can also be beneficial.

As with all patients considering the addition of a medication to their recovery plan, a careful look at the potential risks and benefits is warranted. The patient described in Case 1 on the following page made significant gains after disulfiram was added to her recovery program. There may be several

Table 10.3
Symptoms of Acetaldehyde Toxicity (Ethanol–Disulfiram Reaction)

- Flushing of the skin, particularly the face and upper chest
- Throbbing headache
- Nausea and possibly vomiting
- Sweating
- Hyperventilation and respiratory distress
- Chest pain
- Anxiety and palpitations
- Hypotension

Case 1 (Disulfiram)

Ms. A was a single, middle-aged woman who lived alone. She had maintained steady employment as a secretary and was considered an excellent employee. For many years Ms. A drank alcohol in the evenings after work. The amount she drank gradually increased, and one morning she presented to work smelling of alcohol. Her supervisor had also noticed several absences occurring on Monday mornings. Ms. A was referred to the employee health service at her place of work. She completed an outpatient addiction treatment program, although she soon relapsed. She relapsed once again after completing a residential program. An intensive aftercare program was put into place to include regular attendance at AA and disulfiram 250 mg every morning. Ms. A agreed to have the employee health service dispense the disulfiram every weekday morning. At her 1-year follow-up, Ms. A was doing well.

---

reasons for this improvement. She had limited social supports but daily contact with a concerned person who dispensed the medication and provided social interaction around the issue of her sobriety. Every night when Ms. A went home alone, she did not need to make the decision that she would not drink. By taking her disulfiram, she had already made that decision. Taking disulfiram daily served to remind her that she was committed to sobriety and reinforced the AA slogan that is helpful to many, "One day at a time."

The patient was also informed of the potential for physical illness should she drink with disulfiram in her system; this warning was an effective deterrent to impulse drinking. In essence, this knowledge buys the alcoholic time to consider his or her choice about whether or not to return to a lifestyle dominated by alcohol use. One key to this patient's success was that an outside party monitored the administration of disulfiram. When a patient is given a prescription for the medication that is not accompanied by a comprehensive treatment plan, it is not likely to be as helpful.

In addition to the warning not to drink alcohol, patients are warned to check product labelings for alcohol content. Some patients have reported mild flushing when using alcohol-based paint thinner. Disulfiram may have side effects such as mild drowsiness for a few days, a garlic or metallic-like taste, acne-like skin eruptions, headache, tremor, and rarely a peripheral neuritis or toxic psychosis with delirium. A chemical hepatitis is rare but does warrant examination of liver enzymes after about 1 month's use of disulfiram and again at 3–4 months. If such hepatic dysfunction occurs, it typically arises in the first several months of treatment (Wright & Moore, 1990).

Disulfiram should not be administered until the blood alcohol level has reached zero, and the patient should be warned that a reaction to the ingestion of alcohol can occur as long as 15 days after the last dose of disulfiram (Antabuse package insert, 2005). Disulfiram has been underprescribed by doctors but has the potential to help many patients obtain sobriety as they participate in AA or other treatment modalities. When a patient resists the use of disulfiram, it is instructive to explore his or her concerns; for example, the patient may have a fear of not being able to resist an impulse to drink (and therefore would experience an ethanol–disulfiram reaction); or there may be an unappreciated degree of dependence on using alcohol to cope, which the disulfiram would clearly interrupt. A discussion of these issues often helps the patient recognize his or her dependence on alcohol and possibly strengthen renewed efforts to break this dependency. Some patients object to disulfiram because it is a "crutch." Explaining that a crutch is a device designed to help a person stand up and move forward while healing takes place often suffices to override this objection.

Naltrexone

Naltrexone (Revia) is an example of an anti-craving medication used in the treatment of alcohol dependence. It is a nearly pure opioid antagonist and an analog of the shorter-acting antagonist, naloxone. It does not produce the euphoria that an opioid or an opioid agonist produces, and it does not ameliorate drug craving or prevent withdrawal symptoms. Naltrexone binds to the mu opiate receptor as well as to kappa and delta opiate receptors, reversibly blocking these receptors. The blockage renders the use of opiates such as heroin, meperidine, or hydrocodone "useless" because there is no "room" for the opiate molecule to land at its pharmacological site of action: the opiate receptor. For this reason, naltrexone was initially approved by the FDA for the treatment of opiate dependence, and it has proven very helpful to some people with this problem.

In 1994 naltrexone was approved for alcohol dependence as well. This approval was based on randomized, placebo-controlled trials of naltrexone therapy using the usual dose of 50 mg per day. Several studies found a significantly lower relapse rate in those taking naltrexone when compared with those taking placebo (Volpicelli et al., 1995). Reduced frequency in drinking and a decrease in relapses to heavy drinking, as well as a delay of onset of drinking have been characteristic of patients using naltrexone (Garbutt et al., 1999). There have been at least 25 randomized controlled trials with alcoholic patients across the world who continued to show significant advantages to using naltrexone. The alcoholic person does not become ill, as with disulfiram, if he or she drinks while taking naltrexone. Its mechanism of action in decreasing the craving for alcohol is unclear, though it may work through the brain's natural opioid system (Terenius, 1996).

Naltrexone pills are taken once a day, usually with food. For those who are subject to side effects, the pill may be halved with good results. Common side effects are nausea, headache, dizziness, fatigue, nervousness, insomnia, vomiting, and occasionally somnolence. These typically clear in a short period of time. Occasionally, naltrexone will result in liver enzyme elevation, and liver enzymes should be checked within the first few months of treatment.

Naltrexone is also available in an injectable preparation marketed as Vivitrol. It is long-acting and is given in monthly gluteal injections at doses of 380 mg. It has been shown to be effective in reducing the number of drinking days, heavy drinking days, and sustaining abstinence for six months compared with placebo. Patients must be free of opiates for 7 days prior to taking naltrexone. The most common side effects are nausea, vomiting, headache, dizziness, fatigue, and injection site reactions. The injectable form provides a more consistent blood level than the oral form provides, and is especially useful for patients who have compliance problems (Garbutt, 2005).

If a patient on naltrexone is injured or develops a medical problem (e.g., kidney stones) that would ordinarily require opiate medication, the blockade can be overcome by significantly higher doses of opiates, preferably administered by an anesthesiologist. For this reason, patients on naltrexone should be given a wallet card at a pharmacy stating that they are taking this drug.

As an opioid antagonist, naltrexone's primary action is to block the effects of opioids. For these reasons, it has limited appeal to most opioid addicts. One group of patients who have responded relatively well is healthcare professionals who have a great deal to lose should they relapse, as case 2 demonstrates. These patients typically have better support services and follow-up than street addicts.

Acamprosate

Acamprosate (Campral) reduces neuronal hyperexcitability by acting at glutamate receptors or at calcium channels. The distress of alcohol withdrawal and craving is reduced by acamprosate. The drug has been used for decades in Europe and recently became available in the United States (Mason & Ownby, 2000).

Alcohol both stimulates the GABA inhibiting system and inhibits the brain's major excitability system—glutamate and its receptors. The glutamate receptor, N-methyl-D-aspartate (NMDA), is inhibited by alcohol, which results in decreased anxiety and increased sedation. Chronic alcohol use leads to neuroadaptation in the form of an increased number and increased functioning of NMDA receptors. Thus, when alcohol is removed (withdrawal), the increased glutamatergic action may produce dysphoria, sleep disruption, mood disturbance, and possibly hallucinations and seizures (Littleton, 1998).

Acamprosate inhibits glutamate by reducing its release from the presynaptic nerve terminal and reducing calcium in influx at glutamate receptors. As a result there is an inhibitory modulation of the glutamate system (Wilde & Wagstaff, 1997). Acamprosate has a half-life of 13 hours, is not metabolized, and is excreted in the urine unchanged (Adis R&D Profile, 2002). Hepatic impairment does not modify the pharmokinetics of acamprosate. Common side effects include diarrhea, nausea and vomiting, pruritis, and rash. Dizziness, drowsiness, confusion, and an increase or decrease in libido are less common (Wilde & Wagstaff, 1997).

In one study, acamprosate reduced craving in alcohol-dependent patients who showed significantly increased abstinence rates, compared to placebo, at 6 and 12 months (Whitworth et al., 1996). In another study, compared to placebo, acamprosate resulted in significantly greater time to first relapse, percentage of time abstinent, and complete abstinence (Mason & Ownby, 2000). Acamprosate is generally well tolerated, does not interact with alcohol, and can be stopped abruptly. Dosages range from two to four capsules (333 mg/capsule) per day in a bid or tid schedule. The cost effectiveness of using acamprosate has been demonstrated in European studies (Rychlik et al., 2003).

Acamprosate has the advantage of being excreted through the kidneys without liver involvement and without interaction with other medications. There is no abuse potential with acamprosate, and the major side effect is a mild diarrhea, which often clears with time. Acamprosate, which is the newest medication approved for alcohol dependence, would seem to have a major advantage in reducing the craving that is associated with conditioned withdrawal (Littleton, 1995).

Additional Medications

Three additional medications may prove useful in alcoholism treatment: topiramate, ondansetron, and nalmefene.

TOPIRAMATE

Topiramate is an antiseizure medication that potentiates GABA-ergic transmission and has a blocking effect on subtypes of glutamate receptors. The drug has been shown to be effective in alcohol dependence by blocking the rewarding effects of alcohol. Decreased use of alcohol was found in patients taking up to 300 mg per day of topiramate, compared to those on placebo. The number of continuous abstinent days in topiramate users was also significantly greater than those on placebo (Johnston et al., 2003). Patients should be warned of the increased rate of kidney stones with topiramate and advised to remain adequately hydrated. Common side effects are drowsiness, dizziness, fatigue, psychomotor slowing, and difficulty with concentration.

ONDANSETRON

Ondansetron is a 5HT3 receptor antagonist used for treatment of nausea and vomiting induced by chemotherapy, radiotherapy, or surgery. It has been found to significantly reduce alcohol consumption and increase abstinence rates in patients with early-onset alcoholism (i.e., onset by age 25 or younger). Males predominate in early-onset alcoholism, and there is usually a strong history of familial alcoholism and psychiatric comorbidity. Whether early promising results will hold up remains to be determined (Johnson et al., 2000). Ondansetron is available in 4 and 8 mg tablets as well as an oral suspension. Its use remains off-label for alcoholism treatment. Doses as low as 0.5 mg daily have been effective in treating alcohol abusers (Sellers et al., 1994).

NALMEFENE

Nalmefene is a newer pure opioid antagonist that is similar to naltrexone but has a longer duration of action and acts at mu, delta, and kappa opioid receptors. The drug is currently approved for reversal of acute opioid intoxication and overdose (Mason et al., 1999). Mason and colleagues used 10 or 40 mg bid and found nalmefene to yield significantly fewer relapses to heavy drinking. Common side effects are headache, insomnia, fatigue, and nausea.

Pharmacological Treatment of Opioid Addiction

The number of heroin addicts in the United States is at least as great as it was in the mid-1970s. It is estimated that 1 million people are heroin dependent, and around 200,000 of these receive methadone treatment (Vocci, 2002). Roughly 3 million people have tried heroin (NIDA, 1997). The statistics support the contention that a shocking number of people who try heroin become addicted to it.

The financial expenditure on opioid addiction is great. Heroin dependence is estimated to cost $100 billion annually (Harwood, Fountain, & Livermore, 1998). The person addicted to heroin often requires a broad range of services. Of the medical costs, the portion spent on treatment of the addiction is a relatively small amount. Infectious diseases, especially HIV and hepatitis C, are significant causes of morbidities. Furthermore, heroin addicts are often among those who are unable to handle their health care needs. Homelessness and joblessness are costly problems, as are criminality and incarcerations.

The heroin on the market is a very pure form; a purer product is less costly to users because they need less to get the desired high. Young adults and adolescents are among those who are finding that the "new" heroin is an affordable option (Substance Abuse Mental Health Services Administration, 2000). Using needles to inject drugs is repulsive to many middle-class substance abusers; however, they are willing to smoke or snort a drug, including heroin. They know the dangers of intravenous drug use; however, they do not understand that smoking and snorting the heroin on the market is extremely addictive and dangerous. With this greater purity, overdose deaths have risen sharply, as have emergency room admissions. Because of increased purity and reduced pricing, greater numbers of young people and middle-class users are falling victim to heroin.

Since the 1960s the mainstay of treating heroin addiction has been methadone maintenance. Methadone is dispensed through highly regulated clinics housed outside the mainstream of medicine. In 1994 a longer-acting medication, levo-alpha-acetylmethadol hydrochloride (LAAM), was approved for use through methadone clinics. Though similar to methadone, it offered the advantage of less frequent dosing. LAAM was not well utilized because clinicians were concerned about its safety. The medication has now been taken off the market because of safety concerns about cardiac side effects (U.S. Food and Drug Administration, 2003). Three medications are currently used to treat opioid addiction: buprenorphine, naltrexone, and methadone.

Buprenorphine

In October 2002 the FDA approved buprenorphine for the treatment of opioid dependence. Both the medication and its approval for office-based treatment are unprecedented in the treatment of opioid addiction. Through the Drug Abuse Treatment Act of 2000, outpatient physicians can prescribe buprenorphine to opioid-addicted patients directly from their offices; patients do not need to go to a methadone maintenance clinic. Buprenorphine is a unique drug, a partial agonist, whose chemical structure is sufficiently similar to heroin, methadone, and prescription opioids to ameliorate most drug craving and withdrawal symptoms—and buprenorphine does not produce the euphoria that addicts crave (NIDA, 2002). These advantages address two of the biggest anxieties about methadone treatment: the requirement that a highly regulated free-standing clinic manage treatment and its structure as a full mu agonist, so similar to heroin.

The approval of buprenorphine was long awaited. It was proposed as a treatment for heroin addiction in the 1980s. After close to 20 years of research there was clear evidence that buprenorphine is an effective medication with a wide safety margin (Substance Abuse Mental Health Services Administration, 2000). A reason for its approval as an office-based treatment was the premise that patients addicted to heroin or opioid painkillers would be more comfortable receiving treatment from a doctor's office. In addition to heroin addicts, another group that can benefit from buprenorphine are those who are dependent on prescription drugs. The surge in the use of prescription painkillers such as Oxycontin may have been a factor in making an office-based treatment option available. Case 2 illustrates the use of buprenorphine in a patient addicted to Oxycontin. This patient originally took an analgesic opioid for pain following an orthopedic procedure.

This patient had a number of characteristics that made him an ideal candidate for treatment with buprenorphine. In his favor were his employability, a supportive social network, financial resources, and the fact that he did not abuse other drugs. In brief, there were several areas in which he demonstrated stability. Although he had a history of suicidal ideation, he was psychiatrically and medically stable at the time of treatment with buprenorphine. He also

---

Case 2 (Buprenorphine)

Mr. C was an employed adult from a middle-class family. He took Oxycontin for pain following a surgical procedure. Later he obtained Oxycontin from illicit sources. His use escalated to 80 mg daily, and attempts to discontinue the drug were unsuccessful. Mr. A became distraught at his failure to control his use; hospitalization for suicidal ideation and detoxification soon followed. Thereafter, he was unable to maintain abstinence from Oxycontin. He presented to a general psychiatric outpatient clinic, where treatment with buprenorphine was initiated. On a dose of Suboxone (buprenorphine) 8 mg/2 mg daily, Mr. C did well, with improvements in several life areas.

---

regularly attended a weekly addiction support group. However, patients may do well on buprenorphine even though they have fewer resources than this particular patient.

Some patients do not qualify for buprenorphine treatment. The Substance Abuse and Mental Health Services Administration (SAMHSA), through the Center for Substance Abuse Treatment, released Treatment Indications Protocol (TIP) 40. The document provides valuable information for the appropriate prescribing of buprenorphine, including its contraindications and relative contraindications. Table 10.4 lists some of the concerns and potential side effects associated with prescribing buprenorphine. Before a physician prescribes buprenorphine to a patient who has a condition of concern, the physician should thoroughly understand the possible ramifications of the treatment.

A patient's general stability, home situation, medical and psychiatric conditions, and use of other drugs are areas that must be considered prior to treatment. Some patients on high-dose methadone maintenance may be poor candidates for buprenorphine until they can do well on a lower dose of methadone. Suboxone is too expensive for some patients, so cost may be an unfortunate limiting factor. Buprenorphine is not the treatment of choice for all opioid dependent patients. More research needs to be done to determine whether buprenorphine guidelines can be broadened to include patients who are now seen as poor candidates or whether further restrictions to its use are sensible. Those for whom buprenorphine is not appropriate may be advised to accept a referral for methadone treatment.

Table 10.4
Concerns Associated with Buprenorphine Treatment

Common side effects:

- Sweating

- Headache

- Abdominal pain, nausea, vomiting, constipation

Cautions:

- Pregnancy

- Polysubstance abuse

- Elevated liver enzymes

- Use of medications: antiseizure or HIV antiretroviral

Relative contraindications:

- Use of sedative/hypnotics

- Active alcohol dependence

- Lacks interest in, or motivation for, recovery

- Does not meet DSM-IV-TR diagnosis for opioid dependence

From Center for Substance Abuse Treatment, 2005.

Physicians who want to treat opioid-dependent patients with buprenor-phine from their offices must apply to receive a waiver from SAMHSA. If a waiver is granted, the physician receives a special waiver number from the Drug Enforcement Agency (DEA) that he or she uses when prescribing buprenorphine. Applying for a waiver is a several-step process. No physician can receive a waiver without first having active state and DEA licenses. Most physicians must complete 8 hours of training through one of several medical organizations that provide approved courses. These include the Academy of Addiction Psychiatry, the American Psychiatric Association, the American Society of Addiction Medicine, the American Medical Association, and the American Osteopathic Association. Some physicians are exempt from taking the course if they are certified in addictions or if they have done research on buprenorphine. If in doubt about an exemption from the course requirement, one may communicate with SAMHSA.

The 8 hours of training teaches pharmacology, prescribing protocols, patient selection, and some of the adjunctive treatment needs common to opioid-addicted patients. In addition, physicians must have the capacity to either provide, or refer patients to, psychiatric or substance abuse services. Once the doctor is approved, a special DEA number is issued that allows him or her to prescribe this Schedule III medication. Individual physicians or a group within a single practice facility may treat a maximum of 30 patients with buprenorphine. See Table 10.5 for an outline of the requirements physicians must meet for initial and ongoing certification (Krantz & Mehler, 2004).

By late 2005, the DEA had provided waivers to about 6,000 physicians. This large number speaks to the ease with which an interested doctor can qualify to prescribe buprenorphine. Still, some patients are on a waiting list for 6 months before they can see a buprenorphine provider or receive treatment in a methadone clinic. SAMHSA hopes more physicians will obtain the certification needed to open their offices to opioid-dependent patients in need of care (Daly, 2005).

Some patients and clinicians may be surprised to learn that many medications prescribed for pain control are chemically similar to heroin and methadone, because they act at the same receptor sites within the brain. Among these common medications are codeine, hydrocodone (Vicodin), meperidine (Demerol), morphine, oxycodone (Percodan, Oxycontin), and others. Like heroin and methadone, the active chemical in these drugs attaches to opioid receptors, known as mu receptors. Drugs of this type are called opioid agonists, and they share distinguishing properties.

Depending on a drug's strength—the intensity with which it binds to the receptor and activates it—the drug causes more or less of each property: analgesia, euphoria, sedation, miosis, respiratory depression, habituation, addiction, and a specific withdrawal syndrome. For instance, heroin binds strongly to

Table 10.5
Steps for Obtaining a Waiver to Prescribe Buprenorphine

1. Submit a notification of intent to SAMHSA.
2. Have state and DEA licenses.
3. Complete 8 hours of specialized training.
4. Be able to provide, or refer to, psychosocial services.
5. Adhere to dispensing guidelines and record-keeping.
6. Treat no more than 30 patients at one time.

From Center for Substance Abuse Treatment, 2004.

the mu receptor site and shows a marked degree of these shared properties, whereas codeine, a much weaker drug, shows a low degree of these properties.

As a partial agonist, buprenorphine has a unique pharmacological profile. On one end of the spectrum are the full agonists that bind to and activate the receptor, and on the other end of the spectrum are antagonists that block the receptor. A partial agonist is part agonist and part antagonist; as such, it has advantages as a therapeutic agent. One of these advantages is a ceiling effect, meaning there is a point at which the effect of the drug will not increase even though the dose is increased. There are important ramifications of the ceiling effect for buprenorphine in the treatment of opioid addicts. First, there is less respiratory depression even in overdose, so that deaths should be rare from buprenorphine alone. Second, buprenorphine will not give addicts the satisfying high they want. Third, only mild withdrawal symptoms occur when the drug is discontinued.

NIDA worked with Reckitt & Colman Pharmaceuticals under a Cooperative Research and Development Agreement to bring buprenorphine to market. The difference in the preparations is clinically relevant. Suboxone is a sublingual tablet that combines buprenorphine and naloxone, an antagonist. Taken sublingually, the agonist properties predominate. However, if tablets are crushed and then injected, the naloxone portion overrides buprenorphine. This is important because when the antagonist properties predominate, IV drug users do not get any reinforcement from injecting the Suboxone preparation. Subutex does not contain naloxone, so it does have the potential to produce euphoria if it is injected. Therefore, addiction specialists tend to favor the combination product.

SAMHSA has released TIP 43, which provides a 356-page guide on the treatment of opioid addiction (Center for Substance Abuse Treatment, 2004). Previously released TIP 40 specifically addressed the use of buprenorphine. TIP can be accessed online at www.kap.samhsa.gov.

Other treatments for opiate dependence are available (see Table 10.1). Opiate withdrawal is managed with methadone and buprenorphine, which would be expected because they are opioids. Clonidine is also used because it blocks symptoms of autonomic arousal, although it does not prevent drug craving. Naltrexone and methadone are used to manage opioid dependence.

Naltrexone is an opioid antagonist, and, as noted in the preceding section on medications used in the treatment of alcohol dependence. It too can be prescribed from a physician's office. However, it has less appeal for most opioid addicts than treatment with methadone or buprenorphine because naltrexone has no opioid effect and does not satisfy craving. The individual with an opiate dependence realizes that obtaining or using an opiate is useless because no reinforcing effect will be experienced. Those patients who have access to illicit opioids such as heroin and who have the choice as to whether or not they take naltrexone tend to have a poor response. The urge to gain the euphoria they feel with heroin proves too great. They know that skipping naltrexone will allow them to experience the high they crave.

Patients taking naltrexone for alcohol dependence should also carry a wallet card. Naltrexone should not be administered until 7 days after the last use of an opiate. This delay will avoid an opioid withdrawal syndrome, which will occur if naltrexone is administered while opiates are still in the system. Medical professionals addicted to opioids are considered good candidates for naltrexone, as are others whose livelihoods depend on taking it. Medical licensing boards are an example of a governing body that can mandate that naltrexone be administered to a physician or a nurse as a condition of licensure. Such was the situation in Case 3, below.

This nurse was at risk for losing his license to practice. His employer needed as much assurance as possible that the employee could return to his job with only minimal risk of using opioids. They were willing to give the employee a second chance, with some reticence. This was a "high stakes" situation for the employee, and he needed to maximize the chance that he would succeed in his recovery. The fact that the medication could be administered and supervised at the workplace was an added benefit. Naltexone was a sound choice for this

---

Case 3 (Naltrexone)

A state licensing board referred a 40-year-old nurse for the treatment of opioid dependence. He had stolen opioid analgesics from the nursing unit to which he was assigned. The patient had a distant history of alcohol abuse. The nursing board stipulated that the patient follow treatment recommendations. If he failed to do so or had further work-related problems, he risked losing his nursing license. Aftercare included a recovery group for professionals. The patient also took naltrexone as part of his ongoing recovery plan, which was administered through the health service at his place of employment.

patient. It would block his craving without being an opiate, and it could not give him any high whatsoever. Therefore, he could work drug-free.

Methadone is a cross-tolerant agent used as a substitute for illicit opioids. As noted, methadone maintenance is only available through federally registered clinics and not through the practitioner's office. Methadone can be used by physicians for pain management and detoxification from opiates; however, maintenance requires participation in a formal methadone maintenance clinic. For some addicts, a partial agonist such as buprenorphine is not strong enough. There are good reasons to recommend methadone maintenance for patients who do not qualify for buprenorphine. Criminal activity is curtailed when addicts comply with a methadone maintenance program. Early methadone data showed that death rates for addicts enrolled in programs were reduced. More recent data indicate that both morbidity and mortality from HIV are reduced for heroin addicts who use methadone substitution (Gerada, 2005). Treatment with methadone continues to be criticized, despite its proven effectiveness in curtailing heroin use, decreasing incidents of shared needles, decreasing criminal activity, and restoring functionality. There are detractors that argue against methadone substitution because it is an addictive agent. Some concerns that have been raised are very practical. Clinics may have limited adjunctive services such as psychotherapy and social services. Sometimes the clinics are in high crime areas. There is also a risk that methadone patients will sell their quotas on the street instead of using it as prescribed (an act referred to as *diversion*).

Pharmacological Treatment for Cocaine Addiction

Pharmacological treatments for cocaine have been attempted with marginal success. Tricyclic antidepressants and dopamine agonists such as bromocriptine and amantadine have been tried but have not been consistently effective. The same is true with the anticonvulsant carbamazepine, which enjoyed some brief clinical attention in the mid-90s but has not proven to be effective (Silva DeLima et al., 2002). Currently, two medications are receiving attention in the treatment of cocaine dependence, with some early promising results; disulfiram and modafinil.

Disulfiram, described above for the treatment of alcoholism, has some characteristics that make it an interesting medication to consider in cocaine dependence. Disulfiram not only inhibits acetaldehyde dehydrogenase but also dopamine beta-hydroxylase (DBH); DBH converts dopamine to norepinephrine. Blockade of this enzyme leads to increased dopamine and decreased norepinephrine levels in the brain. As a result, disulfiram has some dopamine agonist-like effects. Cocaine addicts report decreased craving and increased dysphoria if cocaine is used while being on disulfiram. Plasma cocaine levels are increased in the presence of disulfiram, which may contribute to the apparently unpleasant altered cocaine experience (McCance-Katz, Costen, & Jatlow, 1998).

The addition of disulfiram to psychotherapeutic treatment with cocaine users led to a greater reduction in cocaine use (Carroll et al., 1998), and the use of disulfiram in cocaine-dependent individuals who were being maintained on methadone resulted in a significantly greater reduction in the frequency and quantity of cocaine use over a 12-week trial (Petrakis et al., 2000).

Modafinil, approved for the treatment of narcolepsy, is a second promising development in the treatment of cocaine dependence. It increases levels of glutamate, which are depleted with prolonged exposure to cocaine. A double-blind study conducted at the University of Pennsylvania Treatment Research Center found that cocaine-dependent individuals given 400 mg a day of modafinil had fewer cocaine-positive urine samples than the placebo group, and twice as many modafinil patients as placebo patients (33% vs. 13%) abstained from cocaine for 3 weeks or more (Dackis et al., 2005). Possibly modafinil reduces cocaine-induced neurochemical disruptions in the dopamine and glutamate neurons. Modafinil has effects opposite of cocaine withdrawal in that, with cocaine withdrawal there is typically oversleeping, depression, poor concentration, and craving; modafinil curbs oversleeping, generally improves concentration, and, according to the above study, results in less cocaine craving.

This is a new era for the treatment of substance use disorders. Research at multiple levels contributes to our understanding of addiction and our ability to treat patients. No longer are patients as alone with their disease. For physicians and other clinicians new to the field, this is the right time to become more knowledgeable in the identification, diagnosis, and treatment of substance abuse.

Substance Abuse Word List

Acamprosate. This medication gained FDA approval for the treatment of alcohol dependence in 2004. It reduces the craving for alcohol and, in turn, reduces relapse drinking. Chronic alcohol exposure is hypothesized to alter the normal balance between neuronal excitation and inhibition. Evidence suggesting that acamprosate may centrally interact with glutamate and GABA neurotransmitter systems has led to the hypothesis that acamprosate restores this balance.

Action. This is one of the stages of change identified by DiClemente et al. (1991). The patient takes steps toward change.

Addiction. A term sometimes used interchangeably with *substance dependence*. Another interchangeable term that was once popular, now being largely replaced, is *chemical dependency*. This term sounds negative to many people, as does the term *addict*. An addiction implies compulsive use (a drive or intense urge) of a substance and a loss of control when using that substance. It may be helpful to think of addiction as the *inability to consistently control* the use of a substance. This is an important concept because many addicts are able to moderate or discontinue their use for periods of time.

Agonists. Drugs that bind to, and activate, receptor molecules in the brain.

Al-Anon. This is a self-help group for co-dependents, especially spouses of alcoholics. These meetings were designed to follow the 12-step model. Because these meetings are free of charge and often therapeutic to attendees, they are a good option for many people in need of this type of support.

Alcoholics Anonymous (AA). A self-help group that had its beginnings in 1935 when Bill Wilson and Dr. Bob aimed to help each other stop drinking. AA continues to be an effective resource for many. Other self-help groups, also referred to as 12-step programs, include Narcotics Anonymous (NA) and Cocaine Anonymous (CA).

Amotivational syndrome (chronic cannabis syndrome).   The chronic use of cannabis is said to lower goals and leave the user unable to meet life's multitude of obligations. This concept has been strongly debated.

Antagonists.   Drugs that block receptor molecules without activating them; when attached, they prevent other molecules from binding and activating the receptor site.

Blackouts.   This term is sometimes mistakenly linked solely to alcohol. Although blackouts often occur in alcoholics, they are not specific to alcoholism. Blackouts probably occur when a person has rapidly consumed alcohol to the point that memories are not properly stored or recalled.

Buprenorphine.   A partial mu agonist used as an opioid maintenance medication. It can also be used to detoxify patients from full mu agonists. There is less risk of respiratory depression in overdose because of the protective ceiling effect of its partial agonist action. Doctors can treat opioid-addicted patients from their offices once the doctors have obtained a special waiver that allows them to prescribe buprenorphine.

Buproprion.   An antidepressant that is a first-line pharmacological treatment for nicotine dependence (for smoking cessation it is marketed as Zyban). It blocks norepinephrine reuptake, dopamine reuptake, and is an antagonist of high-affinity nicotinic acetylcholine receptors.

CAGE.   An acronym that stands for significant words from each question in a four-question screening tool. Clinicians can use these questions while taking their patients' medical histories. The questions ask about the patient's attempts to *cut down* on substances, their *annoyance* at alcohol-related criticism, their *guilt* about drinking, and their use of *eye-openers*.

Cannabis.   A plant used as a drug since ancient times. Marijuana combines several parts of the plant, and it is commonly rolled in a cigarette or placed in a pipe and smoked. The active ingredient is delta-9-tetrahydrocannabinol. Common effects are mild euphoria, relaxation, heightened sexual interest, hunger, and a distorted sense of time. Cannabis is the most widely used illicit drug and is common choice among adolescent substance abusers.

Carbohydrate deficient transferrin (CDT).   This is a state marker of heavy alcohol consumption that is synthesized in the liver. Normally, carbohydrates bind to transferrin; however, heavy drinking prevents the addition of carbohydrates. CDT levels normalize within approximately 1 month of abstinence. As a marker, CDT levels are useful when monitoring recovering alcoholics for relapse. Sensitivity and specificity of the CDT test are high, and the test's performance is reported to be higher when combined with gamma-glutamyltransferase or the mean corpuscular volume.

Cirrhosis.   The most devastating form of alcohol-induced liver disease is cirrhosis. However, cirrhosis is not caused only from heavy drinking. The cirrhotic liver becomes hard and fibrous, and its function is seriously compromised. In the later stages of liver disease, hepatic encephalopathy portends a poor prognosis.

Clonidine.   An alpha-2 agonist marketed as an antihypertensive medication that can also be effective in ameliorating some opioid withdrawal symptoms. Individual satisfaction with this method of detoxification is variable. A delivery system that is a convenient choice for some patients is the transdermal patch.

"Club drugs."   Drugs that are used as all night parties known as "raves". The most common of these drugs are methylenedioxymethamphetamine (MDMA), ketamine, and gamma-hydroxybutyrate (GHB).

Codependence.   This term refers to the denial of a family member about a loved one's addiction. It is a failure to recognize the problem and a resistance to change the situation.

Comorbidity.   This term refers to the co-occurrence in an individual of both a substance-use disorder and another psychiatric disorder; e.g., a bipolar patient who is also alcohol dependent (*also see* dual diagnosis).

Contemplation.   This is a stage of readiness for change identified by DiClemente et al. (1991). Patients move toward further changes in appreciating the consequences of their addictions.

Contingency management.   A behavioral treatment in which incentives are provided for abstinence.

Crack.   A form of cocaine that is extremely reinforcing because it provides the user with an almost immediate high. Powdered cocaine is processed and dried into small rocks. This hardened cocaine product is vaporized and inhaled.

Crash.   A term that refers to an acute withdrawal reaction from stimulants, especially used to refer to symptoms following cocaine intoxication. Common symptoms of a "crash" are lethargy and depression. Suicidal ideation may also occur, and its presence should be assessed.

Craving.   An intense drive or compulsion to use a substance; craving is often a symptom of addiction.

Cross-tolerance.   This term refers to drugs that are so similar in action that one can substitute for the other in most ways. Cross-tolerant drugs, such as methadone and heroin, are often in the same class. An example of two cross-tolerant substances not in the same class is alcohol and diazepam.

Delirium tremens (DTs).   This is a form of severe alcohol withdrawal that can be fatal, though it is less fatal now than it was in the past because of improved recognition and the availability of treatment. A hallmark of this form of withdrawal syndrome is severe autonomic instability, agitation, and confusion that is often accompanied by hallucinations.

Denial.   An unconscious defense mechanism characterized by refusal to acknowledge painful realities, thoughts, or emotions. The patient using denial struggles to keep anxiety-provoking material from conscious awareness; he or she is not using conscious deceit or lying. The defense of denial may be operating when others can clearly see that a person's difficulties are related to substance use; however, the person does not believe substance use is a problem. In the field of addiction, it is common to refer to such a person as being "in denial."

Determination.   A stage of change in which a decision is made; however, it may be transitory. This is part of the stages of change identified by DiClemente et al. (1991).

Disulfiram (Antabuse).   An aversive agent used to deter alcoholics from drinking, based on their realistic fear of illness should they drink while taking disulfiram. When alcohol is consumed, disulfiram causes an accumulation of acetaldehyde, which is responsible for the toxic reaction that occurs in the presence of alcohol. This agent can be effective if monitored daily and if there is a threat of negative consequences should a daily dose be skipped. Unfortunately, few programs offer such intensive monitoring services.

"Doctor shopping."   This term refers to the act of obtaining medications from multiple clinicians for the purpose of abusing prescription drugs. For this reason it is important to ask patients whether they have more than one prescriber, utilize more than one pharmacy, and if you may speak to those care providers.

Dopamine.   Dopamine is a neurotransmitter within the reward pathway. Pleasurable stimuli, such as drugs of abuse, are responsible for the release of dopamine.

174

Dual diagnosis.   This term is applied when a person has a substance use disorder as well as one or more psychiatric disorders.

Ecstacy.   Methylenedioxymethamphetamine (MDMA), or ecstasy, is a drug that has stimulant and hallucinogenic properties. It is particularly dangerous because it can cause long-term neurotoxic effects.

Enabling.   Doing things for a person with an addiction that seem helpful but actually perpetuate the cycle of addiction. The "enabler" is not able to set appropriate limits on the addict's behavior and becomes mired in the chaos of the addicted lifestyle.

Ethylglucuronide (ETG).   This is a qualitative urine test for ethyl alcohol. It is a sensitive marker that is present in the urine for 2–3 days after alcohol ingestion.

Eye-Opener.   A drink taken in the morning; the implication is that a person drinks in the morning to medicate withdrawal symptoms or to attempt to treat a hangover.

Fagerstrom test for nicotine dependence.   A questionnaire that helps determine the extent of physiological addiction to nicotine. The score is based on the amount of nicotine intake and includes the amount of smoking needed to avoid withdrawal effects.

Fetal alcohol syndrome.   The most common form of mental retardation in the United States, caused by maternal alcohol consumption during pregnancy. Common features include facial stigmata, low birth weight, and small head circumference. Heart malformations and hearing impairment frequently occur.

Flashbacks.   A perceptual phenomenon that occurs after one has used a hallucinogenic drug. It usually involves a reexperiencing of some part of the drug-induced state and is often fleeting.

Flumazenil (Romazicon).   A benzodiazepine antagonist that may be administered intravenously when it is necessary to reverse the effects of a benzodiazepine. Such a situation might occur when multiple sedatives are taken in a serious overdose.

Formication.   The sensation of having bugs under the skin that occurs during intoxication with stimulants, especially noted with cocaine abuse. Also known as "coke bugs."

Gamma-aminobutyric acid (GABA).   The major inhibitory neurotransmitter in the brain that has an important role in mediating the effects of sedatives and alcohol.

Gamma-hydroxybutyrate (GHB).   Since about 1990, GHB has been abused in the United States for its euphoric, sedative, and anabolic effects. It is a central nervous system depressant; one of its precursors has been used as a "date rape" drug.

Gamma-glutamyltransferase (GGT).   A liver enzyme that is sometimes elevated when alcohol is abused. It is more sensitive as a biochemical marker when combined with either carbohydrate-deficient transferring (CDT) or an elevated mean corpuscular volume (MCV).

Gas chromatography-mass spectrometry (GC-MS).   This test is the gold standard for drug abuse. Because it is expensive, it is used only in situations that require a high level of accuracy, such as in employee screening, forensics, or any time confirmation of a less accurate test is needed.

Gateway theory.   A theory that less potent drugs lead to the use of more highly potent and dangerous drugs. This theory is debated on the grounds that not all users of a preceding substance progress to a higher level of use. An example would be that cigarette smoking is very likely to precede marijuana smoking—which is true. However, not all cigarette smokers become marijuana users.

Geriatric syndrome.   A set of symptoms involving falling and dementia, recognized to occur with great frequency in the elderly.

Glutamate.   A major excitatory neurotransmitter that is involved in the drug-seeking behavior seen in addiction.

Hallucinogens.   A class of drugs that are known to enhance perceptual experiences, often sensory in nature. Visual hallucinations are common. The most commonly abused hallucinogen is LSD. Cannabis is sometimes classified as a hallucinogen; however, it is argued that a large dose is required for the user to have a hallucinogenic effect.

Heroin.   Heroin is processed from morphine, a naturally occurring substance extracted from the seedpod of the Asian poppy plant. Heroin usually appears as a white or brown powder. Street names for heroin include "smack," "H," "skag," and "junk."

"Huffing."   Inhalation of fumes from a rag soaked with a product such as gasoline, for the purpose of becoming intoxicated.

Incentivization.   The process whereby one expects a reward and becomes motivated to seek the reward. The addicted or substance-dependent individual will retain an incentive to continue to use a drug even when he or she sincerely is trying to abstain. The experience of incentivization is believed to be mediated by stimulation of the dopamine-rich mesolimbic reward pathway by cues that are associated with prior drug or alcohol use.

Inhalants. Substances used for the purpose of getting "high," containing aliphatic and aromatic hydrocarbons. These substances are in common household products such as gasoline, glue, paint thinners, and spray paints.

Intervention. The act of helping an addict lessen his or her denial about the impact of his or her addiction. Traditionally, a formal intervention has included concerned family, friends, clergy, or counselors. The goal is to clarify ways in which the out-of-control substance use has compromised the addict's values, hurt significant others, and has become a top priority. The intervention is done within an atmosphere of caring and hope.

Loss of control. The inability to predictably regulate the use of a substance; more of the drug is used than intended or is used for longer periods of time than is intended. Loss of control is a classic sign of addiction.

LSD (lysergic acid diethylamide). One of the major drugs making up the hallucinogen class. LSD was discovered in 1938 and is one of the most potent mood-changing chemicals. It is manufactured from lysergic acid, which is found in ergot, a fungus that grows on rye and other grains. LSD is commonly referred to as "acid." Its effects are unpredictable.

Maintenance. This term can have two meanings in the field of substance abuse. It is a stage of change first identified by DiClemente et al. (1991), in which changes in behavior are maintained and can also refer to a form of treatment in which a patient is stable because he or she takes a medication to replace the illicit drug. It usually refers to opioid maintenance with methadone or buprenorphine, or nicotine replacement therapy with the nicotine patch or gum.

Marijuana (*see* cannabis).

Mean corpuscular volume (MCV). An elevated MCV may be indicative of heavy drinking because of the toxic effects of alcohol on erythropoiesis.

Methamphetamine. An addictive stimulant drug that strongly activates certain systems in the brain. It is chemically related to amphetamine, but the central nervous system effects of methamphetamine are greater. It is neurotoxic and can produce a parkinsonian state in the chronic user. It is made in illegal laboratories and has a high potential for abuse and addiction. It can be taken orally, intranasally, through an IV, or smoked as "ice" or "crystal."

Modafinil. This medication may prove promising for the treatment of co-caine dependence; it is approved for the treatment of narcolepsy.

Motivational interviewing. A type of therapeutic interaction in which the therapist utilizes the patient's concern about his or her substance use to challenge discrepancies in the patient's behavior and self-admitted concern. The therapist can use confrontation and empathy in giving feedback to the client.

Nalmefene. A newer pure opioid antagonist that is similar to naltrexone but has a longer duration of action. It may be more effective in reducing al-cohol craving and blocking opiate effects. The drug is currently approved for reversal of acute opioid intoxication and overdose.

Naltrexone. An opiate antagonist that is FDA approved for use in both alcohol and opioid dependence. It reduces alcohol craving. It is also used in highly motivated opioid dependent patients to block the effects of opi-oids. In both types of addiction, naltrexone is most effective when com-bined with recovery support services.

National Institute on Alcohol Abuse and Alcoholism (NIAAA; www. niaaa.nih.gov). Provides leadership in the national effort to reduce alcohol-related problems by conducting and supporting research, collaborating with other research organizations, and translating findings to health care prov-iders as well as other interested parties. The website provides the public with information on a wide variety of alcohol-related topics. NIAAA is a branch of the National Institutes of Health, as is the National Institute on Drug Abuse.

National Institute on Drug Abuse (NIDA; www.nida.nih.gov). The mission of NIDA is to bring the findings of science to bear upon the nation's problem with drug abuse and addiction. NIDA supports research and trans-lates findings for health care professionals and the general public. It was founded in 1974 and became part of the National Institutes of Health in 1992.

Negative reinforcement. The relief that is achieved when a painful state is removed by a particular behavior on the part of an organism. For ex-ample, use of heroin relieves uncomfortable opiate withdrawal symptoms.

Nicotine replacement therapy. Nicotine-containing products used for smoking cessation. Delivery systems include the patch, gum, lozenges, in-halers, and nasal spray.

Nortriptyline.   A tricyclic antidepressant that is used as a second-line agent for smoking cessation.

Nucleus accumbens.   A structure connected to the ventral tegmental area, the amygdala, and the prefrontal cortex. When stimulated, the nucleus accumbens releases dopamine, which is important to the experience of pleasure.

Ondansetron.   An antiemetic used in chemotherapy that has been shown to reduce the use of alcohol in patients with early-onset alcohol dependence.

Partial agonist.   Drugs of this type bind to receptors and activate them, but to a lesser extent than full agonists; antagonist properties predominate once a certain dose is reached.

Phencyclidine (PCP).   This drug belongs to a class of drugs (e.g., ketamine) originally developed as dissociative anesthetics in the 1950s, and which later became substances of abuse. PCP produces an unpredictable response in users; sometimes the response is pleasant but at other times it causes agitation and psychosis.

Polypharmacy.   The use of multiple therapeutic agents, specifically prescription and over-the-counter medications.

Positive reinforcement.   The achievement of a rewarding experience by a particular behavior of an organism. An example is the euphoric/sedative effect of alcohol taken at a social event.

Precontemplation.   One of the stages of change identified by DiClemente et al. (1991). In work with substance abuse patients, it refers to the stage when the patient may not recognize drug or alcohol use as a problem.

Project MATCH.   An important study to determine whether patients with certain characteristics would have a more favorable outcome when matched to a specific type of therapy. This was a large multisite clinical trial that demonstrated the equal efficacy of cognitive–behavioral therapy, motivational enhancement therapy, and 12-step facilitation therapy, regardless of particular client characteristics.

Reward pathway.   This term is used to describe structures within the brain that are linked by dopamine-rich neurons. Drugs and alcohol are examples of stimuli that can increase the activity of the reward pathway.

Quit date.   In many programs and in doctor's offices, smokers are often asked to set a date on which they will stop smoking. Prior to that date, it is helpful for smokers to make environmental and internal modifications to enhance their chances for success.

Relapse.   A return to the use of a substance following an attempt to refrain from using that substance; it is commonly referred to as a "slip."

Rohypnol.   Rohypnol, a trade name for flunitrazepam, belongs to a class of drugs known as benzodiazepines. Rohypnol can incapacitate victims and prevent them from resisting sexual assault. It can also produce "anterograde amnesia," which means individuals may not remember events they experienced while under the effects of the drug.

Self-medication hypothesis.   A proposal that substance abusers begin using and continue using in order to ameliorate uncomfortable emotions. This is a theory that has gained popularity within the addiction field in recent years.

Speedball.   A drug combination of cocaine and heroin.

Standard drink.   A standard drink is defined for hard liquor (1.5 oz.), wine (5 oz.), and beer (12 oz.).

Stages of change.   Identified by DiClemente et al. (1991), the stages are used in motivational therapy to help determine the patient's readiness to change. These stages include precontemplation, contemplation, determination, action, and maintenance (see Chapter 6).

STAR.   An acronym for a guide that can be used to help smokers who are ready to quit. The letters stand for: Set (a quit date); Tell (others of the plan); Anticipate (difficulties); Remove (tobacco products).

Steroids.   Anabolic–androgenic steroids are human-made substances related to male sex hormones. *Anabolic* refers to muscle building, and *androgenic* refers to increased masculine characteristics. Athletes sometimes abuse this class of medications.

Substance.   "A drug of abuse, a medication, or a toxin," according to the American Psychiatric Association's DSM-IV-TR (2000, p. 191), which groups substances into 11 classes. They include the following agents (and for some classes, similar drugs): alcohol, amphetamine, caffeine, cannabis, cocaine, hallucinogens, inhalants, nicotine, opioids, phencyclidine (PCP), sedative/hypnotics.

Substance abuse.   As defined by DSM-IV-TR (2000), "A maladaptive pattern of substance use manifested by recurrent and significant adverse consequences related to the repeated use of substances" (p. 198). A set of criteria in DSM-IV-TR lists specific symptoms that must be present within a 12-month period to qualify for a diagnosis of substance abuse.

Substance dependence. As defined by DSM-IV-TR (2000), "a cluster of cognitive, behavioral, and physiological symptoms indicating that the individual continues use of the substance despite significant substance-related problems" (p. 192). A set of criteria in DSM-IV-TR lists specific symptoms that must be present within a 12-month period to qualify for a diagnosis of substance abuse. Often tolerance, withdrawal, compulsive use, and frequent intoxications are present.

Substance withdrawal. A substance-specific group of symptoms that develops in response to the discontinuation of a substance; withdrawal symptoms may also develop when the amount used is substantially reduced. Symptoms of physiological withdrawal from some substances are the opposite of those seen with intoxication. For instance, sedatives produce sedation whereas sedative withdrawal produces symptoms of arousal, such as alertness and anxiety.

Tolerance. The need to use a much greater amount of a substance to achieve the desired effect. Tolerance is often a symptom of substance dependence, and it suggests chronic use. Another way to conceptualize tolerance is that using the same amount of a substance produces less of an effect over time. An example of tolerance to alcohol is a person who has a blood alcohol concentration above the legal limit but lacks any sign of intoxication.

Topiramate. An antiseizure medication that potentiates GABA-ergic transmission and has a blocking effect on subtypes of glutamate receptors. It has been shown to be effective in alcohol dependence by blocking the rewarding effects of alcohol.

Trigger. A cue or stimulus that prompts a person with a substance use disorder to use that substance.

TWEAK. The acronym of a screening tool used primarily for obstetrics patients who are abusing substances.

Ventral tegmental area. A structure located near the base of the brain that is important to the experience of pleasure through the release of dopamine. It connects to the nucleus accumbens and the prefrontal cortex to form the "reward pathway."

Withdrawal.   Also called an abstinence syndrome, drug or alcohol with-drawal occurs when the substance is quickly discontinued or the amount usually taken is markedly reduced. Withdrawal usually produces physiologi-cal symptoms that are very unpleasant and sometimes dangerous to the sub-stance abuser.

Office-Based Treatment
of Withdrawal

Withdrawal syndromes can be worrisome for clinicians and frightening for patients. However, not all classes of drugs are associated with withdrawal syndromes. These include hallucinogens, inhalants, and the drug phencyclidine. The potential for mild withdrawal symptoms upon discontinuation is debatable in some substances; however, if they do cause withdrawal symptoms, medical intervention is rarely needed. This is the situation for caffeine and cannabis. For caffeine, the biggest problem is the withdrawal headache that can be dealt with by over-the-counter pain relievers, helping headaches to subside in a couple of days. However, caffeine withdrawal can masquerade as a tension-vascular headache or a chronic daily headache. Cannabis, on the other hand, can arguably cause withdrawal symptoms, though its significance is a matter of debate.

It is important to note that the stimulants, cocaine and amphetamines, do produce definite withdrawal symptoms upon discontinuation. However, there is not an approved medical protocol for dealing with those symptoms. Cocaine, in particular, is a drug that can present discomfort and even danger to high-dose users as the drug leaves the body. Whereas the user had been experiencing euphoria, extraordinary energy, and grandiosity, when coming off the drug (also known as a "crash"), there is a risk that an opposite state will develop. The user may become dysphoric and even suicidal. Fatigue, the need for sleep that is sometimes elusive, and an increase in appetite develops. Should the patient become suicidal, hospitalization may be necessary. Otherwise, inter-

---

This Appendix is modified with the permission of the Texas Society of Psychiatric Physicians from material at www.txpsych.org.

ventions depend on the particular symptoms the patient exhibits. Relapse is common so it may be necessary to recommend substance abuse treatment.

The following drug classes outlined in this appendix have withdrawal syndromes for which there are recognized withdrawal protocols: alcohol, anxiolytic/sedative/hypnotics, and opioids. (See Chapter 9 for ways to handle the withdrawal syndrome that accompanies smoking cessation.) Withdrawal from opioids is rarely life threatening; however, patients fear it because of the discomfort it produces. On the other hand, withdrawal syndromes from alcohol and sedative-hypnotics *are* life threatening, and are the most serious abstinence syndromes clinicians see. The following pages contain examples of protocols that are used to treat abstinence from alcohol, anxiolytic/sedative/hypnotics, and opioids.

Alcohol Withdrawal

Alcohol dependence is the most common addiction aside from nicotine dependence. Alcohol can cause withdrawal syndromes that can often be managed outside the hospital setting; however, in cases of complicated withdrawal syndromes, such as those in which patients develop delirium, hospitalization is necessary. Regardless of the setting in which detoxification takes place, the physical examination and laboratory work-up are important components of care. Table A.1 is an example of such an evaluation.

Table A.1
Initiating Detoxification with Exam and Labwork

Physical Exam	Labwork
Heart disease (arrhythmia, congestive heart failure)	Complete blood count Liver enzymes Urine drug screen
Infections	Blood alcohol level
Gastrointestinal bleeding	Electrolytes (potassium, calcium, magnesium, phosphate)
Liver disease	
Pancreatitis	
Nervous system impairment (e.g., signs of head injury, stroke, subdural hematoma)	

There are several reasons why a patient may prefer office-based outpatient detoxification and refuse inpatient or partial hospitalization:

- Has no insurance or has used up previous benefits.
- Fear of stigma if hospitalized or enrolled in a formal treatment program.
- Does not want to lose time from work or wants to minimize time away from work.
- Prefers or needs to stay with family.

The appropriateness, safety, and effectiveness of this procedure will depend on several types of variables. First, those variables that favor office-based out-patient detoxification:

- Demonstrates cooperativeness.
- Lives with, or can be monitored by, a responsible adult.
- No acute medical conditions that would require hospitalization in and of themselves.
- No coexisting psychiatric disorders (Axis I or II) that would require hospitalization in and of themselves.

Variables that weigh against office-based outpatient detoxification:

- A history of being uncooperative with medication schedule.
- Lives alone and has no social network available for assessment.
- Has acute medical problems (e.g., infections, pain symptoms) or unstable chronic medical problem (e.g., hypertension, diabetes mellitus).
- Has a co-occurring psychiatric disorder that may compromise judgment or that requires close monitoring.
- Past pattern of life-threatening complications of alcohol or sedative withdrawal (e.g., repeated seizures, emerging DTs, hyperthermia, hepatic failure, esophageal varices).
- Likelihood of additional withdrawal syndromes due to other substance dependencies.
- Physical and laboratory tests must be available and used, as indicated.

The decision to proceed with office-based outpatient detoxification is a judgment the psychiatrist must make. Knowledge of the patient, consideration of the variables listed above, and ability to monitor the course of treatment will influence the decision. Please keep in mind that detoxification is only the introduction to addiction treatment, and a treatment plan for continuing rehabilitation should be implemented.

Psychoeducation

Educate patient and family member or other supportive persons regarding alcohol withdrawal symptoms and time course (see Table A.2). Point out:

- Need for hospitalization if symptoms of DTs occur (disorientation, confusion, persistent hallucinations).
- Possibility of seizures.

Table A.2
Symptoms of Alcohol Withdrawal (AW)

Time of Appearance	Symptoms (mild to moderate AW)	Symptoms (severe AW)[1]
Start: 6–8 hours	Nausea, insomnia, vomiting, decreased appetite, tremor, pulse increase	Same as mild-to-moderate AW, plus: Visual and auditory hallucinations
Next 1–2 days (intensifies, then diminishes)	Anxiety, headache, irritability, agitation, sensitivity to light and sound, concentration and orientation problems	Seizures[2]
2–4 days		Delirium tremens (DTs): increased agitation, tremulousness, and disorientation; large increases in blood pressure, pulse, and breathing rate; autonomic instability, hyperpyrexia, persistent visual and auditory hallucinations, disorientation
Up to 6 days		Seizures[2]

From Anton & Myrick, 2000.

[1] Emergence of severe AW indicates hospitalization rather than outpatient detoxification. [2] Seizures may not warrant hospitalization, but neurology consultation is indicated.

- Need for further rehabilitation treatment following detoxification.
- Danger of driving or operating dangerous equipment; assess safety of patient's work situation.

Daily Monitoring

Patient should be seen in office as needed; access to physician must be available. In addition:

- Daily monitoring of symptoms (pulse, temperature, blood pressure) by responsible adult; blood pressure monitoring is possible at pharmacies and supermarkets that have blood pressure machines (blood pressure monitoring equipment can also be purchased inexpensively); or visit primary care office for determination of vital signs.
- If pulse, temperature, or diastolic blood pressure exceed 100, report results to physician.

Pharmacotherapy

Once the symptoms of alcohol withdrawal are categorized, pharmacotherapy is essential for the comfort of the patient in order to prevent relief drinking, and to prevent worsening of the withdrawal syndrome. The administration of thiamine and multivitamins has become standard due to the poor nutritional status of many excessive drinkers. Thiamine is given to prevent Wernicke's encephalopathy, a condition characterized by confusion, abnormal eye movements, and ataxia. While standard protocols are useful, it is essential that the protocol not be used in lieu of careful patient monitoring. Adjustments in medications are often needed to prevent sedation or inadequate coverage.

VITAMINS

- Thiamin 100 mg daily 3 × days
- Multivitamin, one daily

BENZODIAZEPINES

Benzodiazepines are the most commonly used agent.

- Advantages
  - √ Well tolerated.
  - √ Proven efficacy.

√ Can be used to treat breakthrough symptoms.

√ Can prevent seizures.

- Disadvantages:

  √ Dangerous if mixed with alcohol.

  √ Side effects include amnesia, sedation, motor incoordination.

  √ Potentially addictive if used for long periods.

Chlordiazepoxide.   Chlordiazepoxide is the preferred regimen.

- Advantages

  √ Long-acting

  √ Unlikely to be abused

- Administration

  √ Day 1: 50 mg po q6 hours

  √ Day 2: 25 mg po q6 hours

  √ Day 3: 25 mg po q6 hours

  √ Day 4: 25 mg po bid (if necessary)

  √ Supplement with 25–50 mg qh if symptoms of withdrawal are not abating.

  √ Decrease dose if patient is oversedated.

Lorazepam.   Lorazepam is the second-line drug.

- Advantage: Can be given even if cirrhotic liver disease present.

- Disadvantage: Short-acting.

- Administration

  √ Day 1: 2 mg po q6h

  √ Day 2: 2 mg po q6h

  √ Day 3: 1 mg po q6h

  √ Day 4: 1 mg po q6h

  √ Day 5: 0.5 mg q6h

  √ Day 6: 0.5 mg q12h

  √ Supplement with 0.5–1.0 mg qh if withdrawal symptoms are not abating.

  √ Decrease dose if patient is oversedated.

Oxazepam.   Oxazepam is another alternative.

- Advantage

  √ Can be given with liver disease

- ✓ Intermedicate acting
- ✓ Unlikely to be abused
- Administration
  - ✓ Day 1: 30 mg q6h
  - ✓ Day 2: 30 mg q6h
  - ✓ Day 3: 15 mg q6h
  - ✓ Day 4: 15 mg q6h
  - ✓ Day 5: 15 mg q12h
  - ✓ Supplement with 15–30 mg qh if symptoms of withdrawal are not abating.
  - ✓ Decrease dose if patient is oversedated.

To avoid benzodiazepine abuse or dependence, prescribe only enough for the number of days of expected use; no refills.

OTHER AGENTS THAT MAY BE USED FOR DETOXIFICATION

Anticonvulsants can also be effective in treating alcohol withdrawal. In most cases it is not necessary to utilize them. However, in cases of prolonged withdrawal they provide another option for controlling symptoms.

Carbamazepine.

- Advantages: No adverse interaction if alcohol ingested.
- Disadvantages
  - ✓ Efficacy not as well documented as benzodiazepines.
  - ✓ Breakthrough symptoms must be treated with benzodiazepines.
  - ✓ Cannot be given if LFTs > 3 × normal.
  - ✓ Not effective for DTs.
- Administration
  - ✓ Day 1–2: 200 mg qid
  - ✓ Day 3–4: 200 mg tid
  - ✓ Day 5–6: 200 mg bid
  - ✓ Day 7–8 200 mg daily

Divalproex sodium.

- Advantages: Can prevent seizures.
- Disadvantages
  - ✓ Efficacy not as well documented as benzodiazepines.
  - ✓ Breakthrough symptoms must be treated with benzodiazepines.
  - ✓ Not effective for DTs.

- Administration
  - √ Day 1: 500 mg po start loading dose, followed by 500 mg po 6 hours later
  - √ Day 2: 500 mg po bid
  - √ Day 3: 500 mg po bid
  - √ Day 4: 250 mg po bid
  - √ Day 5: 250 mg po one dose

Neurontin.   Useful for anxiety or sleep disturbance.

Phenergan suppository.   Administered at 25 or 50 mg, prn, for nausea or vomiting.

Antidiarrheals.   Over-the-counter (e.g., Kaopectate) or prescribed (e.g., Lomotil) antidiarrheals may be useful.

Anxiolytic/Sedative/Hypnotic Withdrawal

Nearly 2% of adults develop a dependence on anxiolytic, sedative, or hypnotic drugs. Benzodiazepine (BZD) dependence is the most common, but barbiturates and musculoskeletal relaxants need to be considered as well.

The same guidelines used for alcohol, apply in determining whether office-based outpatient detoxification is appropriate. Also, obtain a physical exam and laboratory studies; and educate the patient and significant others as to the symptoms and course of withdrawal.

Physiological dependence on BZDs can be expected if they are used for more than 6 months. Short-acting BZDs will have an earlier onset of withdrawal symptoms; longer-acting BZDs will have a later onset. Table A.3 lists common discontinuance or withdrawal symptoms.

Withdrawal Techniques

These techniques are best suited for the chronic BZD user; that is, the patient who has been on a relatively stable dose continuously for 6 months or more.

The patient who has been on a continuous but very variable dose (e.g., 15–20 mg of alprazolam on Sunday but 2–4 mg on Monday and perhaps 6 mg on Tuesday, then 2 mg on Thursday) may be withdrawn using lower doses (preferably at least one-half) than those noted in Table A.4.

Sporadic or intermittent use of anxiolytic/sedative/hypnotics may not require a withdrawal regimen.

Appendix

Table A.3
Benzodiazepine Discontinuance Symptoms

Timing

Symptoms appear within 24 hours for short-acting BZDs; within 2–3 days for intermediate-acting BZDs; and up to 1 week for long-acting BZDs.

Maximum intensity is from 3 days to 2 weeks.

Usually subside by 4 weeks; occasionally last up to 3 months.

- *Very frequent:* Anxiety, agitation, insomnia, irritability, restlessness, muscle tension

- *Common but less frequent:* Nausea, blurred vision, coryza, depression, diaphoresis, nightmares, lethargy, hyperreflexia, hyperacusis, ataxia, aches and pain

- *Uncommon:* Psychosis, confusion, seizures, paranoid delusions, persistent tinnitus, hallucinations

From Ashton, 1995.

Withdrawal from the muscle relaxant carisoprodol is necessary because meprobamate is a metabolite of it.

Diazepam substitution:

- Determine the equivalent dosage of diazepam from Table A.4.
- The longer-acting clonazepam can be used rather than diazepam (5 mg of diazepam = 1 mg of clonazepam).

Calculating dose withdrawal:

- *Divide the daily dose by 5.* For example, as indicated in Table A.4, a patient taking Fioricet would be getting 50 mg of butalbital per capsule. The patient is taking 10 pills of Fioricet per day (500 mg of butalbital). The equivalent in diazepam (10 mg of diazepam is equivalent to 50 mg of butalbital) is 100 mg of diazepam per day. Divide daily dose by 5: 100 mg of diazepam divided by 5 is 20 mg (the dose that is decreased each week). To further illustrate: The diazepam equivalent for a patient taking 6 mg lorazepam per day is 60 mg; 60 mg divided by 5 is 12 mg (the dose that is decreased each week).
- The daily dose of diazepam is divided into three doses per day (last dose at hs). For example, when 60 mg of diazepam is the determined equivalent, the weekly dose will be decreased by 60 ÷ 5 = 12 mg. Week one

Table A.4
Withdrawal Dose Equivalency of 10 mg Diazepam (mgs)

	(mgs)
Barbituates:	
Amobarbital	100
Butobarbital	50
Butalbital	50
Pentobarbital	100
Phenobarbital	30
Secobarbital	100
Other sedative/hypnotics:	
Chloral hydrate	500
Ethychlorvynol	350
Glutethimide	30
Meprobamate	400
Methyprylon	300
Benzodiazepines	
Short-acting (half-life less than 3 hours)	
Triazolam	1
Intermediate-acting (half-life 12–20 hours)	
Alprazolam	1
Lorazepam	1
Oxazepam	30
Temazepam	30
Long-acting (half-life greater than 100 hours)	
Chlorazepate	15
Chlordiazepoxide	25
Clonazepam	2
Diazepam	10
Flurazepam (Dalmane)	30

From Alexander & Perry, 1991.

of withdrawal can start with a daily dose of 48 mg. This is 12 mg/day less than the 60 mg/day calculated to be the predetox level. Therefore, the first week of detox incorporates the first weekly decrease (12 mg in this example). Table A.5 shows an example of a diazepam tapering schedule for anxiolytic/sedative/hypnotic withdrawal.

Table A.5
Diazepam Tapering Schedule

	7:00 A.M.	1:00 A.M.	HS
Week 1	16 mg	16 mg	16 mg
Week 2	12 mg	12 mg	12 mg
Week 3	8 mg	8 mg	8 mg
Week 4	4 mg	4 mg	4 mg
Week 5	2 mg	2 mg	2 mg

Weeks 6, 7, and 8 may require very gradual ½–1 mg taper per week. There is no need to hurry the tapering schedule. A small (2–5 mg) dose may be necessary daily, on an afternoon basis, for some patients as they taper. (Tapering can be slowed as necessary.)

- Trazodone 50–150 mg hs is a useful adjunct.

As the drug taper ends, *rebound symptoms* may appear. *Rebound* is a mixture of prior anxiety symptoms and withdrawal symptoms. These will typically abate after 2 weeks of being drug free. *Relapse* symptoms, which are the reemergence of an anxiety disorder, may also appear. Two drug-free months is sufficient time to determine if reemergence of an anxiety disorder has occurred. Table A.6 shows predictors of benzodiazepine withdrawal.

Table A.6
Predictors of Increased Severity of Benzodiazepine Withdrawal

Drug Variables	Clinical Variables
High dose	Higher pretaper anxiety and depression
Longer duration of treatment	Personality disorders
Shorter half-life	Panic disorders
More rapid taper	History of alcohol and drug abuse

From Benzer, Smith, & Miller, 1995.

Opioid Withdrawal

Dependence on heroin or other opiates affects at least 1 million Americans and is likely to increase in prevalence (Schottenfeld, 2004). The progression from occasional use to dependence is often rapid with heroin but may develop slowly over months or years in prescription painkillers.

Overview

The duration of withdrawal will depend on the half-life of the opiate; symptoms appear 4–12 hours after last dose (see Table A.7).

Signs and symptoms of opiate withdrawal are extensive (see Table A.8).

Table A.7
Temporal Parameters of Opiate Withdrawal Symptoms

Drug	Onset of Withdrawal (hours)	Duration of Withdrawal (days)
Meperidine	8–12	4–5
Heroin	36–72	7–10
Hydromorphone	36–72	7–10
Codeine	36–72	7–10
Hydrocodone	36–72	7–10
Oxycodone	36–72	7–10

from Kleber, 1999.

Clonidine-Aided Detoxification

Clonidine can be a convenient and effective agent in the management of opioid withdrawal. There seem to be individual differences in the acceptance of clonidine for detoxification because it helps control the objective but not the subjective symptoms that are so common in opioid addiction.

- Oral administration
  - √ Day 1: 0.1–0.2 mg orally q4h up to 1 mg
  - √ Days 2–4: 0.1–0.2 mg orally q4h up to 1.2 mg
  - √ Day 5 to completion: Reduce 0.2 mg/day; given in divided doses; the nighttime dose should be reduced last; or reduce total dosage by one-half each day, not to exceed 0.4 mg/day.

Table A.8
Signs and Symptoms of Opioid Withdrawal

Earlier Symptoms	Later Symptoms
Anorexia	Abdominal cramps
Anxiety	Disrupted sleep
Craving	Hot or cold flashes
Dysphoria	Increased blood pressure
Fatigue	Increased pulse
Headache	Low-grade fever
Increased respiratory rate	Muscle and bone pain
Irritability	Muscle spasm (hence the term *kicking the habit*)
Lacrimation	Mydriasis (with dilated, fixed pupils at the peak)
Mydriasis (mild)	Nausea and vomiting
Perspiration	
Piloerection (goose flesh)	
Restlessness	
Rhinorrhea	
Yawning	

from Kleber, 1999.

- Patch administration
  - √ Clonidine patch comes in three strengths (#1, #2, #3) and delivers over 1 week the equivalent of a daily dose of oral clonidine (e.g., #2 patch = 0.2 mg oral clonidine, daily).
  - √ Apply one #2 patch for patients under 100 lbs., two #2 patches if they weigh 100–200 lbs., and three #2 patches for those over 200 lbs.
  - √ On day 1 (the day the patch is applied), oral clonidine may be necessary—0.2 mg q6h for 24 hours, then 0.1 mg q6h for the second 24 hours.
  - √ Patch(es) should be removed if systolic pressure falls below 80 mmHg or diastolic below 50 mmHg.
- Advantages of patch:
  - √ Patients don't have to take pills several times a day.
  - √ Blood levels of medication stay steady.
  - √ Buildup of withdrawal symptoms during night is prevented.

Blood pressure monitoring is important because hypotension can occur, especially in thin patients. Advise patient to take blood pressure before and 20 minutes after a dose of clonidine. If lightheaded or dizzy, patient should lie down. Adequate fluid intake is important. Contact physician if dizziness continues.

Additional Medications for Symptom Control During Opioid Withdrawal

Provide medications over which the patient is allowed to exert some control:

Lomotil 2 tablets qid, prn diarrhea
Kaopectate 30 cc prn after a loose stool
Pro-Banthine 15 mg or Bentyl 20 mg q4h prn abdominal cramps
Tylenol 650 mg q4h prn for headache
Feldene 20 mg daily or Naprosyn 375 mg q8h for back, joint, and bone pain
Mylanta 30 ml q2h prn for indigestion
Phenergan suppositories 25 or 50 mg, prn nausea
Atarax 25 mg q4h prn nausea
Librium 25 mg q4h prn for anxiety
Benadryl 50 mg or temazepam 30 mg hs prn sleep
Doxepin 10–20 mg po hs for insomnia, anxiety, dysphoria

A patient has a right to be informed that alternative treatments to the withdrawal procedure described above are methadone maintenance or outpatient withdrawal using methadone. These procedures can be carried out in licensed Texas Department of Health approved opioid agonist treatment programs.

Cannabis Withdrawal

Cannabis (marijuana) dependence in those who have tried the drug is estimated at 10–15%, and 5% of 18-year-olds are estimated to be daily smokers. Regular use (at least weekly) over several years leads to dependence (using DSM-IV and ICD-10 criteria) in 57–92% of individuals.

In spite of existing dependence criteria cannabis withdrawal is not included in the DSM-IV. That there is withdrawal is suggested, however, by research in both animal and human studies. Human studies are confounded by lack of consistency in time of onset and time of completion of symptoms presumed to be secondary to cannabis withdrawal, as well as by personality variables that influence reporting of symptoms.

The following facts seem to be established (Smith, 2002):

1. Discontinuing cannabis leads to unpleasant effects.
2. The effects are brief, not severe, and usually do not produce "clinically significant distress or impairment" (part of the criteria in DSM-IV for withdrawal states).
3. The most common symptoms are:
   • Insomnia
   • Decreased appetite
   • Agitation (irritability, anxiety)
   • Gastrointestinal distress is less common but may include pain and nausea.
4. Onset of symptoms may begin within 4 hours of last use and last no more than 1 week.

Treatment

The symptoms are mild and brief and may partly reflect the psychological frustration of not having available the desired substance rather than physiologically induced symptoms. Sleep disturbances can be treated with trazodone, zolpidem, or diphenhydramine. Agitation, anxiety, and irritability can be treated briefly (1–2 days) with low doses of clonazepam.

References

Adams WL, Barry KL, Fleming MF. Screening for problem drinking in older primary care patients. *JAMA* 276:1964–7, 1996.

Adis R&D Profile. *Drugs R&D* 3(1):13018, 2002.

AHA (American Hospital Association) News. Substance abuse takes a big bite of health care spending. *AHA News* 37(17): 2001.

Ainslie G. *Breakdown of will.* Cambridge, UK: Cambridge University Press, 2001.

Alexander B, Perry P. Detoxification from benzodiazepines: Schedules and strategies. *J Substance Abuse Treatment* 8:9–17, 1991.

Allen JP, Anthenelli RM. Problem drinking: The case for routine screening. *Current Psychiatry* 2(6):27–44, 2003.

American Psychiatric Association. *Diagnostic and Statistical Manual for Mental Disorders*, 4th ed. Washington, DC: American Psychiatric Association, 1994.

American Psychiatric Association. *Diagnostic and Statistical Manual of Mental Disorders, 4th ed.*, text rev. Washington, DC: American Psychiatric Association, 2000.

American Society of Addiction Medicine. *Patient Placement Criteria for the Treatment of Substance-Related Disorders, 2nd ed.* (ASAM PPC-2). Chevy Chase, MD: American Society of Addiction Medicine, 1996.

Anandrajah G, Hight E. Spirituality and medical practice: Using the HOPE questions as a practical tool for spiritual assessment in office practice. *Am Fam Physicians* 68:81–8, 2001.

Anda RF, Croft JB, Felitti VJ, Nordenberg D, Giles WH, Williamson DF, Giovino GA. Adverse childhood experiences and smoking during adolescence and adulthood. *JAMA* 282:1652–8, 1999.

Antabuse (disulfiram tablets) package insert. Florham Park, NJ: Odyssey Pharmaceuticals, 2005.

Anthony JC, Warner LA, Kessler RC. Comparative epidemiology of dependence on tobacco, alcohol, controlled substances, and inhalants: Basic findings from the National Comorbidity Survey. *Experimental and Clinical Psychopharmacology* 2:224–68, 1994.

Anton RF, Myrick DL. *Pharmacological management of alcohol withdrawal*. 1999 CME Monograph Series sponsored by Dannemiller Memorial Educational Foundation and Alpha and Omega Worldwide, LLC, 2000.

Ascher JA, Cole JD, Colin JN, Feighner JP, Fepris RM, Fibiger HC, et al. Buproprion: A review of its mechanism of antidepressant activity. *J Clin Psychiatry* 56: 395–401, 1995.

Ashton H. Toxicity and adverse consequences of benzodiazepine use. *Psychiatric Annals* 25(3):158–65, 1995.

Azrin NH, McMahon PT, Donohue B, Besalel VA, Lapinski KJ, Kogan ES, et al. Behavior therapy for drug abuse: A controlled treatment outcome study. *Behaviour Research and Therapy* 32:857–66, 1994.

Baille A, Mattick RP, Hall W, Webster P. Meta-analytic review of the efficacy of smoking cessation interventions. *Drug Alcohol Review* 13:157–70, 1994.

Baker-Morissette SL, Gulliver SB, Wiegel M, Barlow DH. Prevalence of smoking in anxiety disorders uncomplicated by co-morbid alcohol or substance abuse. *J of Psychopathology & Behavioral Assessment* 26(2):107–12, 2004.

Barry KL, Fleming MF. The Alcohol Use Disorders Identification Test (AUDIT) and the SMAST-13: Predictive validity in a rural primary care sample. *Alcohol and Alcoholism* 28(1):33–42, 1993.

Bean P, Daniel P. CDT current facts and future projection for the insurance industry. *On the Risk* 12:43–8, 1996.

Benjamin D, Grant ER, Pohorecky LA. Naltrexone reverses ethanol-induced dopamine release in the nucleus accumbens in awake, freely moving rats. *Brain Res* 621(1):137–40, 1993.

Benzer DO, Smith DE, Miller NS. Detoxification from benzodiazepine use: Strategies and schedules for clinical practice. *Psychiatric Annals* 25(3):180–185, 1995.

Biederman J, Wilens T, Mick E, Spencer T, Faraone SV. Pharmacotherapy of attention deficit/hyperactivity disorder reduces risk for substance use disorder. *Pediatrics* 104(20):293–4, 1999.

Bien TH, Miller WR, Tonigan JC. Brief interventions for alcohol problems: A review. *Addiction* 88:315–36, 1993.

Blazer DG, Steffens DC, Busse EW. *American Psychiatric Publishing Textbook of Geriatric Psychiatry*, 3rd ed. Arlington, VA: American Psychiatric Publishing, 2004.

Bowles TM, Sommi RW, Amiri M. Successful management of prolonged gamma-hydroxybutyrate and alcohol withdrawal. *Pharmacotherapy* 21(2):254–7, 2001.

Boyle P, Maisonneuve P. Lung cancer and tobacco smoking. *Lung Cancer* 12:167–81, 1995.

Brady KT. Substance dependence and anxiety disorders. In Kranzler HR & Tinsley JA (Eds.), *Dual diagnosis and psychiatric treatment*, 2nd ed. New York: Marcel Dekker, 2004.

Breslau N, Peterson EL, Schultz LR, Chilcoat HD, Andreski P. Major depression and stages of smoking: A longitudinal investigation. *Arch General Psychiatry* 55:161–6, 1998.

Brook JS, Gordon AS, Brook A, Brook DW. The consequences of marijuana use on intrapersonal and interpersonal functioning in black and white adolescents. *Genetic, Social, and General Psychology Monographs* 115(3):349–69, 1988.

Brook JS, Nomura C, Cohen P. Prenatal, perinatal, and early childhood risk factors and drug involvement in adolescents. *Genetic, Social, and General Psychology Monographs* 115(2):221–41, 1988.

Brown RA, Kahler CW, Niaura R, Abrams DB, Sales SD, Ramsey SE, et al. Cognitive behavioral treatment for depression in smoking cessation. *J Consult Clin Psychology* 69:471–80, 2001.

Burke KC, Burke JD, Rae DS. Increased rates of drug abuse and dependence after onset of mood or anxiety disorders in adolescence. *Hosp Community Psychiatry* 45(5):451–5, 1994.

Cacciola JS, Alterman AI, McKay JR, Rutherford MJ. Psychiatric co-morbidity in patients with substance use disorders: Do not forget Axis II disorders. *Psychiatric Annals* 31(5):321–31, 2001.

Carroll KM, Nich C, Ball SA, McCance E, Rounsaville BJ. Treatment of cocaine and alcohol dependence with psychotherapy and disulfiram. *Addiction* 93(5):713–27, 1998.

Cassell EJ. *The nature of suffering and the goals of medicine*. New York: Oxford University Press, 1991.

Cavanaugh RM, Henneberger PK. Talking to teens about family problems: An opportunity for prevention. *Clin Pediatr* 35:67–71, 1996.

Centers for Disease Control and Prevention. Youth tobacco surveillance—United States, 2000. *MMWR Morbidity and Mortality Weekly Report* 50(SS04):1–84, 2001.

Center for Substance Abuse Treatment. *Medication-assisted treatment for opioid addiction in opioid treatment programs*. Treatment improvement protocol (TIP) Series 43. DHHS Publication No. (SMA) 05-4048. Rockville, MD: Substance Abuse and Mental Health Services Administration.

Center for Substance Abuse Treatment. *Clinical guidelines for the use of buprenorphine in the treatment of opioid addiction*. Treatment Improvement Protocol (TIP) Series 40. DHHS Publication No. (SMA) 04-3939. Rockville, MD: Substance Abuse and Mental Health Services Administration, 2004.

Chan AW, Pristach EA, Welte JW, Russell M. Use of the TWEAK test in screening for alcoholism/heavy drinking in three populations. *Alcohol Clin Exp Res* 17(6): 1188–92, 1993.

Chermock ST, Singer K, Beresford TP. Screening for alcoholism among medical inpatients: How important is corroboration of patient self-report? *Alcohol Clin Exp Res* 22:1393–8, 1998.

Cherputel CJ, Sogholians K, Hurley LB. Alcohol-related health services use and identifications of patients in the emergency department. *Am Emerg Med* 28: 418–23, 1996.

Ciraulo D, Nace E. Benzodiazepine treatment of anxiety or insomnia in substance abuse patients. *Am J Addictions* 9:276–84, 2000.

Chiba M, Masironi R. Toxic and trace elements in tobacco and tobacco smoke. *Bulletin World Health Organ* 70:270–6, 1992.

Claassen C, Adinoff B. Alcohol withdrawal syndrome: Guidelines for management. *CNS Drugs* 12(4):279–91, 1999.

Cloninger CR. Neurogenetic adaptive mechanisms in alcoholism. *Science* 236:410–16, 1987.

Craig K, Gomez HF, McManus JL, Bania TC. Severe gamma-hydroxybutyrate withdrawal: A case report and literature review. *J Emerg Med* 18(1):65–70, 2000.

Crawford MJ, Patton R, Touquet R, Drummond C, Byford S, Barrett B, et al. Screening and referral for brief intervention of alcohol-misusing patients in an emergency department: A pragmatic randomized controlled trial. *Lancet* 364:1334–9, 2004.

Cyr MG, Wartman SA. The effectiveness of routine screening questions in the detection of alcoholism. *JAMA* 259:51–4, 1988.

Dackis CA, Kampman KM, Lynch KG, Pettinati HM, O'Brien CP. A double-blind, placebo-controlled trial of modanfinil for cocaine dependence. *Neuropsychopharmacology* 30(1):205–11, 2005.

Dallas Fraternal Order of Police. *Crime Prevention Community Service Journal*, 2004.

Daly R. Protocol guides medication treatment of addiction. *Psychiatric News* 40(23):17, 2005.

Dias PJ. Adolescent substance abuse assessment in the office. *Pediatric Clinics of North America* 49:269–300, 2002.

Dick DM, Foroud T. Candidate genes for alcohol dependence: A review of genetic evidence from human studies. *Alcohol Clin Exp Res* 27(5):868–79, 2003.

DiClemente CC, Prochaska JO, Fairhurst SK, Velicer WF, Velasquez MM, Rossi JS. The process of smoking cessation: An analysis of precontemplation, contemplation, and preparation stages of change. *J Consult Clin Psychol* 59:295–304, 1991.

Drake RE, Mercer-McFadden C, Mueser KT, McHugo GJ, Bond GR. Review of integrated mental health and substance abuse treatment for patients with drug disorders. *Schizophrenia Bulletin* 24(4):589–608, 1998.

Drake RE, Mueser KT. Co-occurring alcohol use disorder and schizophrenia. *Alcohol Research and Health* 26(2):99–102, 2002.

Dupont RL. A practical approach to benzodiazepine discontinuation. *J Psychiatric Res* 24(Suppl. 2):81–90, 1990.

Eckardt MJ, Martin PR. Clinical assessment of cognition in alcoholism. *Alcohol Clin Exp Res* 10(2):123–7, 1986.

Eliopoulos C, Klein J, Phan MK, Knie B, Greenwald M, Chitayat D, Koren G. Hair concentrations of nicotine and cotinine in women and their newborn infants. *JAMA* 271:621–3, 1994.

Emrick CD, Tonigan JS, Montgomery H, Little L. Alcoholics Anonymous: What is currently known? In McCrady BS & Miller WR (Eds.), Research on Alcoholics Anonymous: Opportunities and Alternatives. New Brunswick, NJ: Rutgers Center of Alcohol Studies, 1993.

Enoch MA, Goldman D. Genetics of alcoholism in substance abuse. *Psychiatric Clinics of North America* 22:289–99, 1999.

Erikson, EH. *A way of looking at things: Selected papers from 1930–1980.* New York: Norton, 1987.

Ewing JA. Detecting alcoholism: The CAGE questionnaire. *JAMA* 252:1905–7, 1984.

Fagerstrom KO, Schneider NG. Measuring nicotine dependence: A review of the Fagerstrom Tolerance Questionnaire. *J of Behavioral Medicine* 12(2):159–81, 1989.

Farnsworth MG. Benzodiazepine abuse and dependence: Misconceptions and facts. *Journal of Family Practice* 31(4):393–400, 1990.

Farrell, M. Cannabis dependence and withdrawal. *Addiction* 94(9):1277–8, 1999.

Finlayson RE, Davis LJ. Prescription drug dependence in the elderly population: Demographic and clinical features of 100 patients. *Mayo Clinic Proceedings* 69(12):1215–7, 1994.

Fiore MC, Jorenby DE, Schensky AE, Smith SS, Baver RR, Baker TB. Smoking status as the new vital sign: Effect on assessment and intervention in patients who smoke. *Mayo Clinic Prac* 70(3):209–13, 1995.

Fiore MC, Bailey WC, Cohen ST, Dorfman SF, Goldstein MG, Gritz ER, et al. Smoking cessation: Clinical practice guidelines No 18. Rockville, MD: U.S. Department of Health and Human Services, Public Health Service Agency of Health Care Policy and Research, AHCPR Publication No. 96-0692, 1996.

Fiore MC, Bailey WC, Cohen ST, Dorfman SF, Goldstein MG, Gritz ER, et al. *Treating tobacco use and dependence: Clinical practice guidelines.* Rockville, MD: U.S. Department of Health and Human Services, Public Health Services, June 2000.

Fleming MF, Barry KL, Manwell LB, Johnson K, London R. Brief physician advice for problem alcohol drinkers: A randomized controlled test in community based primary care practices. *JAMA* 227:1039–45, 1997.

Fleming MF, Mundt MP, French MT, Manwell LB, Stauffacher EA, Barry KL. Brief physician advice for problem drinkers: Long-term efficacy and benefit–cost analysis. *Alcohol Clin Exp Res* 26:36–43, 2002.

Franklin JE, Frances RJ. Alcohol and other psychoactive substance use disorders. In Hales RE & Yudofsky SC (Eds.), *Essentials of clinical psychiatry* (pp. 189–192). Washington, DC: American Psychiatric Association, 1999.

French SA, Jeffrey RW. Weight concerns and smoking: A literature review. *Ann Behav Med* 17:234–44, 1995.

Gambert SR. Substance abuse in the elderly. In Lowinson JH, Ruiz P, Millman RB (Eds), *Substance abuse: A comprehensive textbook*. Baltimore, MD: Williams & Wilkins, 1992.

GAP Committee on Alcoholism and the Addictions. *Addiction treatment: Avoiding the pitfalls—A case approach*. Washington, DC: American Psychiatric Association, 1998.

Garbutt JC, Kranzler HR, O'Malley SS, Gastfriend DR, Pettinati HM, Silverman BL, et al. Efficacy and tolerability of long-acting injectable naltrexone for alcohol dependence: A randomized controlled trial. *JAMA* 293:1617–25, 2005.

Garbutt JC, West SL, Carrey TS, Lohr KN, Crews FT. Pharmacological treatment of alcohol dependence: A review of the evidence. *JAMA* 281:1318–25, 1999.

Garofalo R, Wolf RC, Kessel S, Palfrey J, DuRant RH. The association between health risk behaviors and sexual orientation among a school-based sample of adolescents. *Pediatrics* 101:895–902, 1998.

Geller G, Levine DM, Momon JA, Moore, RD, Bone LR, Stokes EJ. Knowledge, attitude, and reported practices of medical students and house staff regarding the diagnosis and treatment of alcoholism. *JAMA* 261:3115–20, 1989.

Gerada C. Drug misuse: A review of treatments. *Clinical Medicine* 5(1):69–73, 2005.

Gerstein DR, Harwood H, Suter N. *Evaluating recovery services: The California Drug and Alcohol Treatment Assessment (Caldata)*. California Department of Alcohol and Drug Programs Executive Summary: Publications No. ADP 94-628, 1994.

Gilpin E, Chol WS, Berry C, Pierce JP. How many adolescents start smoking each day in the United States? *J Adolesc Health* 25:248–55, 1999.

Giovino GA. Epidemiology of tobacco use in the United States. *Oncogene* 21:7326–40, 2002.

Giovino GA, Henningfield JE, Tomar SL, Escobedo LG, Slade J. Epidemiology of tobacco use and dependence. *Epidemiology Review* 17(1) 48–65, 1995.

Glassman AH. Cigarette smoking: Implications for psychiatric illness. *Am J Psychiatry* 150:546–53, 1993.

Goldenring J, Cohen E. Getting into adolescents' heads. *Contemporary Pediatrics* 5:75, 1988.

Goldstein RZ, Volkow ND. Drug addiction and its underlying neurobiological basis: Neuroimaging evidence for the involvement of the frontal cortex. *Am J Psychiatry* 159:1642–52, 2002.

Grant BF, Dawson DA. Age of onset of alcohol use and its association with DSM-IV alcohol abuse and dependence: Results from the National Longitudinal Alcohol Epidemiologic Survey. *J Substance Abuse* 9:103–10, 1997.

Grant BF, Hassin DS, Chou P, Stinson FS, Dawson DA. Nicotine dependence and psychiatric disorders in the United States: Results from the National Epidemiologic Survey on Alcohol and Related Conditions. *Arch Gen Psychiatry* 61:1107–15, 2004a.

Grant BF, Stinson FS, Dawson DA, Chou P, Ruan WJ, Pickering RP. Co-occurrence of 12-month alcohol and drug use disorders and personality disorders in the United States: Results from National Epidemiologic Survey on Alcohol and Related Conditions. *Arch Gen Psychiatry* 61(4):361–8, 2004b.

Grant M, Ritson EB. International review of treatment and rehabilitation services for alcoholism and alcohol abuse. In Institute of Medicine's *Broadening the Base of Treatment for Alcohol Problems* (pp. 550–78). Washington, DC: National Academy Press, 1990.

Greenfield SF, Manwani SG, Nagiso JE. Epidemiology of substance use disorders in women. *Obstet Gynecol Clin North Am* 30:413–46, 2003.

Group for the Advancement of Psychiatry. *Addiction treatment: Avoiding pitfalls—A case approach*, Report No. 142. Washington, DC: American Psychiatric Association, 1998.

Hall SM, Killen JD. Psychological and pharmacological approaches to smoking relapse prevention. In Grabowski J & Hall SM (Eds.), *Pharmacological adjuncts in smoking cessation*, NIDA Research Monograph 53 (pp. 131–143). Washington, DC: U.S. Department of Health and Human Services, 1985.

Hall SM, Turnstall CD, Vila KL, Duffy K. Weight gain prevention and smoking cessation: Cautionary findings. *Am J Public Health,* 82:799–803, 1992.

Haney M, Ward A, Comer S, Foltin R, Fischman M. Abstinence symptoms following smoked marijuana in humans. *Psychopharmacology* 141(4):395, 1999.

Harwood H. *Updating estimates of the economic costs of alcohol abuse in the United States: Estimates, update methods, and data.* Report prepared by the Levin Group for the National Institute on Alcohol Abuse and Alcoholism, 2000.

Harwood HJ, Fountain D, Livermore G. Economic costs of alcohol abuse and alcoholism. *Recent Dev Alcohol* 14:307–30, 1998.

Hasin D, Nunes E, Meydan J. Comorbidity of alcohol, drug, and psychiatric disorders: Epidemiology. In Kranzler HR & Tinsley JA (Eds.), *Dual diagnosis and psychiatric treatment: Substance abuse and comorbid disorders* (pp. 1–34). New York: Marcel Dekker, 2004.

Heishman S, Singleton E, Liguori A. Marijuana craving questionnaire: Development and initial validation of a self-report instrument. *Addiction* 96:1034, 2001.

Helzer J, Pryzbeck T. The co-occurrence of alcoholism with other psychiatric disorders in the general population and its impact on treatment. *J Stud Alcohol* 49:210–24, 1988.

Hollenback KA, Barrett-Connor E, Edelstein SL, Holbrook T. Cigarette smoking and bone mineral density in older men and women. *Am J Public Health* 83:1265–70, 1993.

Hser YI, Grella CE, Hubbard RL, Hsieh SC, Fletcher BW, Brown BS. An evaluation of drug treatment for adolescents in four U.S. cities. *Arch Gen Psychiatry* 58(7):689–95, 2001.

Hughes JR, Hatsukami DK, Mitchell JE, Dahlgreen LA. Prevalence of smoking among psychiatric outpatients. *Am J Psychiatry* 143:993–7, 1986.

Hughes JR, Hatsukami DK. The nicotine withdrawal syndrome: A brief review and update. *Int J Smoking Cessation* 1:21–6, 1992.

Hughes JR, Lesmes GR, Hatsukami DK, Richmond RL, Lichtenstei E, Jorenby DE, et al. Are higher doses of nicotine replacement more effective for smoking cessation? *Nicotine Tob Res* 1(2):169–74, 1999.

Hurt RD, Eberman KM, Croghan IT, Offord KP, Davis LJ, Morse RM, et al. Nicotine dependence treatment during inpatient treatment for other addictions: A prospective intervention trial. *Alcoholism Clin Exp Res* 18(4):867–72, 1994.

Hymowitz N, Cummings MD, Hyland A, Lynn, WR, Pechacek TS, Hartwell TD. Predictors of smoking cessation in a "cohort" of adult smokers followed for five years. *Tobacco Control* 6 (Suppl. 2):S57–S62, 1997.

Jacob T, Sher KJ, Bucholz KK, True WT, Sirevaag EJ, Rohrbaugh J, et al. An integrative approach for studying the etiology of alcoholism and other addictions. *Twin Res* 4(2):103–18, 2001.

Johnson BA, Ait-Daoud N, Bowden CL, DiClemente CC, Roache JD, Lawson K, et al. Oral topiramate for treatment of alcohol dependence: A randomized controlled trial. *Lancet* 361:1677–85, 2003.

John U, Meyer C, Hans–Jurgen R, Hapke U. Depressive disorders are related to nicotine dependence in the population but do not necessarily hamper smoking cessation. *J Clin Psychiatry* 65:169–76, 2004.

Johnson BA, Roache JD, Javors MA, DiClemente CC, Cloninger CR, Prikoda TJ, et al. Odansetron for reduction of drinking among biologically predisposed alcoholic patients: A randomized controlled trial. *JAMA* 284:963–71, 2000.

Johnston LD, O'Malley PM, Bachman JG. *Monitoring the future: National Survey results on drug use* (1975–2002). Bethesda, MD: National Institute on Drug Abuse, 2003.

Judd LL, Akiskal HS. Depressive episode and symptoms dominate the longitudinal course of bipolar disorder. *Curr Psychiatry Rep* 5:417–8, 2003.

Kalivas PW, Volkow ND. The neural basis of addiction: A pathology of motivation and choice. *Am J Psychiatry* 162:(8)1403–13, 2005.

Kalman D, Baker-Morissette S, George T. Co-morbidity of smoking in patients with psychiatric and substance use disorders. *Am J Addictions* 14:106–23, 2005.

Kaminer Y. Adolescent substance abuse treatment: Where do we go from here? *Psychiatric Services* 52:147–9, 2001.

Kaminer Y, Bukstein OG. Treating adolescent substance abuse. In Frances RJ, Miller SI, Mach AH (Eds.), *Clinical textbook of addictive disorders*, 3rd ed. (pp. 559–87). New York: Guilford Press, 2005.

Kandel DB. Does marijuana cause the use of other drugs? *JAMA* 289:482–3, 2003.

Kaplan RF. The neuropsychology of alcoholism: Effects of premorbid and comorbid disorders. In Kranzler HR & Tinsley JA (Eds.), *Dual diagnosis and psychiatric treatment: Substance abuse and comorbid disorders*, 2nd ed. New York: Marcel Dekker, 2004.

Kendler KS, Karkowski LM, Neale MC, Prescott CA. Illicit psychoactive substance use, heavy use, abuse, and dependence in a U.S. population-based sample of male twins. *Arch Gen Psychiatry* 57(3):261–9, 2000.

Kessler RC, McGonagle KA, Zhas S, Nelson CB, Hughes M, Eshleman S, et al. Lifetime and 12-month prevalence of DSM-III-R psychiatric disorders in the United States: Results from the National Comorbidity Survey. *Arch Gen Psychiatry* 51:8–19, 1994.

Kessler RC, Nelson CB, McGonagle, KA, Edlund MJ, Frank RG, Leaf PJ. The epidemiology of co-occurring addictive and mental disorders: Implications for prevention and service utilization. *Am J Orthopsychiatry* 66:17–31, 1996.

Khantzian EJ. The self-medication hypotheses of substance use disorders: A reconsideration and recent applications. *Hammond Review of Psychiatry* 4:231–44, 1997.

Kinnunen T, Doherty K, Militello FS, Garvey AJ. Depression and smoking cessation: Characteristics of depressed smokers and effects of nicotine replacement. *J Consult Clin Psychol* 64 (4):791–8, 1996.

Kipniss L, Miller NS. Smoking cessation treatment calls for an individualized approach. *Psychiatric Annals* 33(9):573–81, 2003.

Kleber HS. Opioids: Detoxification. In Galanter M & Kleber HD (Eds.), *Textbook of substance abuse treatment*, 2nd ed. (pp. 251–269). Washington, DC: American Psychiatric Press, 1999.

Klesges RC, Meyers AW, Klesges LM, La Vasque ME. Smoking, body weight, and their effects on smoking behavior: A comprehensive review of the literature. *Psychol Bull* 106:204–30, 1989.

Knight JR, Shrier LA, Bravender RO, Farrell M, Vanderbelt J, Shaffer HJ. A new brief screen for adolescent substance abuse. *Arch Pediatr Adolesc Med* 153:591–6, 1999.

Koback KA, Taylor LH, Dottle SL, Greist JH, Jefferson JW, Burroughs D, et al. A computer-administered telephone interview to identify mental disorders. *JAMA* 278(11):905–10, 1997.

Koob, GF. Neuroadeptive mechanisms of addiction: Studies on the extended amygdala. *European Neuropsychopharmacology* 13:442–52, 2003.

Krall EA, Dawson-Hughes B. Smoking and bone loss among post-menopausal women. *J Bone Miner Res* 6:331–8, 1991.

Krantz MJ, Mehler PS. Treating opioid dependence: Growing implications for primary care. *Arch Internal Medicine* 164(3):277–88, 2004.

Kreek MJ, Koob GF. Drug dependence: Stress and dysregulation of brain reward pathways. *Drug and Alcohol Dependence* 51:230–47, 1998.

Kristenson H, Ohlin H, Holten-Nosslin MB, Trell E, Hood B. Identification and intervention of heavy drinking on middle-aged men: Results and follow-up of 24–60 months on long-term studies with randomized centers. *Alcohol: Clinical and Experimental Research* 7:203–9, 1983.

Lasser K, Boyd JW, Woolhander S, Himmelstein DU, McCormick D, Bor DH. Smoking and mental illness: A population-based prevalence study. *JAMA* 284: 2606–10, 2000.

Lewis DC, Gordon AJ. Alcoholism and the general hospital: The Roger Williams Intervention Program. *Bull NY Acad Medicine* 59(2):181–97, 1983.

Liepman MR, Calles JL, Kizilbash L, Nazeer A, Sheikh S. Genetic and non-genetic factors influencing substance use by adolescents. *Adolescent Medicine* 13(2): 375–402, 2002.

Littleton J. Acamprosate in alcohol dependence: How does it work? *Addiction* 90:1179–88, 1995.

Littleton J. Neurochemical mechanisms underlying alcohol withdrawal. *Alcohol Health and Research World* 22:13–24, 1998.

Mason BJ, Ownby RL. Acamprosate for the treatment of alcohol dependence: A review of double-blind, placebo controlled trials. *CNS Spectrums* 5:58–69, 2000.

Mason BJ, Salvato FR, Williams LD, Ritvo EC, Cutler RB. A double-blind placebo-controlled study of oral nalmefene for alcohol dependence. *Arch Gen Psychiatry* 56:719–24, 1999.

Mayfield D et al. The CAGE questionnaire: Validation of a new alcoholism screening instrument. *Am J Psychiatry* 131:1121, 1974.

McCance-Katz EF, Costen TR, Jatlow P. Disulfiram effects on acute cocaine administration. *Drug Alcohol Dependence* 52(1):27–39, 1998.

McFall M, Saxon A, Thompson C, Yoshimoto D, Malte C, Straits-Troster K, et al. Improving the rates of quitting smoking for veterans with posttraumatic stress disorder. *Am J Psychiatry* 162(7):1311–19, 2005.

McFarland K, Lopisk CC, Kalivas PW. Prefrontal glutamate release into the core of the nucleus accumbens mediates cocaine-induced reinstatement of drug-seeking behavior. *J Neuroscience* 23:351–3, 2003.

McLellan AJ, Davis DC, O'Brien CP, Kleber HD. Drug dependence: A chronic medical illness. *JAMA* 284:1689–94, 2000.

Mendenhall C, Roselle GA, Moritz T, VA, Cooperative Study Groups 119 and 275. Relationship of protein calorie malnutrition to alcoholic liver disease: A reexamination of data from two Veterans Administration Cooperative Studies. *Alcohol Clin Exp Res* 19(3):635–41, 1995.

Middleman AB, Faulkner AH, Woods ER. High-risk behaviors among high school students in Massachusetts who use anabolic steroids. *Pediatrics* 96:268–72, 1995.

Mikhailidis DP, Ganotakis ES, Papadakis JA, Jeremy JY. Smoking and urological disease. *J Royal Society of Health* 118(4):210–12, 1998.

Miller WR, Rollnick S. Motivational approach. In Rogers F, Keller DS, & Margenstern J (Eds.), *Treating substance abuse: Theory and techniques* (pp. 266–85). New York: Guilford Press, 1996.

Miotto K, Darakjian J, Basch J, Murray S, Zogg J, Rawson R. Gamma-hydroxybutyric acid: Patterns of use, effects, and withdrawal. *Am. J Addict* 10(3):232–41, 2001.

Modesto-Lowe V, Pierucci-Lagna A, Kranzler HR. Substance abuse and mood disorders. In Kranzler HR & Tinsley JA (Eds.), *Dual diagnosis and psychiatric treatment: Substance abuse and comorbid disorders,* 2nd ed. (pp. 157–91). New York: Marcel Dekker, 2004.

Monitoring the Future. Available at www.samsha.gov, 2000.

Monitoring the Future. Available at www.monitoringthefuture.org, 2003.

Monitoring the Future. Available at www.monitoringthefuture.org, 2005.

Moore RD, Bone LR, Geller G, Mamon JA, Stokes EJ, Levine DM. Prevalence, detection, and treatment of alcoholism in hospital patients. *JAMA* 261:403–7, 1989.

Mullen JBM, Wigs BR, Wright JL, Hogg JC, Pare PD. Non-specific airway reactivity in cigarette smokers: Relationship to airway pathology and baseline lung function. *Am Rev Resp Dis* 133:120–5, 1986.

Murphy JM, Horton NJ, Mohson RR, Laird NM, Sobol AM, Leighton AH. Cigarette smoking in relation to depression: Historical trends from the Stirling County Study. *Am J Psychiatry* 160:1663–9, 2003.

Murray CJL, Lopez AD (Eds.). *The global burden of disease and injury series, Volume 1: A comprehensive assessment of mortality and disability from diseases, injuries, and risk factors in 1990 and projected in 2020.* Cambridge, MA: Harvard University Press, 1996.

Nace EP. *The treatment of alcoholism.* New York: Brunner/Mazel, 1987.

Nace EP, Davis C, Gaspari JD. Axis II comorbidity in a substance abuse sample. *Am J Psychiatry* 148:118–20, 1991.

Narrow WE, Rae DS, Robins LN, Regier DA. Revised prevalence estimates of mental disorders in the United States. *Arch Gen Psychiatry* 59:115–23, 2002.

National Household Survey on Drug Abuse (NHSDA). Washington, DC: Substance Abuse and Mental Health Services Administration (SAMHSA), 1999.

Nestler EJ. Genes and addiction. *Nat Genet* 26(3):227–81, 2000.

Nestler EJ. Molecular basis of long term plasticity underlying addiction. *Neuroscience* 2(2):119–28, 2001a.

Nestler EJ. Molecular neurobiology of addiction. *Am J Addictions* 10:201–17, 2001b.

NIAAA. *Make a difference: Talk to your child about alcohol.* NIH Publication No. 00-4313. U.S. Department of Health and Human Services Public Health Service, 2000.

NIAAA. *The physician's guide to helping patients with alcohol problems.* NIH Publication No. 95-3769. U.S. Department of Health and Human Services Public Health Service, 1995.

NIAAA. *Helping patients who drink too much: A clinician's guide.* NIH Publication No. 05-3769. U.S. Department of Health and Human Services Public Health Service, 2005.

NIDA. NIDA research and SAMHSA physician training combine to put care for opiate dependence in hands of family doctor. *NIDA Newsroom,* October 9, 2002.

NIDA. *NIDA Notes,* Vol. 12. www.nida.nih.gov/CEWG/DAWN.html, 1997.

NIDA. *Heroin abuse and addiction, research report series.* Washington, DC: National Institutes of Health, 1997.

Novack DH, Suchman AL, Clark W, Epstein RM, Najhery E, Kapton C. Calibrating the physician: Personal awareness and effects patient care. *JAMA* 278(6):502–9, 1997.

O'Brien CP. Myths about the treatment of addiction. *Lancet* 347:237–40, 1996.

Offer B, Offer JB. *From teenage to young manhood: A psychological study.* New York: Basic Books, 1975.

Office of Health and Environmental Assessment. *Respiratory health effects of passive smoking: Lung cancer and other disorders.* Washington, DC: U.S. Government Printing Office, 1992.

Olde Rikkert MG, Rigaud AS, van Hoeyweghen RJ, de Graaf J. Geriatric syndromes: Medical misnomer or progress in geriatrics? *Netherlands Journal of Medicine* 61(3):83–87, 2003.

O'Malley SS, Jaffe AJ, Chang G, Rode S, Schottenfeld RS, Meyer RE, Rounsaville BJ. Six-month follow-up of naltrexone and psychotherapy for alcohol dependence. *Arch Gen Psychiatry* 53:217–24, 1996.

Paavola M, Vartiainen E, Puska P. Smoking cessation between teenage years and adulthood. *Health Education Research* 16(1):49–57, 2001.

Pataki CS. Normal adolescence. In Sadock BJ & Sadock VA (Eds.), *Kaplan & Sadock's Comprehensive Textbook of Psychiatry*, 8th ed. Philadelphia, PA: Lippincott, Williams & Wilkins, 2005.

Perkins K. Issues in the prevention of weight gain after smoking cessation. *Ann Behav Med* 16:46–52, 1994.

Petrakis IL, Carroll KM, Nich C, Gordon LT, McCance-Katz EF, Frankforter T, et al. Disulfiram treatment for cocaine dependence in methadone-maintained opioid addicts. *Addiction* 95(2):219–28, 2000.

Petrakis IL, Gonzales G, Rosenheck R, Krystal JH. Comorbidity of alcoholism and psychiatric disorders: An overview. *Alcohol Research and Health* 26(2):81–9, 2002.

Pfefferbaum A, Sullivan EF, Mathalon DH, Lim KO. Frontal lobe volume loss observed with magnetic resonance imagining in older chronic alcoholics. *Alcohol Clin Exp Res* 21:521–9, 1997.

Pincus HA, Zarin DA, Tanielian TL, Johnson JL, West JC, Petit AR, et al. Psychiatric patients and treatments in 1997. *Arch Gen Psychiatry* 56:441–9, 1999.

Plomin R, Owen MJ, McGuffin P. The genetic basis of complex human behaviors. *Science* 264:1733–9, 1994.

Pontieri FE, Tanda G, Orzi F. Effects of nicotine on the nucleus accumbens and similarity to those of addictive drugs. *Nature* 382:255–7, 1996.

Preslau N, Johnson EO, Hiripi E, Kessler R. Nicotine dependence in the United States: Prevalence, trends, and smoking persistence. *Arch Gen Psychiatry* 58:810–16, 2001.

Project MATCH Research Group. Matching alcoholism treatments to client heterogeniety: Project MATCH post-treatment drinking outcomes. *Journal of Studies on Alcohol* 58:7–29, 1997.

Project MATCH Reseach Group. Matching alcoholism treatment to client heterogeneity: Project MATCH three-year drinking outcomes. *Alcohol Clin Exp Res* 22:1300–11, 1998.

Rakel RE, Bope ET. *Conn's current therapy*. Philadelphia, PA. Elsevier Saunders, 2005.

Regier DA, Farmer ME, Rae DS, Locke BZ, Keith SJ, Judd LL, et al. Comorbidity of mental disorders with alcohol and other drug abuse: Results from the Epidemiologic Catchment Area (ECA) study. *JAMA* 264:2511–18, 1990.

Regier DA, Narrow WE, Rae DS, Manderscheid RW, Locke BZ, Goodwin FK. The defacto U.S. mental and addictive disorders service system: Epidemiologic Catchment Area prospective one-year prevalence rates of disorders and services. *Arch Gen Psychiatry* 50:85–94, 1993.

Reynaud M, Schwan R, Loiseaux-Meuner M, Albuisson E, Deteis P. Patients admitted to emergency services for drunkenness: Moderate alcohol users or harmful drinkers? *Am J Psychiatry* 158:96–9, 2001.

Richards JW. Words as therapy-smoking cessation. *Journal of Family Practice* 34(6):687–92, 1992.

Rigotti NA, Pasternak RC. Cigarette smoking and coronary heart disease: Risks and management. *Cardiology Clinics* 14(1):51–67, 1996.

Rinaldi RC, Steindler EM, Wilford BB, Goodwin D. Clarification and standardization of substance abuse terminology. *JAMA* 259:555–7, 1988.

Robbins AS, Manson JE, Lee IM, Satterfield S, Hennekens CH. Cigarette smoking and stroke in a cohort of U.S. male physicians. *Annals of Internal Medicine* 120(6): 458–62, 1994.

Robinson TE, Berridge KC. The psychology and neurobiology of addiction: An incentive–sensitization view. *Addiction* 95(Suppl. 2):91–117, 2000.

Robinson TE, Berridge KC. Incentive–sensitization and addiction. *Addiction* 96(1):103–14, 2001.

Robinson TE, Kolb B. Persistent structural modifications in nucleus accumbens and prefrontal cortex neurons produced by previous experience with amphetamine. *Journal of Neuroscience* 17:8491–7, 1997.

Rohman ME, Cleary PD, Warburg M, Dellbanes TL, Aronson MD. The response of primary care physicians to problem drinkers. *Am J Alcohol Abuse* 13:199–209, 1987.

Rustin TA. Incorporating nicotine dependence into addiction treatment. *J Addict Dis* 17(1):83–108, 1998.

Rychlik R, Siedentop H, Pfeil T, Daniel D. Cost-effectiveness of adjuvant treatment with acamprosate in maintaining abstinence in alcohol dependent patients. *Eur Addict Res* 9:59–64, 2003.

Rydon P, Redman S, Sanson-Fisher RW, Reid AL. Detection of alcohol-related problems in general practice. *Journal of Studies on Alcohol* 53(3):197–202, 1992.

Sadock BJ, Sadock VA (2005). *Kaplan and Sadock's comprehensive textbook of psychiatry*, 8th ed. Philadelphia, PA. Lippincott, Williams and Wilkins.

Salloum IM, Douaihy A, Ndimbit OK, Kirisci L. Concurrent alcohol and cocaine dependence impact on physical health among psychiatric patients. *Journal of Addictive Disorders* 23(2):71–81, 2004.

Satcher D, Eriksen M. The paradox of tobacco control. *JAMA* 271(8):627–8, 1994.

Schneir AB, Ly BT, Clark RF. A case of withdrawal from the GHB precursors gamma-butyrolactone and 1,4-butanediol. *J Emerg Med* 21(1):31–3, 2001.

Schottenfeld RS. Opioids: Maintenance treatment. In Galanter M & Kleber HD (Eds.), *Textbook of Substance Abuse Treatment*, 3rd ed. (pp. 291–304). Washington, DC: The American Psychiatric Publishing Inc., 2004.

Schroader SA. What to do with a patient who smokes. *JAMA* 294:482–7, 2005.

Schweizer E, Rickels K. Benzodiazepine dependence and withdrawal: A review of the syndrome and its clinical management. *Acta Psychiatr Scand* 98 (Suppl. 393):95–101, 1998.

Secretary of Health and Human Services. *Alcohol and health special report to the U.S. Congress on alcohol and health, 9th ed. Effects of alcohol on fetal and postnatal development.* Washington DC: National Institutes of Health, 1997.

Secretary of Health and Human Services. *Special report to the U.S. Congress on alcohol and health, 10th ed. Alcohol and the brain: Neuroscience and neurobehavior.* Washington, DC: National Institute on Alcohol Abuse and Alcoholism, 2000.

Secretary of Health and Human Services. *Special report to the U.S. Congress on alcohol and health, 10th ed. Alcohol involvement over the life course.* Washington, DC: National Institute on Alcohol Abuse and Alcoholism, 2000.

Sellers EM, Toneatto T, Romach MK, Somer GR, Sobell LC, Sobell MB. Clinical efficacy of the 5-HT3 antagonist ondansetron in alcohol abuse and dependence. *Alcoholism in Clinical and Experimental Research* 18:879–85, 1994.

Shaef A. *Codependence misunderstood/mistreated.* New York: Harper and Row, 1986.

Shapiro T, Hertzig ME: Normal child and adolescent development. In Hales RE & Yudofsky SC (Eds.), *Essentials of clinical psychiatry*, 3rd ed. Washington, DC: American Psychiatric Association, 1999.

Sharkey J, Brennan D, Cumon P. The pattern of alcohol consumption of a general hospital population in North Belfast. *Alcohol and Alcoholism* 31(3):279–85, 1996.

Sillanauber P. Lab markers of alcohol abuse. *Alcohol and Alcoholism* 31(6):613–16, 1996.

Silva DeLima M, Garcia D, Oliveira Soares B, Alves Pereira Reisser A, Farrell M. Pharmacological treatment of cocaine dependence: A systematic review. *Addiction* 97:931–49, 2002.

Slemmer JE, Martin BR, Damaj MI. Buproprion is a nicotine antagonist. *J Pharmacol Exp Ther,* 295:321–7, 2000.

Smith N. A review of the published literature into cannabis withdrawal symptoms in human users. *Addiction* 97:621–632, 2002.

Sokol RJ, Martier S, Ager JW. The T-ACE questions: Practical prenatal detection of risk-drinking. *Am J Obstet Gynecol* 160(4):863–70, 1989.

Spitzer, RL, Williams JB, Kroenke K, Linzer M, deGruy FV III, Hahn SR, et al. Utility of a new procedure for diagnosing mental disorders in primary care: The PRIME-MD 1000 study. *JAMA* 272(22):1749–56, 1994.

Stuyt EB. Recovery rates after treatment for alcohol/drug dependence: Tobacco users vs. non-tobacco users. *Am J Addict* 6(2):159–67, 1997.

Stuyt EB, Order-Connors B, Ziedonis D. Addressing tobacco through program and system change in mental health and addiction settings. *Psychiatric Annals* 33(7): 447–56, 2003.

Substance Abuse and Mental Health Services Administration (SAMSHA). *Buprenorphine clinical practice guidelines*. Washington, DC: U.S. DHHS, 2000.

Terenius L. Alcohol addiction (alcoholism) and the opioid system. *Alcohol* 13:31–34, 1996.

Tinsley JA, Juergens SM. Chemical dependency. In Lemcke D, Pattison J, Marshall LA, Cowley DS (Eds.), *Current care of women: Diagnosis and treatment*. New York: Lange Medical Books/McGraw-Hill, 2004.

Tomar SL, Husten CG, Manley MW. Do dentists and physicians advise tobacco users to quit? *J Am Dental Assoc* 127(2):259–65, 1996.

Upadhyaya HP, Brady KT, Wharton M, Liao J. Psychiatric disorders and cigarette smoking among child and adolescent psychiatry inpatients. *Am J Addict* 12:144–52, 2003.

Upadhyaya H, Deas D, Brady K. How to help nicotine dependent adolescents quit smoking. *Current Psychiatry* 3(9):41–54, 2004.

U.S. Department of Health, Education, and Welfare. *Surgeon General's Report on Smoking and Health*. Washington, DC: U.S. Public Health Service, 1964.

U.S. Department of Health and Human Services. *The Economic Costs of Alcohol and Drug Abuse in the United States, 1992*. Washington, DC: U.S. Government Printing Office, 1998.

U.S. Department of Health and Human Services. *Clinical guidelines for the use of buprenorphine in the treatment of opioid addiction, TIP 40*. Washington, DC: Department of Health and Human Services, 2005.

U.S. Department of Health and Human Services. *Monitoring the Future: National Results on Adolescent Drug Use, Overview of Key Findings, 2001*. NIH Publications No. 02-5105. Bethesda, MD: National Institutes of Health, 2002.

U.S. Food and Drug Administration. Product discontinuation notice: ORLAMM. www.fda.gov/cder/drug/shortages/orlaam.htm, August 23, 2003.

van den Bree MB, Pickworth WB. Risk factors predicting changes in marijuana involvement in teenagers. *Arch Gen Psychiatry* 62:34–9, 2005.

Vocci F. Buprenorphine approval expands options for addiction treatment. *NIDA Notes* 17(4): 2002.

Volkow ND, Fowler JS, Wang GJ. Imaging studies on the role of dopamine in cocaine reinforcement and addiction in humans. *J Psychopharmacol* 13(4):337–45, 1999.

Volkow ND, Fowler JS, Wang GJ, Hitzemann R, Logan J, Schlyer D, et al. Decreased dopamine D2 receptor availability is associated with the reduced frontal metabolism in cocaine abusers. *Synapse* 14:169–77, 1993.

Volkow ND, Fowler JS, Wang GJ, Swanson JM. Dopamine in drug abuse and addiction: Results from imaging studies and treatment implications. *Mol Psychiatry* 9:557–69, 2004.

Volkow ND, Wang GJ, Fowler JS, Hitzemann R, Angrist B, Gatley SJ, et al. Association of methylphenidate-induced craving with drugs in right striato–orbitofrontal metabolism in cocaine abusers: Implications in addiction. *Am J Psychiatry* 156:19–26, 1999.

Volpicelli JR, Alterman AI, Hayashida M, O'Brien CP. Naltrexone in the treatment of alcohol dependence. *Arch Gen Psychiatry* 49(11):876–80, 1992.

Volpicelli JR, Clay KL, Watson NT, O'Brian CP. Naltrexone in the treatment of alcoholism: Predicting response to naltrexone. *J Clin Psychiatry* 56(Suppl. 7): 39–44, 1995.

Wadland WC, Stoffelmayr B, Berger E, Crombach A, Ives K. Enhancing smoking cessation rates in primary care. *J Family Practice* 48:711–18, 1999.

Walsh RA, Redman S, Brinsmead MW, Byrne JM, Melmeth A. A smoking cessation program at a public antenatal clinic. *Am J Public Health* 87(7):1201–4, 1997.

Wechsler H, Levine S, Idelson RK, Schor EL, Coakley E. The physician's role in health promotion revisited: A survey of primary care practitioners. *N Engl J Med* 334(15):996–8, 1996.

Wechsler H, Lee JE, Kuo M, Lee H. College binge drinking in the 1990's: A continuing problem. Results of the Harvard School of Public Health 1999 College Alcohol Study. *Journal of American College Health* 48:199–210, 2000.

Wiesbeck G, Schuckit M. An evaluation of the history of a marijuana withdrawal syndrome in a large population. *Addiction* 91(10):1469, 1996.

Whitworth AB, Fischer F, Lesch OM, Nimmerrichter A, Oberbauer H, Platz T, et al. Comparison of acamprosate and placebo and long-term treatment of alcohol dependence. *Lancet* 347:1438–42, 1996.

Wilde MI, Wagstaff AJ. Acamprosate: A review of its pharmacology and clinical potential in the management of alcohol dependence after detoxification. *Drugs* 53:1038–53, 1997.

Wisborg K, Henriksen TB, Obel C, Skajaa E. Smoking during pregnancy and hospitalization of the child. *Pediatrics* 104(4):46, 1999.

Wright C, Moore RD. Disulfiram treatment of alcoholism. *Am J Medicine* 88:647–55, 1990.

Ziedonis DM, William JM. Management of smoking in people with psychiatric disorders. *Current Opinion in Psychiatry* 16(3):305–15, 2003.

Zvosec DL, Smith SW, McCutcheon JR, Spillane J, Hall BJ, Peacock EA. Adverse events, including death, associated with the use of 1,4-butanediol. *N Engl J Med* 344(2):87–94, 2001.

Index

abstinence
  brain recovery and, 87, 121, 130
  case example of, 44
  "gray" zone and, 71
  inability for, 31–32, 33, 35
  intensity of care and, 84, 86
  investigating reasons for, 43–44
  low-risk drinking vs., 97
  medications maintaining, 152
  syndrome, *see* withdrawal
Academy of Addiction Psychiatry, 165
acamprosate, 4, 27, 151, 160–61, 171
accountability, 20, 143
acetaldehyde toxicity, 156
action stage, 91, 92, 142, 171
addiction(s)
  brain and, *see* separate entry
  challenges of treating, 5
  consequences of, facing, 91
  etiology of, 2
  psychiatric symptoms and, 53–54
  research on, 20–22
  specialist, 88–89
  terms, 2, 69, 171
  see also specific addictions
adolescence/adolescents, 6, 10
  alcohol/substance use during, 102–4, 105–6, 109–110
  behavior changes in, 61, 106
  developmental factors, 102–3
  diagnostic considerations in, 70, 101, 104–5
  smoking during, 105, 106, 109
  treatment options for, 110–13
Adult Children of Alcoholics, 60
advice, 92
agonists
  definition, 171
  opioid, 166
  partial, 179

Al-non, 57, 60, 63, 98, 113, 171
alcohol(ism)
  adolescent use of, *see* adolescence
  case example of, 42, 84, 122, 123, 125
  comorbid drugs and, 75
  and depression, 76
  elderly, use of, 118, 119–121
  motor vehicle accidents and, 103
  neurotransmitters affected by, 22
  pharmacological treatment of, 155–162
  polyneuropathy from, 120–21, 123
  quantifying the amount of, 46, 47, 96–98
  -related symptoms, 42
  and smoking rates, 75, 137
  social drinking turns into, 124, 125
  types of, 111, 112
  withdrawal, office based, 184–190
Alcoholics Anonymous (AA), 4, 57, 61, 62, 63, 86–87,
    88, 89, 93, 98, 130, 153, 154, 155, 158, 171
Alexander, B., 192
alliance, 72
Alzheimer's disease, 121
American Academy of Addiction Psychiatry
    (AAAP), 88
American Board of Medical Specialties, 89
American Medical Association, 165
American Osteopathic Association, 165
American Psychiatric Association, 14, 165
American Society of Addiction Medicine
    (ASAM), 82, 165
amnesia/amnestic disorders, 45, 48, 66, 106, 110
amotivational syndrome, 172
amphetamines, 106, 183
amygdala, role in mediating addictions, 19, 20, 21
anorexia nervosa, 146
Antabuse, *see* disulfiram
antagonists
  definition, 172
  opioid, 26–27, 153, 158, 159, 161, 167

217